PRINCIPLES OF ECONOMICS

Principles

of

Economics

Carl Menger

Translated by James Dingwall and Bert F. Hoselitz

With an Introduction by F. A. Hayek

Libertarian Press, Inc.
P.O. Box 309, 401 Erie Street
Grove City, PA 16127

Library of Congress Cataloging in Publication Data

Menger, Carl, 1840—1921.
  Principles of Economics

  Translation of Grundsätze der Volkswirtschaftslehre.
  No more published.
  "The Institute for Humane Studies Series in Economic Theory."
  Includes bibliographical references and index.
    1. Economics. I. Dingwall, James.   II. Hoselitz,
Berthold Frank, 1913-   III. Title.
ISBN 0-910884-27-7

Manufactured in the United States of America

CONTENTS

INTRODUCTION | **BY F.A. HAYEK**

CARL MENGER[1]

T HE HISTORY of economics is full of tales of forgotten fore-runners, men whose work had no effect and was only rediscovered after their main ideas had been made popular by others, of remarkable coincidences of simultaneous discoveries, and of the peculiar fate of individual books. But there must be few instances, in economics or any other branch of knowledge, where the works of an author who revolutionised the body of an already well-developed science and who has been generally recognised to have done so, have remained so little

1. This biographical study was written as an Introduction to the Reprint of Menger's *Grundsätze der Volkswirtschaftslehre* which constitutes the first of a series of four Reprints embodying Menger's chief published contributions to Economic Science and which were published by the London School of Economics as Numbers 17 to 20 of its *Series of Reprints of Scarce Works in Economics and Political Science.*

known as those of Carl Menger. It is difficult to think of a parallel case where a work such as the *Grundsätze* has exercised a lasting and persistent influence but has yet, as a result of purely accidental circumstances, had so extremely restricted a circulation.

There can be no doubt among competent historians that if, during the last sixty years, the Austrian School has occupied an almost unique position in the development of economic science, this is entirely due to the foundations laid by this one man. The reputation of the School in the outside world and the development of its system at important points were due to the efforts of his brilliant followers, Eugen von Böhm-Bawerk and Friedrich von Wieser. But it is not unduly to detract from the merits of these writers to say that its fundamental ideas belong fully and wholly to Carl Menger. If he had not found these principles he might have remained comparatively unknown, might even have shared the fate of the many brilliant men who anticipated him and were forgotten, and almost certainly would for a long time have remained little known outside the countries of the German tongue. But what is common to the members of the Austrian School, what constitutes their peculiarity and provided the foundations for their later contributions is their acceptance of the teaching of Carl Menger.

The independent and practically simultaneous discovery of the principle of marginal utility by William Stanley Jevons, Carl Menger, and Léon Walras is too well known to require retelling. The year 1871, in which both Jevons' *Theory of Political Economy* and Menger's *Grundsätze* appeared, is now generally and with justice regarded as the beginning of the modern period in the development of economics. Jevons had outlined his fundamental ideas nine years earlier in a lecture (published in 1866) which, however, attracted little attention, and Walras began to publish his contribution only in 1874, but the complete independence of the work of the three founders is quite certain. And indeed, although their central positions, the point in their system to which they and their contemporaries naturally attached the greatest importance, are the same, their work is so clearly distinct in general character and background that the most interesting problem is really how so different routes should have led to such similar results.

To understand the intellectual background of the work of Carl Menger, a few words on the general position of economics at that time are required. Although the quarter of a century between about 1848, the date of J.S. Mill's *Principles*, and the emergence of the new school saw in many ways the greatest triumphs of the classical political economy in the applied fields, its foundations, particularly its theory of value, had become more and more discredited. Perhaps the systematic exposition in J.S. Mill's *Principles* itself, in spite or because of his complacent satisfaction about the perfected state of the theory of value, together with his later retractions on other essential points of the doctrine, did as much as anything else to show the deficiencies of the classical system. In any case, critical attacks and attempts at reconstruction multiplied in most countries.

Nowhere, however, had the decline of the classical school of economists been more rapid and complete than in Germany. Under the onslaughts of the Historical School not only were the classical doctrines completely abandoned—they had never taken very firm root in that part of the world—but any attempt at theoretical analysis came to be regarded with deep distrust. This was partly due to methodological considerations. But even more it was due to an intense dislike of the practical conclusions of the classical English School—which stood in the way of the reforming zeal of the new group which prided itself on the name of the "ethical school." In England the progress of economic theory only stagnated. In Germany a second generation of historical economists grew up who had not only never become really acquainted with the one well-developed system of theory that existed, but had also learnt to regard theoretical speculations of any sort as useless if not positively harmful.

The doctrines of the classical school were probably too much discredited to provide a possible basis of reconstruction for those who were still interested in problems of theory. But there were elements in the writings of the German economists of the first half of the century which contained the germs for a possible new development.[1] One of the reasons why the classical doctrines had never firmly established themselves in Germany was that German economists had always remained conscious of certain contradictions inherent in any cost or labour theory of value. Owing, perhaps, partly to the influence of Condillac and other French and Italian authors of the eighteenth century a tradition had been kept alive which refused to separate value entirely from utility. From the early years of the century into the 'fifties and 'sixties a succession of writers, of whom Hermann was probably the outstanding and most influential figure (the wholly successful Gossen remaining unnoticed), tried to combine the ideas of utility and scarcity into an explanation of value, often coming very

---

1. The same is largely true of France. Even in England there was a kind of unorthodox tradition, of which the same may be said, but it was completely obscured by the dominant classical school. It is, however, important here because the work of its outstanding representative, Longfield, had through the intermediaryship of Hearn no doubt some influence on Jevons.

near to the solution provided by Menger. It is to these speculations, which to the more practical minds of the contemporary English economists must have appeared useless excursions into philosophy, that Menger owed most. A glance through the extensive footnotes in his *Grundsätze*, or the author's index which has been added to the present edition, will show how extraordinarily wide a knowledge he possessed of these German authors and also of the French and Italian writers, and how small a rôle the writers of the classical English school plays in comparison.

But while Menger probably surpassed all his fellow-founders of the marginal utility doctrine in the width of his knowledge of the literature—and only from a passionate book collector inspired by the example of the encyclopaedic Roscher could one expect a similar knowledge at the early age the *Grundsätze* was written—there are curious gaps in the list of authors to whom he refers which go far to explain the difference of his approach from that of Jevons and Walras.[1] Particularly significant is his apparent ignorance, at the time when he wrote the *Grundsätze*, of the work of Cournot, to whom all the other founders of modern economics, Walras, Marshall, and very possibly Jevons[2], seem to have been directly or indirectly indebted. Even more surprising, however, is the fact that at that time Menger does not seem to have known the work of von Thünen, which one would have expected him to find particularly congenial. While it can be said, therefore, that he worked in an atmosphere distinctly favourable to an analysis on utility lines, he had nothing so definite on which to build a modern theory of price as his fellows in the same field, all of whom came under the influence of Cournot, to which must be added, in the case of Walras, that of Dupuit[3] and, in the case of Marshall, that of von Thünen.

It is an interesting speculation to think what direction the development of Menger's thought would have taken if he had been acquainted with these founders of mathematical analysis. It is a curious

1. It is hardly surprising that he did not know his immediate German predecessor H.H. Gossen, but neither did Jevons or Walras when they first published their ideas. The first book which did justice at all to Gossen's work, F.A. Lange's *Arbeiterfrage* (2nd ed.), appeared in 1870 when Menger's *Grundsätze* was probably already being set up in print.

2. Dr. Hicks tells me that he has some reason to believe that Lardner's diagrammatic exposition of the theory of monoply, by which Jevons according to his own testimony was mainly influenced, derives from Cournot. On this point see Dr. Hicks's article on Léon Walras which is to appear in one of the next issues of *Econometrica*.

3. Menger did, however, know the work of Leon Walras's father, A.A. Walras, whom he quotes on p. 54 of the *Grundsätze*.

fact that, so far as I am aware, he has nowhere commented on the value of mathematics as a tool of economic analysis. There is no reason to assume that he lacked either the technical equipment or the inclination. On the contrary, his interest in the natural sciences is beyond doubt, and a strong bias in favour of their methods is evident throughout his work. And the fact that his brothers, particularly Anton, are known to have been intensely interested in mathematics, and that his son Karl became a noted mathematician, may probably be taken as evidence of a definite mathematical strain in the family. But although he knew later not only the work of Jevons and Walras, but also that of his compatriots Auspitz and Lieben, he does not even refer to the mathematical method in any of his writings on methodology.[1] Must we conclude that he felt rather sceptical about its usefulness?

Among the influences to which Menger must have been subject during the formative period of his thought there is a complete absence of influence of Austrian economists, for the simple reason that, in the earlier part of the nineteenth century in Austria, there were practically no native economists. At the universities where Menger studied, political economy was taught as part of the law curriculum, mostly by economists imported from Germany. And though Menger, like all the later Austrian economists, proceeded to the degree of Doctor of Law, there is no reason to believe that he was really stimulated by his teachers in economics. This, however, leads us to his personal history.

Born on February 28, 1840, in Neu-Sandec, Galicia, the territory of the present Poland, the son of a lawyer, he came from an old family of Austrian craftsmen, musicians, civil servants and army officers, who had, only a generation before, moved from the German parts of Bohemia to the Eastern provinces. His mother's father,[2] a Bohemian merchant who had made a fortune during the Napoleonic wars,

1. The only exception to this statement, a review of R. Auspitz and R. Lieben, *Untersuchungen über die Theorie des Preises*, in a daily newspaper (the *Wiener Zeitung* of July 8th, 1889), can hardly be called an exception, as he expressly says that he does not want to comment there on the value of mathematical exposition of economic doctrines. The general tone of the review as well as his objection to the fact that the authors in his opinion "use the mathematical method not only as a means of exposition but as a means of research" confirms the general impression that he did not consider it as particularly useful.

2. Anton Menger, the father of Carl, was the son of another Anton Menger, who came from an old German family that had in 1623 emigrated to Eger in Bohemia, and of Anna *née* Müller. His wife, Caroline, was the daughter of Josef Gerzabek, merchant in Hohenmaut, and of Therese, *née* Kalaus, whose ancestors can be traced in the register of baptism of Hohenmaut back into the 17th and 18th centuries respectively.

bought a large estate in Western Galicia where Carl Menger spent a great part of his boyhood, and before 1848 still saw the conditions of semi-servitude of the peasants which, in this part of Austria had persisted longer than in any part of Europe outside Russia. With his two brothers, Anton, later the well-known writer on law and socialism, author of the *Right to the Whole Produce of Labour*, and Carl's colleague at the faculty of law of the University of Vienna, and Max, in his days a well-known Austrian parliamentarian and writer on social problems, he went to the Universities of Vienna (1859-60) and Prague (1860-3). After taking his doctor's degree at the University of Cracow he devoted himself first to journalism, writing for papers in Lemberg and later in Vienna, on economic questions. After a few years he entered the Civil Service in the press department of the Austrian "Ministerratspräsidium," an office which had always retained a very special position in the Austrian Civil Service and attracted many men of great talent.

Wieser reports that Menger once told him that it was one of his duties to write surveys of the state of the markets for an official newspaper, the *Wiener Zeitung*, and that it was in studying the market reports that he was struck by the glaring contrast between the traditional theories of price and the facts which experienced practical men considered as decisive for the determination of prices. Whether this was really the original cause which led Menger to the study of the determination of prices or whether, which seems more likely, it only gave a definite direction to studies which he had been pursuing since he had left the university, we do not know. There can be little doubt, however, that during the years intervening between the date when he left the university and the publication of the *Grundsätze* he must have worked intensely on these problems, delaying publication until his system was fully worked out in his mind.[1]

He is said to have once remarked that he wrote the *Grundsätze* in a state of morbid excitement. This can hardly mean that this book was the product of a sudden inspiration, planned and written in great haste. Few books can have been more carefully planned; rarely has the first exposition of an idea been more painstakingly developed and followed up in all its ramifications. The slender volume which appeared early in 1871 was intended as a first, introductory part of a comprehensive treatise. It dealt with the fundamental questions, on which he disagreed with accepted opinion, with the exhaustiveness necessary to satisfy the author that he was building on absolutely firm ground. The problems treated in this "First, General Part," as it is

1. The earliest manuscript notes on the theory of value which have been preserved date from the year 1867.

described on the title page, were the general conditions which led to economic activity, value exchange, price, and money. From manuscript notes communicated by his son more than fifty years later, in the introduction to the second edition, we know that the second part was to treat "interest, wages, rent, income, credit, and paper money," a third "applied" part the theory of production and commerce, while a fourth part was to discuss criticism of the present economic system and proposals for economic reform.

His main aim, as he says in the preface, was a uniform theory of price which would explain all price phenomena and in particular also interest, wages, and rent by one leading idea. But more than half of the volume is devoted to matters which only prepare the way for that main task—to the concept which gave the new school its special character, *i.e.* value in its subjective, personal sense. And even this is not reached before a thorough examination of the main concepts with which economic analysis has to work.

The influence of the earlier German writers with their predilection for somewhat pedantic classifications and long-winded definitions of concepts is here clearly noticeable. But in Menger's hands the time-honoured "fundamental concepts" of the traditional German textbook assume new life. Instead of a dry enumeration and definition they become the powerful instrument of an analysis in which every step seems to result with inevitable necessity from the preceding one. And though Menger's exposition still lacks many of the more impressive phrases and elegant formulations of the writings of Böhm-Bawerk and Wieser, it is in substance hardly inferior and in many respects definitely superior to these later works.

It is not the purpose of the present introduction to give a connected outline of Menger's argument. But there are certain less known, somewhat surprising, aspects of his treatment which deserve special mention. The careful initial investigation of the causal relationship between human needs and the means for their satisfaction, which within the first few pages leads him to the now celebrated distinction between goods of the first, second, third and higher orders, and the now equally familiar concept of complementarity between different goods, is typical of the particular attention which, the widespread impression to the contrary notwithstanding, the Austrian School has always given to the technical structure of production—an attention which finds its clearest systematic expression in the elaborate "vorwerttheoretischer Teil" which precedes the discussion of the theory of value in Wieser's late work, the *Theory of Social Economy*, 1914.

Even more remarkable is the prominent rôle which the element of time plays from the very beginning. There is a very general impression that the earlier representatives of modern economics were inclined to neglect this factor. In so far as the originators of the mathematical exposition of modern equilibrium theory are concerned, this impression is probably justified. Not so with Menger. To him economic activity is essentially planning for the future, and his discussion of the period, or rather different periods, to which human forethought extends as regards different wants has a definitely modern ring.

It is somewhat difficult to believe now that Menger was the first to base the distinction between free and economic goods on the idea of scarcity. But, as he himself says, while the very concept was not known in the English literature, the German authors who had used it before him, and particularly Hermann, had all been trying to base the distinction on the presence or absence of cost in the sense of effort. But, very characteristically, while all of Menger's analysis is grounded on the idea of scarcity, this simple term is nowhere used. "Insufficient quantity" or "das ökonomische Mengenverhältnis" are the very exact but somewhat cumbersome expressions which he uses instead.

It is characteristic of his work as a whole that he attaches more importance to a careful description of a phenomenon than to giving it a short and fitting name. This frequently prevents his exposition from being as effective as might have been wished. But it also protects him against a certain one-sidedness and a tendency towards oversimplification to which a brief formula so easily leads. The classic instance of this is, of course, the fact that Menger did not originate— nor, so far as I know, ever use—the term marginal utility introduced by Wieser, but always explained value by the somewhat clumsy but precise phrase, "the importance which concrete goods, or quantities of goods, receive for us from the fact that we are conscious of being dependent on our disposal over them for the satisfaction of our wants," and describes the magnitude of this value as equal to the importance which attached to the least important satisfaction which is secured by a single unit of the available quantity of the commodity.

Another, perhaps less important but not insignificant instance of Menger's refusal to condense explanations in a single formula, occurs even earlier in the discussion of the decreasing intensity of individual wants with increasing satisfaction. This physiological fact, which later under the name of "Gossen's law of the satisfaction of wants" was to assume a somewhat disproportionate position in the exposition of the theory of value, and was even hailed by Wieser as Menger's main discovery, takes in Menger's system the more appropriate minor position as one of the factors which enable us to arrange the different individual sensations of want in order of their importance.

On yet another and a more interesting point in connection with the pure theory of subjective value Menger's views are remarkably modern. Although he speaks occasionally of value as measurable, his exposition makes it quite clear that by this he means no more than that the value of any one commodity can be expressed by naming another commodity of equal value. Of the figures which he uses to represent the scales of utility he says expressly that they are not intended to represent the absolute, but only the relative importance of the wants, and the very examples he gives when he first introduces them makes it perfectly clear that he thinks of them not as cardinal but as ordinal figures.[1]

Next to the general principle which enabled him to base the explanation of value on utility the most important of Menger's contributions is probably the application of this principle to the case where more than one good is required to secure the satisfaction of any want. It is here that the painstaking analysis of the causal relationship between goods and wants in the opening chapters and the concepts of complementarity and of goods or different orders bears its fruits. Even to-day it is hardly recognised that Menger answered the problem of the distribution of the utility of a final product between the several co-operating commodities of a higher order—the problem of imputation as it was later called by Wieser—by a fairly developed theory of marginal productivity. He distinguishes clearly between the case where the proportions in which two or more factors can be used in the production of any commodity are variable and the case where they are fixed. He answers the problem of imputation in the first case by saying that such quantities of the different factors as can be substituted for each other in order to get the same additional quantity of the product must have equal value, while in the case of fixed proportions he points out that the value of the different factors is determined by their utility in alternative uses.

In this first part of his book, which is devoted to the theory of subjective value, and compares well with the later exposition by Wieser, Böhm-Bawerk and others, there is really only one major point on which Menger's exposition leaves a serious gap. A theory of value can hardly be called complete and will certainly never be quite convincing if the rôle that cost of production plays in determining the relative value of different commodities is not explicitly explained.

---

1. Further aspects of Menger's treatment of the general theory of value which might be mentioned are his persistent emphasis on the necessity to classify the different commodities on economic rather than technical grounds, his distinct anticipation of the Böhm-Bawerkian doctrine of the underestimation of future wants, and his careful analysis of the process by which the accumulation of capital turns gradually more and more of the originally free factors into scarce goods.

At an early point of his exposition Menger indicates that he sees the problem and promises a later answer. But this promise is never fulfilled. It was left to Wieser to develop what later became known as the principle of opportunity cost or "Wieser's Law," *i.e.* the principle that the other uses competing for the factors will limit the quantity available for any one line of production in such a way that the value of the product will not fall below the sum of the value which all the factors used in its production obtain in these competing uses.

It has sometimes been suggested that Menger and his school were so pleased with their discovery of the principles governing value in the economy of an individual that they were inclined to apply the same principles in an all too rapid and over-simplified way to the explanation of price. There may be some justification for such a suggestion so far as the works of some of Menger's followers, particularly the younger Wieser, are concerned. But it certainly cannot be said of Menger's own work. His exposition completely conforms to the rule later so much emphasized by Böhm-Bawerk, that any satisfactory explanation of price would have to consist of two distinct and separate stages of which the explanation of subjective value is only the first. It only provides the basis for an explanation of the causes and limits of exchanges between two or more persons. Menger's arrangement in the *Grundsätze* is exemplary in this respect. The chapter on exchange which precedes that on price makes the influence of value in the subjective sense on the objective exchange relationships quite clear without postulating any greater degree of correspondence than is actually justified by the assumptions.

The chapter on price itself, with its careful investigation of how the relative valuations of the individual participants in the exchange themselves will affect the ratios of exchange in the case of an isolated exchange of two individuals, under conditions of monopoly and finally under conditions of competition, is the third and probably the least known of the main contributions of the *Grundsätze*. Yet it is only in reading this chapter that one realises the essential unity of his thought, the clear aim which directs his exposition from the beginning to this crowning achievement.

On the final chapters, which deal with the effects of production for a market, the technical meaning of the term "commodity" *(Ware)* as distinguished from the simple "good," their different degrees of saleability leading up to the introduction and discussion of money, little need be said at this point. The ideas contained here and the fragmentary remarks on capital contained in earlier sections are the only sections of this first work which were developed further in his printed work later on. Although they embody contributions, of lasting influence, it was mainly in their later, more elaborate exposition that they became known.

The considerable space devoted here to the discussion of the contents of the *Grundsätze* is justified by the outstanding character of this work among Menger's publications and, indeed, among all the books which have laid the foundations of modern economics. It is, perhaps, appropriate to quote in this connection the judgment of the scholar best qualified to assess the relative merits of the different variants of the modern school, of Knut Wicksell who was the first, and hitherto the most successful, to combine what is best in the teaching of the different groups. "His fame," he says, "rests on this work and through it his name will go down to posterity, for one can safely say that since Ricardo's *Principles* there has been no book—not even excepting Jevon's brilliant if rather aphoristic achievement and Walras's unfortunately difficult work—which has exercised such great influence on the development of economics as Menger's *Grundsätze*."[1]

But the immediate reception of the book can hardly be called encouraging. None of the reviewers in the German journals seem to have realised the nature of its main contribution.[2] At home Menger's attempt to obtain, on the strength of this work, a lectureship *(Privatdozentur)* at the University of Vienna succeeded only after some difficulty. He can scarcely have known that, just before he began his lectures, there had just left the University two young men who immediately recognised that his work provided the "Archimedian point," as Wieser called it, by which the existing systems of economic theory could be lifted out of their hinges. Böhm-Bawerk and Wieser, his first and most enthusiastic disciples, were never his direct pupils, and their attempt to popularise Menger's doctrines in the seminars of the leaders of the older historical school, Knies, Roscher, and Hildebrand was fruitless.[3] But Menger gradually succeeded in gaining considerable influence at home. Soon after his promotion to the rank

---

1. *Ekonomisk Tidskrift*, 1921, p. 118.
2. An exception should, perhaps, be made for Hack's review in the *Zeitschrift für die gesamte Staatswissenschaft*, 1872, who not only emphasized the excellence of the book and the novelty of its method of approach, but also pointed out as opposed to Menger that the economically relevant relationship between commodities and wants was not that of cause and effect but one of means and end.
3. It might not be altogether out of place to correct a wrong impression which may be created by A. Marshall's assertion that between the years 1870 and 1874, when he developed the details of his theoretical position, "Böhm-Bawerk and Wieser were still lads at school or college...." *(Memorials of Alfred Marshall*, p. 417). Both had left the University together and entered civil service in 1872, and in 1876 were already in a position to expound in reports to Knies's seminar in Heidelberg the main elements of their later contribution.

of *professor extraordinarius* in 1873 he resigned from his position in the prime minister's office, to the great surprise of his chief, Prince Auersperg, who found it difficult to understand that anybody should want to exchange a position with prospects to satisfy the greatest ambition for an academic career.[1] But this did not yet mean Menger's final *adieu* to the world of affairs. In 1876 he was appointed one of the tutors to the ill-fated Crown Prince Rudolph, then eighteen years of age, and accompanied him during the next two years on his extensive travels through the greater part of Europe, including England, Scotland, Ireland, France and Germany. After his return he was appointed in 1879 to the chair of political economy in Vienna, and thenceforward he settled down to the secluded and quiet life of the scholar which was to be so characteristic of the second half of his long life.

By this time the doctrines of his first book—apart from a few short reviews of books he had published nothing in the intervening period—were beginning to attract wider attention. Rightly or wrongly, with Jevons and Walras it was the mathematical form rather than the substance of their teaching which appeared to be their main innovation, and which contributed the chief obstacle to their acceptance. But there were no obstacles of this sort to an understanding of Menger's exposition of the new theory of value. During the second decade after the publication of the book, its influence began to extend with great rapidity. At the same time Menger began to acquire considerable reputation as a teacher, and to attract to his lectures and seminars an increasing number of students, many of whom soon became economists of considerable reputation. In addition to those already noted, among the early members of his school his contemporaries Emil Sax and Johann von Komorzynski, and his students Robery Meyer, Robert Zuckerkandl, Gustav Gross, and—at a somewhat later date—H. von Schullern-Schrattenhofen, Richard Reisch and Richard Schüller deserve special mention.

But, while at home a definite school was forming, in Germany, even more than in other foreign countries, economists maintained a hostile attitude. It was at this time that the younger Historical School, under the leadership of Schmoller, was gaining the greatest influence in that country. The *"Volkswirtschaftliche Kongress,"* which had preserved the classical tradition, was superseded by the newly founded *"Verein für Sozialpolitik."* Indeed the teaching of economic theory was more and more excluded from German universities. Thus

1. Menger had at that time already declined the offer of professorships in Karlsruhe (1872), Basel (1873), and a little later also declined an offer of a professorship in the Zürich Polytechnic with prospects to a simultaneous professorship at the University.

Menger's work was neglected, not because the German economists thought that he was wrong, but because they considered the kind of analysis he attempted was useless.

Under these conditions it was only natural that Menger should consider it more important to defend the method he had adopted against the claims of the Historical School to possess the only appropriate instrument of research, than to continue the work on the *Grundsätze*. It is to this situation that his second great work, the *Untersuchungen über die Methode der Socialwissenschaften und der politischen Oekonomie insbesondere* is due. It is well to remember that in 1875 when Menger started to work on that book, and even in 1883 when it was published, the rich crop of works by his disciples which definitely established the position of the school, had not yet begun to mature, and that he might well have thought that it would be wasted effort to continue while the question of principle was not decided.

In their way the *Untersuchungen* are hardly less an achievement than the *Grundsätze*. As a polemic against the claims of the Historical School to an exclusive right to treat economic problems the book can hardly be surpassed. Whether the merits of its positive exposition of the nature of theoretical analysis can be rated as high is, perhaps, not quite certain. If this were, indeed, its main title to fame there might be something in the suggestion occasionally heard among Menger's admirers that it was unfortunate that he was drawn away from his works on the concrete problems of economics. This is not to mean that what he said on the character of the theoretical or abstract method is not of very great importance or that it had not very great influence. Probably it did more than any other single book to make clear the peculiar character of the scientific method in the social sciences, and it had a very considerable effect on professional "methodologists" among German philosophers. But to me, at any rate, its main interest to the economist in our days seems to lie in the extraordinary insight into the nature of social phenomena which is revealed incidentally in the discussion of problems mentioned to exemplify different methods of approach, and in the light shed by his discussion of the development of the concepts with which the social sciences have to work. Discussions of somewhat obsolete views, as that of the organic or perhaps better physiological interpretation of social phenomena, give him an opportunity for an elucidation of the origin and character of social institutions which might, with advantage, be read by present-day economists and sociologists.

Of the central contentions of the book only one may be singled out for further comment; his emphasis on the necessity of a strictly individualistic or, as he generally says, atomistic method of analysis. It has been said of him by one of his most distinguished followers that "he himself always remained an individualist in the sense of the classical economists. His successors ceased to be so." It is doubtful whether this statement is true of more than one or two instances. But in any case it fails signally to give Menger full credit for the method he actually employed. What with the classical economists had remained something of a mixture between an ethical postulate and a methodological tool, was developed by him systematically in the latter direction. And if emphasis on the subjective element has been fuller and more convincing in the writings of the members of the Austrian School than in those of any other of the founders of modern economics, this is largely due to Menger's brilliant vindication in this book.

Menger had failed to arouse the German econoists with his first book. But he could not complain of neglect of his second. The direct attack on what was the only approved doctrine attracted immediate attention and provoked, among other hostile reviews, a magisterial rebuke from Gustav Schmoller, the head of the school—a rebuke couched in a tone more than usually offensive.[1] Menger accepted the challenge and replied in a passionate pamphlet, *Irrthümer des Historismus in der deutschen Nationalokönomie*, written in the form of letters to a friend, in which he ruthlessly demolished Schmoller's position. The pamphlet adds little in substance to the *Untersuchungen*. But it is the best instance of the extraordinary power and brilliance of expression which Menger could achieve when he was engaged, not on building up an academic and complicated argument, but on driving home the points of a straightforward debate.

The encounter between the masters was soon imitated by their disciples. A degree of hostility not often equalled in scientific controversy was created. The crowning offence from the Austrian point of view was given by Schmoller himself who, on the appearance of Menger's pamphlet, took the probably unprecedented step of announcing in his journal that, although he had received a copy of the book for review, he was unable to review it because he had immediately returned it to the author, and reprinting the insulting letter with which the returned copy had been accompanied.

It is necessary to realise fully the passion which this controversy aroused, and what the break with the ruling school in Germany

1. "Zur Methodologie der Staats-und Sozialwissenschaften," in *Jahrbuch für Gesetzgebung, Verwaltung und Volkswirtschaft im deutschen Reich*, 1883. In the reprint of this article in Schmoller's *Zur Litteraturgeschichte der Staats-und Sozialwissenschaften*, 1888, the most offensive passages have been mitigated.

meant to Menger and his followers, if we are to understand why the problem of the adequate methods remained the dominating concern of most of Menger's later life. Schmoller, indeed, went so far as to declare publicly that members of the "abstract" school were unfit to fill a teaching position in a German university, and his influence was quite sufficient to make this equivalent to a complete exclusion of all adherents to Menger's doctrines from academic positions in Germany. Even thirty years after the close of the controversy Germany was still less affected by the new ideas now triumphant elsewhere, than any other important country in the world.

In spite of these attacks, however, in the six years from 1884 to 1889 there appeared in rapid succession the books which finally established the reputation of the Austrian School the world over. Böhm-Bawerk, indeed, had already in 1881 published his small but important study on *Rechte und Verhältnisse vom Standpunkt der wirtschaftlichen Güterlehre*, but it was only with the simultaneous publications of the first part of his work on capital, the *Geschichte und Kritik der Kapitalzinstheorien*, and of Wieser's *Ursprung und Hauptgesetze des wirtschaftlichen Wertes* in 1884 that it became apparent how powerful a support to Menger's doctrines had arisen in this quarter. Of these two works Wieser's was undoubtedly the more important for the further development of Menger's fundamental ideas, since it contained the essential application to the cost phenomenon, now known as Wieser's law of cost, to which reference has already been made. But two years later appeared Böhm-Bawerk's *Grundzüge einer Theorie des wirtschaftlichen Güterwertes*[1] which, although it adds little except by way of casuistic elaboration to the work of Menger and Wieser, by the great lucidity and force of its argument has probably done more than any other single work to popularise the marginal utility doctrine. In the year 1884 two of Menger's immediate pupils, V. Mataja and G. Gross, had published their interesting books on profits, and E. Sax contributed a small but acute study on the question of method in which he supported Menger in his fundamental attitude but criticised him on some points of detail.[2] In 1887 Sax made his main contribution to the development of the Austrian School by the publication of his *Grundlegung der theoretischen Staatswirtschaft*, the first and most exhaustive attempt

---

1. Originally a series of articles in (Conrad's) *Jahrbücher* it has recently been reprinted as No. 11 of the *Series of Reprints of Scarce Tracts in Economics and Political Science*, published by the London School of Economics (1932).
2. V. Mataja, *Der Unternehmergewinn*, Vienna, 1884; G. Gross, *Lehre vom Unternehmergewinn*, Leipzig, 1884; E. Sax, *Das Wesen und die Aufgaben der Nationalökonomie*, Vienna, 1884.

to apply the marginal utility principle to the problems of public finance, and in the same year another of Menger's early students, Robert Meyer, entered the field with his investigation of the somewhat cognate problem of the nature of income.[1]

But the richest crop was that of the year 1889. In this year was published Böhm-Bawerk's *Positive Theorie des Kapitalzinses*, Wieser's *Natürlicher Wert*, Zuckerkandl's *Zur Theorie des Preises*, Komorzynski's *Wert in der isolierten Wirtschaft*, Sax's *Neueste Fortschritte der nationalökonomischen Theorie*, and H. von Schullern-Schrattenhofen's *Untersuchungen über Begriff und Wesen der Grundrente.*[2]

Perhaps the most successful early exposition of the doctrines of the Austrian School in a foreign language was M. Pantalconi's *Pure Economics* which appeared first in the same year.[3] Of other Italian economists L. Cossa, A. Graziani and G. Mazzola accepted most or all of Menger's doctrines. Similar success attended these doctrines in Holland where the acceptance by the great Dutch economist, N.G. Pierson, of the marginal utility doctrine in his textbook (1884-1889), published later in English under the title *Principles of Economics*, had also considerable influence. In France Ch. Gide, E. Villey, Ch. Secrétan and M. Block spread the new doctrine, and in the United States S.N. Patten and Professor Richard Ely had received it with great sympathy. Even the first edition of A. Marshall's *Principles*, which appeared in 1890, showed a considerably stronger influence of Menger and his group than readers of the later editions of that great work would suspect. And in the next few years Smart and Dr. Bonar, who had already earlier shown their adherence to the school, widely popularised the work of the Austrian School in the English-speaking

1. Robert Meyer, *Das Wesen des Einkommens*, Berlin, 1887.
2. In the same year two other Viennese economists, R. Auspitz and R. Lieben, published their *Untersuchungen über die Theorie des Preises*, still one of the most important works of mathematical economics. But although they were strongly influenced by the work of Menger and his group, they build rather on the foundations laid by Cournot and Thünen, Gossen, Jevons and Walras than on the work of their compatriots.
3. Maffeo Pantaleoni, *Principii di Economia Pura*, Firenze, 1889 (2nd ed. 1894), English translation, London, 1894. An unjust remark in the Italian edition accusing Menger of plagiarism of Cournot, Gossen, Jennings, and Jevons was eliminated in the English edition and Pantaleoni later made amends by editing, with an introduction from his pen, an Italian translation of the *Grundsätze*, cf. C. Menger, *Principii fondamentali di economia pura*, con prefazione di Maffeo Pantaleoni, Imola, 1909 (first published as a supplement to the *Giornale degli Economisti* in 1906 and 1907 without the preface of Pantaleoni). The preface is also reprinted in the Italian translation of the second edition of the *Grundsätze* (to be mentioned below) which was published at Bari, 1925.

world.[1] But, and this brings us back to the special position of Menger's work, it was now not so much his writings as those of his pupils which continuously gained in popularity. The main reason for this was simply that Menger's *Grundsätze* had for some time been out of print and difficult to procure, and that Menger refused to permit either a reprint or a translation. He hoped to replace it soon by a much more elaborate "system" of economics and was, in any case, unwilling to have the work republished without considerable revision. But other tasks claimed his prior attention, and for years led to a continual postponement of this plan.

Menger's direct controversy with Schmoller had come to an abrupt end in 1884. But the *Methodenstreit* was carried on by others, and the problems involved continued to claim his main attention. The next occasion which induced him to make a public pronouncement on these questions was the publication, in 1885 and 1886, of a new edition of Schönberg's *Handbuch der politischen Oekonomie*, a collective work in which a number of German economists, most of them not convinced adherents to the Historical School, had combined to produce a systematic exposition of the whole field of political economy. Menger reviewed the work for a Viennese legal journal in an article which also appeared as a separate pamphlet under the title *Zur Kritik der politischen Oekonomie* (1887).[2] Its second half is largely devoted to the discussion of the classification of the different disciplines commonly grouped together under the name of political economy, a theme which, two years later, he treated more exhaustively in another article entitled *Grundzüge einer Klassifikation der Wirtschaftswissenschaften*.[3] In the intervening year, however, he published one of his two further contributions to the substance—as ddistinguished from the methodology—of economic theory, his important study, *Zur Theorie des Kapitals*.[4]

It is pretty certain that we owe this article to the fact that Menger did not quite agree with the definition of the term capital which was implied in the first, historical part of Böhm-Bawerk's *Capital and Interest*. The discussion is not polemical. Böhm-Bawerk's book is

1. Cf. particularly J. Bonar, "The Austrian Economists and their Views on Value," *Quarterly Journal of Economics*, 1888, and "The Positive Theory of Capital," *ibid*, 1889.
2. The original review article appeared in (Grünhut's) *Zeitschrift für das Privatund öffentliche Recht der Gegenwart*, vol. xiv, the separate pamphlet, Vienna, 1887.
3. See (Conrad's) *Jahrbücher für Nationalökonomie und Statistik*, N F., vol. xiv, Jena, 1889.
4. In the same journal, N.F., vol. xvii, Jena, 1888. An abridged French translation, by Ch. Secrétan appeared in the same year in the *Revue d'Économie Politique* under the title "Contribution a la théorie du capital."

mentioned only to commend it. But its main aim is clearly to rehabilitate the abstract concept of capital as the money value of the property devoted to acquisitive purposes against the Smithian concept of the "produced means of production." His main argument that the distinction of the historical origin of a commodity is irrelevant from an economic point of view, as well as his emphasis on the necessity of clearly distinguishing between the rent obtained from already existing instruments of production and interest proper, refer to points which, even to-day, have not yet received quite the attention they deserve.

It was at about the same time, in 1889, that Menger was almost persuaded by his friends not to postpone further the publication of a new edition of the *Grundsätze*. But although he actually wrote a new preface to that new edition (excerpts from which have been printed more than thirty years later by his son in the introduction to the actual second edition), nevertheless publication was again postponed. Soon after a new set of publications emerged, which absorbed his main attention and occupied him for the next two years.

Towards the end of the 'eighties the perennial Austrian currency problem had assumed a form where a drastic final reform seemed to become both possible and necessary. In 1878 and 1879 the fall of the price of silver had first brought the depreciated paper currency back to its silver parity and soon afterwards made it necessary to discontinue the free coinage of silver; since then the Austrian paper money had gradually appreciated in terms of silver and fluctuated in terms of gold. The situation during that period—in many respects one of the most interesting in monetary history—was more and more regarded as unsatisfactory, and as the financial position of Austria seemed for the first time for a long period strong enough to promise a period of stability, the Government was generally expected to take matters in hand. Moreover, the treaty concluded with Hungary in 1887 actually provided that a commission should immediately be appointed to discuss the preparatory measures necessary to make the resumption of specie payments possible. After considerable delay, due to the usual political difficulties between the two parts of the dual monarchy, the commission, or rather commisions, one for Austria and one for Hungary, were appointed and met in March 1892, in Vienna and Budapest respectively.

The discussions of the Austrian "Währungs-Enquete-Commission," of which Menger was the most eminent member, are of considerable interest quite apart from the special historical situation with which they had to deal. As the basis of their transactions the Austrian Ministry of Finance had prepared with extraordinary care three voluminous memoranda, which contain probably the most complete collection available of documentary material for monetary history of the preceding period which has appeared in any publication.[1] Among the members besides Menger there were other well-known economists, such as Sax, Lieben and Mataja, and a number of journalists, bankers and industrialists, such as Benedikt, Hertzka and Taussig, all of whom had a more than ordinary knowledge of monetary problems, while Böhm-Bawerk, then in the Ministry of Finance, was one of the Government representatives and vice-chairman. The task of the commission was not to prepare a report, but to hear and discuss the views of its members on a number of questions put to them by the Government.[2] These questions concerned the basis of the future currency, the retention, in the case of the adoption of the Gold Standard, of the existing silver and paper circulation, the ratio of exchange between the existing paper florin and gold, and the nature of the new unit to be adopted.

Menger's mastery of the problem, no less than his gift of clear exposition, gave him immediately a leading position in the commission and his statement attracted the widest attention. It even achieved what, for an economist, was perhaps the unique distinction of causing a temporary slump on the stock exchange. His contribution consisted not so much in his discussion of the general question of the choice of the standard—here he agreed with practically all the members of the commission that the adoption of the Gold Standard was the only practical course—but in his careful discussion on the practical problems of the exact parity to be chosen and the moment of time to be selected for the transition. It is mainly for his evaluation of these practical difficulties connected with any transition to a new standard of currency, and the survey of the different considerations that have to be taken into account, that his evidence is rightly celebrated. It has extraordinarily topical interest to-day, where similar problems have to be faced by almost all countries.[3]

1. *Denkschrift über den Gang der Währungsfrage seit dem Jahre 1867.—Denkschrift über das Papiergeldwesen der österreichisch-ungarischen Monarchie.—Statistische Tabellen zur Währungsfrage der österreichisch-ungarischen Monarchie.* All published by the k.k. Finanzministerium, Vienna, 1892.

2. Cf. *Stenographische Protokolle über die vom 8. bis 17. Marz 1892 abgehaltenen Sitzungen der nach Wien einberufenen Währungs-Enquete-Commission.* Wien, k.k. Hof- und Staatsdruckerei, 1892. Shortly before the commission met Menger had already outlined the main problems in a public lecture, "Von unserer Valuta," which appeared in the *Allgemeine Juristen Zeitung*, Nos. 12 and 13 of the volume for 1892.

3. It is unfortunately impossible, within the scope of this introduction, to devote to this important episode in currency history the space it deserves because of its close

This evidence, the first of a series of contributions to monetary problems, was the final and mature product of several years of concentration on these questions. The results of these were published in rapid succession in the course of the same year—a year during which there appeared a greater number of publications from Menger's hand than at any other period of his life. The results of his investigations into the special problems of Austria appeared as two separate pamphlets. The first, entitled *Beiträge zur Währungsfrage in Oesterreich-Ungarn*, and dealing with the history and the peculiarities of the Austrian currency problem and the general question of the standard to be adopted, is a revised reprint of a series of articles which appeared earlier in the year in Conrad's *Jahrbücher* under a different title.[1] The second, called *Der Uebergang zur Goldwährung. Untersuchungen über die Wertprobleme der österreichisch-ungarischen Valutareform* (Vienna, 1892), treats essentially the technical problems connected with the adoption of a Gold Standard, particularly the choice of the appropriate parity and the factors likely to affect the value of the currency once the transition had been made.

But the same year also saw the publication of a much more general treatment of the problems of money which was not directly concerned with the special question of the day, and which must be ranked as the third and last of Menger's main contributions to economic theory. This was the article on money in volume iii of the first edition of the *Handwörterbuch der Staatswissenschaften* which was then in the process of publication. It was his preoccupation with the extensive investigations carried out in connection with the preparation of this elaborate exposition of the general theory of money, investigations which must have occupied him for the preceding two or three years, which brought it about that the beginning of the discussion of the special Austrian problems found Menger so singularly equipped to deal with them. He had, of course, always been strongly interested in monetary problems. The last chapter of the *Grundsätze* and parts of the *Untersuchungen über die Methode* contain important contributions, particularly on the question of the origin of money. It should also be noted that, among the numerous review articles which Menger used to write for daily newspapers, particularly in his early

connection with Menger and his school and because of the general interest of the problems which were discussed. It would be well worth a special study and it is very regrettable that no history of the discussions and measures of that period exists. In addition to the official publications mentioned before, the writings of Menger provide the most important material for such a study.

1. "Die Valutaregulierung in Oesterreich-Ungarn," (Conrad's) *Jahrbücher für Nationalökonomie und Statistik*, III, F., vols. iii and iv, 1892.

years, there are two in 1873 which deal in great detail with J.E.
Cairnes's *Essays* on the effects of the gold discoveries: in some respects
Menger's later views are nearly related to those of Cairnes.[1] But while
Menger's earlier contributions, particularly the introduction of the
concepts of the different degrees of "saleability" of commodities as
the basis for the understanding of the functions of money, would have
secured him an honourable position in the history of monetary
doctrines, it was only in this last major publication that he made his
main contribution to the central problem of the value of money.
Until the work of Professor Mises twenty years later, the direct continuation of Menger's work, this article remained the main
contribution of the "Austrian School" to the theory of money. It is
worth while dwelling a little on the nature of this contribution, for it
is a matter on which there is still much misunderstanding. It is often
thought that the Austrian contribution consists only of a somewhat
mechanical attempt to apply the marginal utility principle to the
problem of the value of money. But this is not so. The main Austrian
achievement in this field is the consistent application to the theory of
money of the peculiar subjective or individualistic approach which,
indeed, underlies the marginal utility analysis, but which has a much
wider and more universal significance. Such an achievement springs
directly from Menger. His exposition of the meaning of the different
concepts of the value of money, the causes of changes and the possibility of a measurement of this value, as well as his discussion of the
factors determining the demand for money, all seem to me to represent a most significant advance beyond the traditional treatment of
the quantity theory in terms of aggregates and averages. And even
where, as in the case of his familiar distinction between the "inner"
and the "outer" value *(innerer und äusserer Tauschwert)* of money,
the actual terms employed are somewhat misleading—the distinction
does not, as would appear from the terms, refer to different kinds of
value but to the different forces which affect prices—the underlying
concept of the problem is extraordinarily modern.

With the publications of the year 1892[2] the list of Menger's major
works which appeared during his lifetime comes to an abrupt end.

---

1. These articles appeared in the *Wiener Abendpost* (a supplement to the *Wiener
   Zeitung)* of April 30th and June 19th, 1873. As is the case with all the early
   journalistic work of Menger, they are anonymous.
2. In addition to those already mentioned there appeared in the same year a French
   article, "La Monnaie Mesure de la Valeur," in the *Revue d'Économie Politique*
   (vol. vi) and an English article, "On the Origin of Money," in the *Economic
   Journal* (vol. ii).

During the remaining three decades of his life he only published occasional small articles, a complete list of which will be found in the bibliography of his writings at the end of the last volume of the present edition of his collected works. For a few years these publications were still mainly concerned with money. Of these, his lecture on *Das Goldagio und der heutige Stand der Valutareform* (1893), his article on money and coinage in Austria since 1857 in the *Oesterreichische Staatswörterbuch* (1897), and particularly the thoroughly revised edition of his article on money in volume four of the second edition of the *Handwörterbuch der Staatswissenschaften* (1900),[1] ought to be specially mentioned. The latter publications are mainly of the character of reviews, biographical notes or introductions to works published by his pupils. His last published article is an obituary of his disciple Böhm-Bawerk, who died in 1914.

The reason for this apparent inactivity is clear. Menger now wanted to concentrate entirely on the major tasks which he had set himself—the long postponed systematic work on economics, and beyond this a comprehensive treatise on the character and methods of the social sciences in general. It was to the completion of this work that his main energy was devoted and in the late 'nineties he looked forward to a publication in the near future and considerable parts were ready in a definite form. But his interests and the scope of the proposed work continued to expand to wider and wider circles. He found it necessary to go far in the study of other disciplines. Philosophy, psychology and ethnography claimed more and more of his time, and the publication of the work was again and again postponed. In 1903 he went so far as to resign from his chair at the comparatively early age of 63 in order to be able to devote himself entirely to his work.[2] But he was never satisfied and seems to have continued to work on it in the increasing seclusion of his old age until he died in 1921 at the advanced age of 81. An inspection of his manuscript has shown that, at one time, considerable parts of the work must have been ready for publication. But even after his powers had begun to fail he continued to revise and rearrange the manuscripts to such an extent that any attempt to reconstruct this would be a very difficult, if not an impossible task. Some of the material dealing with the subject-matter of the *Grundsätze* and partly

---

1. The reprint of the same article in vol. iv of the third edition of the *Handwörterbuch* (1909) contains only small stylistic changes compared with the second edition.
2. In consequence, almost all the living representatives of the "Austrian School," like Professors H. Mayer, L. von Mises and J. Schumpeter, were not direct pupils of Menger but of Böhm-Bawerk or Wieser.

intended for a new edition of this work, has been incorporated by his son in a second edition of this work, published in 1923.[1] Much more, however, remains in the form of voluminous but fragmentary and disordered manuscripts, which only the prolonged and patient efforts of a very skillful editor could made accessible. For the present, at any rate, the results of the work of Menger's later years must be regarded as lost.

•   •   •   •   •

For one who can hardly claim to have known Carl Menger in person it is a hazardous undertaking to add to this sketch of his scientific career an appreciation of his character and personality. But as so little about him is generally known to the present generation of economists, and since there is no comprehensive literary portrait available,[2] an attempt to piece together some of the impressions recorded by his friends and students, or preserved by the oral tradition in Vienna, may not be altogether out of place. Such impressions naturally relate to the second half of his life, to the period when he had ceased to be in active contact with the world of affairs, and when he had already taken to the quiet and retired life of the scholar, divided only between his teaching and his research.

The impression left on a young man by one of those rare occasions when the almost legendary figure became accessible is well reproduced in the well-known engraving of F. Schmutzer. It is possible, indeed, that one's image of Menger owes as much to this masterly portrait as to memory. The massive, well-modelled head, with the clossal forehead and the strong but clear lines there delineated are not easily forgotten. Tall, with a wealth of hair and full beard, in his prime Menger must have been a man of extraordinarily impressive appearance.

In the years after his retirement it became a tradition that young economists entering upon an academic career undertook the pilgrimage to his home. They would be genially received by Menger among his books and drawn into conversation about the life which he had known so well, and from which he had withdrawn after it had given him all he had wanted. In a detached way he preserved a keen interest

---

1. *Grundsätze der Volkswirtschaftslehre* von Carl Menger, Zweite Auflage mit einem Geleitwort von Richard Schüller aus dem Nachlass herausgegeben von Karl Menger, Wien, 1923. A full discussion of the changes and additions made in this edition will be found in F.X. Weiss, "Zur zweiten Auflage von Carl Mengers Grundsätzen," *Zeitschrift für Volkswirtschaft und Sozialpolitik*, N.F., vol. iv, 1924.

2. Of shorter sketches those by F. von Wieser in the *Neue österreichische* Biographie, 1923, and by R. Zuckerkandl in the *Zeitschrfit für Volkswirtschaft, Sozialpolitik und Verwaltung*, vol. xix, 1911, ought to be specially mentioned.

in economics and university life to the end and when, in the later years, failing eyesight had defeated the indefatigable reader, he would expect to be informed by the visitor about the work he had done. In these late years he gave the impression of a man who, after a long active life, continued his pursuits not to carry out any duty or self-imposed task, but for the sheer intellectual pleasure of moving in the element which had become his own. In his later life, perhaps, he conformed somewhat to the popular conception of the scholar who has no contact with real life. But this was not due to any limitation of his outlook. It was the result of a deliberate choice at a mature age and after rich and varied experience.

For Menger had lacked neither the opportunity nor the external signs of distinction to make him a most influential figure in public life, if he had cared. In 1900 he had been made a life member of the upper chamber of the Austrian Parliament. But he did not care sufficiently to take a very active part in its deliberations. To him the world was a subject for study much more than for action, and it was for this reason only that he had intensely enjoyed watching it at close range. In his written work one can search in vain for any expressions of his political views. Actually, he tended to conservatism or liberalism of the old type. He was not without sympathy for the movement for social reform, but social enthusiasm would never interfere with his cold reasoning. In this, as in other respects, he seems to have presented a curious contrast to his more passionate brother Anton.[1] Hence it is mainly as one of the most successful teachers at the

---

1. The two brothers were regular members of a group which met in the 'eighties and 'nineties almost daily in a coffee-house opposite the University and which consisted originally mainly of journalists and business men, but later increasingly of Carl Menger's former pupils and students. It was through this circle that, at least until his retirement from the University, he mainly retained contact with, and exercised some influence on, current affairs. The contrast between the two brothers is well described by one of his most distinguished pupils, R. Sieghart. (Cf. the latter's *Die letzen Jahrzehnte einer Grossmacht*, Berlin, 1932, p. 21): "Wahrlich ein seltsames und seltenes Brüderpaar die beiden Menger; Carl, Begründer der österreichischen Schule der Nationalökonomie, Entdecker des wirtschaftspsychologischen Gesetzes vom Grenznutzen, Lehrer des Kronprinzen Rudolf, in den Anfängen seiner Laufbahn auch Journalist, die grosse Welt kennend wenn auch fliehend, seine Wissenschaft revolutionierend, aber als Politiker eher konservativ; auf der anderen Seite Anton, weltfremd, seinem eigenen Fach, dem bürgerlichen Recht und Zivilprozess, bei glänzender Beherrschung der Materie immer mehr abgewandt, dafür zunehmend mit sozialen Problemen und ihrer Lösung durch den Staat befasst, glühend eingenommen von den Fragen des Sozialismus. Carl völlig klar, jederman verständlich, nach Ranke's Art abgeklärt; Anton schwieriger zu verfolgen, aber sozialen Problemen in allen ihren Erscheinungsformen—im bürgerlichen Recht, in Wirtschaft und Staat—zugewandt. Ich habe von Carl Menger die nationalökonomische Methode gelernt, aber die Probleme, die ich mir stellte, kamen aus Anton Mengers Hand."

University that Menger is best remembered by generations of students, and that he has indirectly had enormous influence on Austrian public life.[1] All reports agree in the praise of his transparent lucidity of exposition. The following account of his impression by a young American economist who attended Menger's lectures in the winter 1892-93 may be reproduced here as representative: "Professor Menger carries his fifty-three years lightly enough. In lecturing he rarely uses his notes except to verify a quotation or a date. His ideas seem to come to him as he speaks and are expressed in language so clear and simple, and emphasised with gestures so appropriate, that it is a pleasure to follow him. The student feels that he is being led instead of driven, and when a conclusion is reached it comes into his mind not as something from without, but as the obvious consequence of his own mental process. It is said that those who attend Professor Menger's lectures regularly need no other preparation for their final examination in political economy, and I can readily believe it. I have seldom, if ever, heard a lecturer who possessed the same talent for combining clearness and simplicity of statement with philosophical breadth of view. His lectures are seldom 'over the heads' of his dullest students, and yet always contain instruction for the brightest."[2] All his students retain a particularly vivid memory of the sympathetic and thorough treatment of the history of economic doctrines, and mimeographed copies of his lectures on public finance were still sought after by the student twenty years after he had retired, as the best preparation for the examinations.

His great gifts as a teacher were, however, best shown in his seminar where a select circle of advanced students and many men who had long ago taken their doctor's degree assembled. Sometimes, when practical questions were discussed, the seminar was organised on parliamentary lines with appointed main speakers *pro* and *contra* a measure. More frequently, however, a carefully prepared paper by one of the members was the basis of long discussions. Menger left the students to do most of the talking, but he took infinite pains in assisting in the preparations of the papers. Not only would he put his library completely at the disposal of the students, and even bought for

1. The number of men who at one time or another, belonged to the more intimate circle of Menger's pupils and later made a mark in Austrian public life is extra- orindarily large. To mention only a few of those who have also contributed some form to the technical literature of economics, the names of K. Adler, St. Bauer, M. Dub, M. Ettinger, M. Garr, V. Graetz, I. von Gruber-Menninger, A. Krasny, G. Kunwald, J. Landesberger, W. Rosenberg, H. Schwarzwald, E. Schwiedland, R. Sieghart, E. Seidler and R. Thurnwald may be added to those mentioned earlier in the text.

2. H. R. Seager, "Economics at Berlin and Vienna," *Journal of Political Economy*, vol. i, March, 1893, reprinted in *Labor and other Essays*, New York, 1931.

them books specially needed, but he would go through the manuscript with them many times, discussing not only the main questions and the organisation of the paper, but even "teaching them elocution and the technique of breathing."[1]

For newcomers it was, at first, difficult to get into closer contact with Menger. But once he had recognised a special talent and received the student into the select circle of the seminar he would spare no pains to help him on with his work. The contact between Menger and his seminar was not confined to academic discussions. He frequently invited the seminar to a Sunday excursion into the country or asked individual students to accompany him on his fishing expeditions. Fishing, in fact, was the only pastime in which he indulged. Even here he approached the subject in the scientific spirit he brought to everything else, trying to master every detail of its technique and to be familiar with its literature.

It would be difficult to think of Menger as having a real passion which was not in some way connected with the dominating purpose of his life, the study of economics. Outside the direct study of his subject, however, there was a further preoccupation hardly less absorbing, the collection and preservation of his library. So far as its economic section is concerned this library must be ranked as one of the three or four greatest libraries ever formed by a private collector. But it comprised by no means only economics, and its collections on ethnography and philosophy were nearly as rich. After his death the greater part of this library, including all economics and ethnography, went to Japan and is now preserved as a separate part of the library of the school of economics in Tokyo. That part of the published catalogue which deals with economics alone contains more than 20,000 entries.[2]

It was not given to Menger to realise the ambition of his later years and to finish the great treatise which, he hoped, would be the crowning achievement of his work. But he had the satisfaction of seeing his great early work bearing the richest fruit, and to the end he retained an intense and never flagging enthusiasm for the chosen object of his study. The man who is able to say, as it is reported he once said, that if he had seven sons, they should all study economics, must have been extraordinarily happy in his work. That he had the gift to inspire a similar enthusiasm in his pupils is witnessed by the host of distinguished economists who were proud to call him their master.

1. Cf. V. Graetz, "Carl Menger," *Neues Wiener Tagblatt*, February 27th, 1921.

2. *Katalog der Carl Menger-Bibliothek in der Handelsuniversität Tokio.* Erster Teil. Sozialwissenschaften. Tokio, 1926 (731 pp).

To ANYONE barely acquainted with the development of present-day economic theory we need hardly explain why we undertook the task of translating Carl Menger's *Grundsätze der Volkwirthschaftslehre*. In this work Menger first stated the central propositions that were to form the theoretical core around which the economics of the Austrian School developed. His work served as the basic text of successive generations of Austrian students and scholars. That economists in Sweden and Italy found direct inspiration in the *Grundsätze* (both in the original German and in translation) goes some distance, moreover, toward explaining the excellence of economic theorizing in these two countries. But English-speaking economists were not so fortunate in this respect. Relying upon second-hand expositions of Menger's ideas, and lacking direct contact with his treatise in a language that could be read by more than a few, they failed to obtain the full benefit of his innovations. From the vantage point of the present day, this fact must be regretted. Menger's chief contribution to economics was his statement of marginal utility theory and his integration of it into value and price theory, and it is readily granted that this function was performed in England largely by the works of Jevons and Marshall. But some of the blind spots of English economics might have been avoided if Menger's treatment of bilateral monopoly, of the relation of monopoly to competition, and of the marketability of commodities as a foundation for the theory of money had been easily available to English-speaking scholars. As it was, imperfect competition and the role of liquidity in monetary theory became explicit theoretical concerns of English-speaking writers only in the 1930's.

The fact that the *Grundsätze* has remained untranslated into English for almost 80 years must therefore be considered a mystery. While we are unable to offer a complete solution to this mystery, we nevertheless feel (and most acutely!) that we have earned the right to offer at least a partial solution. For Menger's book is more than normally difficult to translate, and it seems possible, to us at any rate, that this fact may well have discouraged earlier attempts to translate it.

The difficulties we have encountered may be attributed in part to the fact that Menger was a pioneer attempting to express ideas and concepts for which he could find no exact words in the German economic literature of his day. He therefore coined a considerable number of new expressions, many of which have been superseded by more modern terms—this is not to imply that his *ideas* had only a transitory influence, but merely that a more apt terminology for their expression was later devised. In a number of instances these expressions were untranslatable compounds or words for which no exact English equivalents exist. A more serious difficulty was the fact that Menger's style is unusually cumbersome, even for German. His constructions form complicated patterns of clauses within clauses; they are filled with pronominal referents to these clauses; and they abound in agglomerations of adverbial fillers. Many of his sentences run half a page or more and expound several independent thoughts which, due to the tight grammatical fusion, can be separated by a translator only with the expenditure of much effort and ingenuity. It is suggested that these peculiarities of Menger's style may in part be attributed to his exposure to the heavy officialese current in his day among Austrian civil servants.

The translation presented here is a complete rendering of the first edition of the *Grundsätze* which was published in Vienna in 1871. A second German edition was published in Vienna in 1923, two years after Menger's death. We rejected the possibility of a *variorum* translation because it was the first edition only that influenced the development of economic doctrine, because of the posthumous character of the second edition, and because the numerous differences between the two editions make a *variorum* translation impractical.

While our translation is complete, we have eliminated Menger's excessively long footnotes (several of which occupy from three to five pages each) by transferring the material of these notes either to appendices or to the text itself. All such transfers have been indicated in notes at the appropriate points. In general, we have placed footnotes of a bibliographical character in appendices, and have placed in the text only material that is really an integral part of it. There were no appendices in the original. The titles of the appendices have been supplied by us.

Menger's bibliographical references and citations posed a special problem. In his time, not only was there no standardized method of giving citations, but a quite general spirit of carelessness prevailed. Menger was neither more nor less guilty in this respect than the bulk of his contemporaries. If we had given his citations without verification and without change, they would have been unreliable and to some extent useless. Moreover, the editions of standard authors used by Menger are now, in many instances, unavailable or extremely scarce. We have checked all citations and references, and were successful in verifying all but some half dozen which we have noted as they occur. We have substituted references to modern standard editions for all references given by Menger to inaccessible editions. Thus all references to Adam Smith, Ricardo, and Roscher are given in terms of the Modern Library edition of the *Wealth of Nations,* the Gonner edition of Ricardo's *Principles,* and the twentieth edition of Roscher's *System.*

Another problem was posed by the fact that Menger gives verbatim quotations from other writers in several different languages, principally German, French, and Latin. We have preferred to leave these quotations in the original languages in which they were given, but have supplied English translations in footnotes whenever it appeared that a translation might prove helpful.

Translators' footnotes have all been labeled as such in order to avoid any possible confusion between Menger's notes and our own. We have attempted to keep our own notes to a minimum. Most of them record the transfers already mentioned of material from the overlong footnotes of the original to appendices or to the text, or explain the translations we have given to especially troublesome words. In only a few instances have we taken the liberty of commenting upon the text, and in these instances we did so because we felt that some obscurity could thereby be eliminated.

We have prepared an index which we hope may prove useful. Although we have in general used Menger's terms in the selection of entry headings, there were a number of instances in which we felt that strict adherence to this rule would unduly limit the usefulness of the index to present-day readers. We do not, therefore, necessarily represent any index heading as a term used by Menger himself.

We wish to thank Professor Frank H. Knight for his introduction to our translation and Professor Friedrich A. von Hayek for his constant encouragement. We are indebted to Mrs. Edna Dombrovsky, Mr. E. L. Pattullo, and Miss Elizabeth Sterenberg for the typing of the manuscript, to Miss Elizabeth Sterenberg in addition for her assistance in the location of references, and to the Social Science Research Committee of the University of Chicago for a grant to finance the typing of the manuscript.

JAMES DINGWALL
BERT F. HOSELITZ

PRINCIPLES OF ECONOMICS

Dedicated by the author
with respectful esteem
to
DR. WILHELM ROSCHER
Royal Saxonian Councillor
Professor of Political and Cameral Sciences
at the
University of Leipzig

THE IMPARTIAL observer can have no doubt about the reason our generation pays general and enthusiastic tribute to progress in the field of the natural sciences, while economic science receives little attention and its value is seriously questioned by the very men in society to whom it should provide a guide for practical action.

Never was there an age that placed economic interests higher than does our own. Never was the need of a scientific foundation for economic affairs felt more generally or more acutely. And never was the ability of practical men to utilize the achievements of science, in all fields of human activity, greater than in our day. If practical men, therefore, rely wholly on their own experience, and disregard our science in its present

45

state of development, it cannot be due to a lack of serious interest or ability on their part. Nor can their disregard be the result of a haughty rejection of the deeper insight a true science would give into the circumstances and relationships determining the outcome of their activity. The cause of such remarkable indifference must not be sought elsewhere than in the present state of our science itself, in the sterility of all past endeavors to find its empirical foundations.

Every new attempt in this direction, however modest the effort, contains its own justification. To aim at the discovery of the fundamentals of our science is to devote one's abilities to the solution of a problem that is directly related to human welfare, to serve a public interest of the highest importance, and to enter a path where even error is not entirely without merit.

In order to avoid any justifiable doubts on the part of experts, we must not, in such an enterprise, neglect to pay careful attention to past work in all the fields of our science thus far explored. Nor can we abstain from applying criticism, with full independence of judgment, to the opinions of our predecessors, and even to doctrines until now considered definitive attainments of our science. Were we to fail in the first task, we would abandon lightly the whole sum of experience collected by the many excellent minds of all peoples and of all times who have attempted to achieve the same end. Should we fail in the second, we would renounce from the beginning any hope of a fundamental reform of the foundations of our science. These dangers can be evaded by making the views of our predecessors our own, though only after an unhesitating examination, and by appealing from doctrine to experience, from the thoughts of men to the nature of things.

This is the ground on which I [1] stand. In what follows I have endeavored to reduce the complex phenomena of human economic activity to the simplest elements that can still be subjected to accurate observation, to apply to these elements the measure corresponding to their nature, and constantly adhering to this measure, to investigate the manner in which the

1. Menger uses an editorial "we" throughout. In conformity with modern usage, we have converted Menger's references to himself from the first person plural to the first person singular.—TR.

more complex economic phenomena evolve from their elements according to definite principles.

This method of research, attaining universal acceptance in the natural sciences, led to very great results, and on this account came mistakenly to be called the natural-scientific method. It is, in reality, a method common to all fields of empirical knowledge, and should properly be called the empirical method. The distinction is important because every method of investigation acquires its own specific character from the nature of the field of knowledge to which it is applied. It would be improper, accordingly, to attempt a natural-scientific orientation of our science.

Past attempts to carry over the peculiarities of the natural-scientific method of investigation uncritically into economics have led to most serious methodological errors, and to idle play with external analogies between the phenomena of economics and those of nature. Bacon said of scholars of this description: "Magna cum vanitate et desipientia inanes similitudines et sympathias rerum describunt atque etiam quandoque affingunt," [2, 3] a statement which, strangely enough, is still true today of precisely those writers on economic subjects who continue to call themselves disciples of Bacon while they completely misunderstand the spirit of his method.

If it is stated, in justification of these efforts, that the task of our age is to establish the interconnections between all fields of science and to unify their most important principles, I should like to question seriously the qualifications of our contemporaries to solve this problem. I believe that scholars in the various fields of science can never lose sight of this common goal of their endeavors without damage to their research. But the solution of this problem can be taken up successfully only when the several fields of knowledge have been examined most carefully, and when the laws peculiar to each field have been discovered.

2. Francis Bacon, *Novum Organum*, II, 27.
3. In *The Philosophical Works of Francis Bacon*, translated by Ellis and Spedding, edited by John M. Robertson, London, 1905, pp. 334-5, this passage reads as follows: "similitudes and sympathies of things that have no reality, . . . they describe and sometimes invent with great vanity and folly."—TR.

It is now the task of the reader to judge to what results the method of investigation I have adopted has led, and whether I have been able to demonstrate successfully that the phenomena of economic life, like those of nature, are ordered strictly in accordance with definite laws. Before closing, however, I wish to contest the opinion of those who question the existence of laws of economic behavior by referring to human free will, since their argument would deny economics altogether the status of an exact science.

Whether and under what conditions a thing is *useful* to me, whether and under what conditions it is a *good*, whether and under what conditions it is an *economic good*, whether and under what conditions it possesses *value* for me and how large the *measure* of this value is for me, whether and under what conditions an *economic exchange* of goods will take place between two economizing individuals, and the limits within which a *price* can be established if an exchange does occur—these and many other matters are fully as independent of my will as any law of chemistry is of the will of the practicing chemist. The view adopted by these persons rests, therefore, on an easily discernible error about the proper field of our science. For economic theory is concerned, not with practical rules for economic *activity*, but with the *conditions* under which men engage in provident activity directed to the satisfaction of their needs.

Economic theory is related to the practical activities of economizing men [4] in much the same way that chemistry is related to the operations of the practical chemist. Although reference to freedom of the human will may well be legitimate as an objection to the complete predictability of economic activity, it can never have force as a denial of the conformity to definite laws of phenomena that condition the outcome of the economic activity of men and are entirely independent of the human will.

4. The terms *"wirtschaftender Mensch," "wirtschaftendes Individuum,"* and *"wirtschaftende Person"* occur continually throughout the work. The adjective *"wirtschaftend"* does not refer to the properties or motives of individuals but to the activity in which they are engaged. More specifically, it does not refer to "the profit motive" or to "the pursuit of self-interest," but to the act of economizing.—TR.

It is precisely phenomena of this description, however, which are the objects of study in our science.

I have devoted special attention to the investigation of the causal connections between economic phenomena involving products and the corresponding agents of production, not only for the purpose of establishing a price theory based upon reality and placing all price phenomena (including interest, wages, ground rent, etc.) together under one unified point of view, but also because of the important insights we thereby gain into many other economic processes heretofore completely misunderstood. This is the very branch of our science, moreover, in which the events of economic life most distinctly appear to obey regular laws.

It was a special pleasure to me that the field here treated, comprising the most general principles of our science, is in no small degree so truly the product of recent development in German political economy, and that the reform of the most important principles of our science here attempted is therefore built upon a foundation laid by previous work that was produced almost entirely by the industry of German scholars.

Let this work be regarded, therefore, as a friendly greeting from a collaborator in Austria, and as a faint echo of the scientific suggestions so abundantly lavished on us Austrians by Germany through the many outstanding scholars she has sent us and through her excellent publications.

Dr. Carl Menger

CHAPTER I | THE GENERAL THEORY OF THE GOOD

ALL THINGS are subject to the law of cause and effect. This great principle knows no exception, and we would search in vain in the realm of experience for an example to the contrary. Human progress has no tendency to cast it in doubt, but rather the effect of confirming it and of always further widening knowledge of the scope of its validity. Its continued and growing recognition is therefore closely linked to human progress.

One's own person, moreover, and any of its states are links in this great universal structure of relationships. It is impossible to conceive of a change of one's person from one state to another in any way other than one subject to the law of causality. If, therefore, one passes from a state of need to a state in which

51

the need is satisfied, sufficient causes for this change must exist. There must be forces in operation within one's organism that remedy the disturbed state, or there must be external things acting upon it that by their nature are capable of producing the state we call satisfaction of our needs.

Things that can be placed in a causal connection with the satisfaction of human needs we term *useful things*.[1] If, however, we both recognize this causal connection, and have the power actually to direct the useful things to the satisfaction of our needs, we call them *goods*.[2]

If a thing is to become a good, or in other words, if it is to acquire goods-character, all four of the following prerequisites must be simultaneously present:

1. A human need.

2. Such properties as render the thing capable of being brought into a causal connection with the satisfaction of this need.

3. Human knowledge of this causal connection.

4. Command of the thing sufficient to direct it to the satisfaction of the need.

Only when all four of these prerequisites are present simultaneously can a thing become a good. When even one of them is absent, a thing cannot acquire goods-character,[3] and a thing already possessing goods-character would lose it at once if but one of the four prerequisites ceased to be present.[4]

Hence a thing loses its goods-character: (1) if, owing to a change in human needs, the particular needs disappear that the

1. *"Nützlichkeiten."*—TR.

2. See the first three paragraphs of Appendix A (p. 286) for the material originally appearing here as a footnote.—TR.

3. *Güterqualität.* Later Menger uses such terms as *"Waarencharakter"* (commodity-character), *"ökonomischer Charakter"* (economic character), *"nichtökonomischer Charakter"* (noneconomic character), *"Geldcharakter"* (money-character), etc. It is only in the present instance that he uses *"Qualität"* instead of *"Charakter."* Since the meanings are the same, we have chosen the translation "goods-character" to make the constructions parallel.—TR

4. From this it is evident that goods-character is nothing inherent in goods and not a property of goods, but merely a relationship between certain things and men, the things obviously ceasing to be goods with the disappearance of this relationship.

thing is capable of satisfying, (2) whenever the capacity of the thing to be placed in a causal connection with the satisfaction of human needs is lost as the result of a change in its own properties, (3) if knowledge of the causal connection between the thing and the satisfaction of human needs disappears, or (4) if men lose command of it so completely that they can no longer apply it directly to the satisfaction of their needs and have no means of reëstablishing their power to do so.

A special situation can be observed whenever things that are incapable of being placed in any kind of causal connection with the satisfaction of human needs are nevertheless treated by men as goods. This occurs (1) when attributes, and therefore capacities, are erroneously ascribed to things that do not really possess them, or (2) when non-existent human needs are mistakenly assumed to exist. In both cases we have to deal with things that do not, in reality, stand in the relationship already described as determining the goods-character of things, but do so only in the opinions of people. Among things of the first class are most cosmetics, all charms, the majority of medicines administered to the sick by peoples of early civilizations and by primitives even today, divining rods, love potions, etc. For all these things are incapable of actually satisfying the needs they are supposed to serve. Among things of the second class are medicines for diseases that do not actually exist, the implements, statues, buildings, etc., used by pagan people for the worship of idols, instruments of torture, and the like. Such things, therefore, as derive their goods-character merely from properties they are imagined to possess or from needs merely imagined by men may appropriately be called *imaginary* goods.[5]

As a people attains higher levels of civilization, and as men penetrate more deeply into the true constitution of things and of their own nature, the number of true goods becomes constantly larger, and as can easily be understood, the number of imaginary goods becomes progressively smaller. It is not unimportant evidence of the connection between accurate knowledge and human welfare that the number of so-called imagi-

5. Aristotle (*De Anima* iii.10. 433ᵃ 25-38) already distinguished between true and imaginary goods according to whether the needs arise from rational deliberation or are irrational.

nary goods is shown by experience to be usually greatest among peoples who are poorest in true goods.

Of special scientific interest are the goods that have been treated by some writers in our discipline as a special class of goods called "relationships." [6] In this category are firms, goodwill, monopolies, copyrights, patents, trade licenses, authors' rights, and also, according to some writers, family connections, friendship, love, religious and scientific fellowships, etc. It may readily be conceded that a number of these relationships do not allow a rigorous test of their goods-character. But that many of them, such as firms, monopolies, copyrights, customer good-will, and the like, are actually goods is shown, even without appeal to further proof, by the fact that we often encounter them as objects of commerce. Nevertheless, if the theorist who has devoted himself most closely to this topic [7, 8] admits that the classification of these relationships as goods has something strange about it, and appears to the unprejudiced eye as an anomaly, there must, in my opinion, be a somewhat deeper reason for such doubts than the unconscious working of the materialistic bias of our time which rgeards only materials and forces (tangible objects and labor services) as things and, therefore, also as goods.

It has been pointed out several times by students of law that our language has no term for "useful actions" in general, but only one for "labor services." Yet there is a whole series of actions, and even of mere inactions, which cannot be called labor services but which are nevertheless decidedly useful to certain persons, for whom they may even have considerable economic value. That someone buys commodities from me, or uses my legal services, is certainly no labor service on his part, but it is

6. "Verhältnisse." There is no English word or phrase that is capable of expressing the same meaning as "Verhältnisse" in this context. The English terms "intangibles" and "claims" are closest, but less broad in meaning. We have chosen the English word "relationships" as corresponding most closely to the primary meaning of "Verhältnisse." The reader can obtain the full meaning of the term, however, only from the text itself.—TR.

7. A. E. F. Schäffle, Die national-ökonomische Theorie der ausschliessenden Absazverhältnisse, Tübingen, 1867, p. 2.

8. See the last paragraph of Appendix A (p. 288) for the material originally appearing here as a footnote.—TR.

nevertheless an action beneficial to me. That a well-to-do doctor ceases the practice of medicine in a small country town in which there is only one other doctor in addition to himself can with still less justice be called a labor service. But it is certainly an inaction of considerable benefit to the remaining doctor who thereby becomes a monopolist.

Whether a larger or smaller number of persons regularly performs actions that are beneficial to someone (a number of customers with respect to a merchant, for instance) does not alter the nature of these actions. And whether certain inactions on the part of some or all of the inhabitants of a city or state which are useful to someone come about voluntarily or through legal compulsion (natural or legal monopolies, copyrights, trade marks, etc.), does not alter in any way the nature of these useful inactions. From an economic standpoint, therefore, what are called clienteles, good-will, monopolies, etc., are the useful actions or inactions of other people, or (as in the case of *firms,* for example) aggregates of material goods, labor services, and other useful actions and inactions. Even relationships of friendship and love, religious fellowships, and the like, consist obviously of actions or inactions of other persons that are beneficial to us.

If, as is true of customer good-will, firms, monopoly rights, etc., these useful actions or inactions are of such a kind that we can dispose of them, there is no reason why we should not classify them as goods, without finding it necessary to resort to the obscure concept of "relationships," and without bringing these "relationships" into contrast with all other goods as a special category. On the contrary, all goods can, I think, be divided into the two classes of *material goods* (including all forces of nature insofar as they are goods) and of *useful human actions* (and inactions), the most important of which are labor services.

2. THE CAUSAL CONNECTIONS BETWEEN GOODS

Before proceeding to other topics, it appears to me to be of preëminent importance to our science that we should become clear about the causal connections between goods. In our own, as in all other sciences, true and lasting progress will be made only when we no longer regard the objects of our scientific observations merely as unrelated occurrences, but attempt to discover their *causal connections* and the laws to which they are subject. The bread we eat, the flour from which we bake the bread, the grain that we mill into flour, and the field on which the grain is grown—all these things are goods. But knowledge of this fact is not sufficient for our purposes. On the contrary, it is necessary in the manner of all other empirical sciences, to attempt to classify the various goods according to their inherent characteristics, to learn the place that each good occupies in the causal nexus of goods, and finally, to discover the economic laws to which they are subject.

Our well-being at any given time, to the extent that it depends upon the satisfaction of our needs, is assured if we have at our disposal the goods required for their direct satisfaction. If, for example, we have the necessary amount of bread, we are in a position to satisfy our need for food directly. The causal connection between bread and the satisfaction of one of our needs is thus a direct one, and a testing of the goods-character of bread according to the principles laid down in the preceding section presents no difficulty. The same applies to all other goods that may be used directly for the satisfaction of our needs, such as beverages, clothes, jewelry, etc.

But we have not yet exhausted the list of things whose goods-character we recognize. For in addition to goods that serve our needs directly (and which will, for the sake of brevity, henceforth be called "goods of first order") we find a large number of other things in our economy that cannot be put in any direct causal connection with the satisfaction of our needs, but which possess goods-character no less certainly than goods of first order. In our markets, next to bread and other goods capable of satisfying human needs directly, we also see quantities of flour, fuel, and salt. We find that implements and tools for the production of bread, and the skilled labor services necessary for their use, are regularly traded. All these things, or at any rate by far the greater number of them, are incapable of satisfying human needs in any direct way—for what human need could be satis-

fied by a specific labor service of a journeyman baker, by a bak-
ing utensil, or even by a quantity of ordinary flour? That these
things are nevertheless treated as goods in human economy, just
like goods of first order, is due to the fact that they serve to produce bread and other goods of first order, and hence are indirectly, even if not directly, capable of satisfying human needs.
The same is true of thousands of other things that do not have
the capacity to satisfy human needs directly, but which are
nevertheless used for the production of goods of first order, and
can thus be put in an indirect causal connection with the satisfaction of human needs. These considerations prove that the relationship responsible for the goods-character of these things,
which we will call goods of *second* order, is fundamentally the
same as that of goods of first order. The fact that goods of first
order have a direct and goods of second order an indirect causal
relation with the satisfaction of our needs gives rise to no difference in the essence of that relationship, since the requirement for the acquisition of goods-character is the existence of
some causal connection, but not necessarily one that is direct,
between things and the satisfaction of human needs.

At this point, it could easily be shown that even with these
goods we have not exhausted the list of things whose goods-
character we recognize, and that, to continue our earlier example, the grain mills, wheat, rye, and labor services applied to
the production of flour, etc., appear as goods of *third* order,
while the fields, the instruments and appliances necessary for
their cultivation, and the specific labor services of farmers, appear as goods of *fourth* order. I think, however, that the idea I
have been presenting is already sufficiently clear.

In the previous section, we saw that a causal relationship between a thing and the satisfaction of human needs is one of the
prerequisites of its goods-character. The thought developed in
this section may be summarized in the proposition that it is not
a requirement of the goods-character of a thing that it be capable of being placed in *direct* causal connection with the satisfaction of human needs. It has been shown that goods having
an indirect causal relationship with the satisfaction of human
needs differ in the closeness of this relationship. But it has also
been shown that this difference does not affect the essence of

goods-character in any way. In this connection, a distinction was made between goods of first, second, third, fourth, and higher orders.

Again it is necessary that we guard ourselves, from the beginning, from a faulty interpretation of what has been said. In the general discussion of goods-character, I have already pointed out that goods-character is not a property inherent in the goods themselves. The same warning must also be given here, where we are dealing with the order or place that a good occupies in the causal nexus of goods. To designate the order of a particular good is to indicate only that this good, in some particular employment, has a closer or more distant causal relationship with the satisfaction of a human need. Hence the order of a good is nothing inherent in the good itself and still less a property of it.

Thus I do not attach any special weight to the orders assigned to goods, either here or in the following exposition of the laws governing goods, although the assignment of these orders will, if they are correctly understood, become an important aid in the exposition of a difficult and important subject. But I do wish especially to stress the importance of understanding the causal relation between goods and the satisfaction of human needs and, depending upon the nature of this relation in particular cases, the more or less direct causal connection of the goods with these needs.

3. THE LAWS GOVERNING GOODS-CHARACTER

A. *The goods-character of goods of higher order is dependent on command of corresponding complementary goods.*

When we have goods of first order at our disposal, it is in our power to use them directly for the satisfaction of our needs. If we have the corresponding goods of second order at our disposal, it is in our power to transform them into goods of first order, and thus to make use of them in an indirect manner for the satisfaction of our needs. Similarly, should we have only goods of third order at our disposal, we would have the power to transform them into the corresponding goods of second order, and these in turn into corresponding goods of first order. Hence we would have the power to utilize goods of third order for the satisfaction of our needs, even though this power must be exercised by transforming them into goods of successively lower orders. The same proposition holds true with all goods of higher order, and we cannot doubt that they possess goods-character if it is in our power actually to utilize them for the satisfaction of our needs.

This last requirement, however, contains a limitation of no slight importance with respect to goods of higher order. For it is never in our power to make use of any particular good of higher order for the satisfaction of our needs unless we also have command of the other (complementary) goods of higher order.

Let us assume, for instance, that an economizing individual possesses no bread directly, but has at his command all the goods of second order necessary to produce it. There can be no doubt that he will nevertheless have the power to satisfy his need for bread. Suppose, however, that the same person has command of the flour, salt, yeast, labor services, and even all the tools and appliances necessary for the production of bread, but lacks both fuel and water. In this second case, it is clear that he no longer has the power to utilize the goods of second order in his possession for the satisfaction of his need, since bread cannot be made without fuel and water, even if all the other necessary goods are at hand. Hence the goods of second order will, in this case, immediately lose their goods-character with respect to the need for bread, since one of the four prerequisites for the existence of their goods-character (in this case the fourth prerequisite) is lacking.

It is possible for the things whose goods-character has been lost with respect to the need for bread to retain their goods-character with respect to other needs if their owner has the power to utilize them for the satisfaction of other needs than his need for bread, or if they are capable, by themselves, of directly or indirectly satisfying a human need in spite of the lack of one or more complementary goods. But if the lack of one or more complementary goods makes it impossible for the available goods of second order to be utilized, either by themselves alone or in combination with other available goods, for the satisfaction of any human need whatsoever, they will lose their goods-character completely. For economizing men will no longer have the power to direct the goods in question to the satisfaction of their needs, and one of the essential prerequisites of their goods-character is therefore missing.

Our investigation thus far yields, as a first result, the proposition that the goods-character of goods of *second* order is dependent upon complementary goods of the same order being available to men with respect to the production of at least one good of first order.

The question of the dependence of the goods-character of goods of higher order than the second upon the availability of complementary goods is more complex. But the additional complexity by no means lies in the relationship of the goods of higher order to the corresponding goods of the next lower order (the relationship of goods of third order to the corresponding goods of second order, or of goods of fifth order to those of fourth order, for example). For the briefest consideration of the causal relationship between these goods provides a complete analogy to the relationship just demonstrated between goods of second order and goods of the next lower (first) order. The principle of the previous paragraph may be extended quite naturally to the proposition that the goods-character of goods of higher order is directly dependent upon complementary goods of the same order being available with respect to the production of at least one good of the next lower order.

The additional complexity arising with goods of higher than second order lies rather in the fact that even command of all the goods required for the production of a good of the next lower order does not necessarily establish their goods-character unless men also have command of all their complementary goods of this next and of all still lower orders. Assume that someone has command of all the goods of third order that are required to produce a good of second order, but does not have the other complementary goods of second order at his command. In this case, even command of all the goods of third order required for the production of a single good of second order will not give him the power actually to direct these goods of third order to the satisfaction of human needs. Although he has the power to transform the goods of third order (whose goods-character is here in question) into goods of second order, he does not have the power to transform the goods of second order into the corresponding goods of first order. He will therefore not have the power to direct the goods of third order to the satisfaction of his needs, and because he has lost this power, the goods of third order lose their goods character immediately.

It is evident, therefore, that the principle stated above—the goods-character of goods of higher order is directly dependent upon complementary goods of the same order being available with respect to the production of at least one good of the next lower order—does not include all the prerequisites for the establishment of the goods-character of things, since command of all complementary goods of the same order does not by itself give us the power to direct these things to the satisfaction of our needs. If we have goods of third order at our disposal, their goods-character is indeed directly dependent on our being able to transform them into goods of second order. But a further requirement for their goods-character is our ability to transform the goods of second order in turn into goods of first order, which involves the still further requirement that we must have command of certain complementary goods of second order.

The relationships of goods of fourth, fifth, and still higher orders are quite analogous. Here again the goods-character of things so remote from the satisfaction of human needs is directly dependent on the availability of complementary goods of the same order. But it is dependent also upon our having command of the complementary goods of the next lower order, in turn of the complementary goods of the order below this, and so on, in such a way that it is in our power actually to direct the goods of higher order to the production of a good of first order, and thereby finally to the satisfaction of a human need. If we designate the whole sum of goods that are required to utilize a good of higher order for the production of a good of first order as its complementary goods in the wider sense of the term, we obtain the general principle that *the goods-character of goods of higher order depends on our being able to command their complementary goods in this wider sense of the term.*

Nothing can place the great causal interconnection between goods more vividly before our eyes than this principle of the mutual interdependence of goods.

When, in 1862, the American Civil War dried up Europe's most important source of cotton, thousands of other goods that were complementary to cotton lost their goods-character. I refer in particular to the labor services of English and continental cottonmill workers who then, for the greater part, became unemployed and were forced to ask public charity. The labor services (of which these capable workers had command) remained the same, but large quantities of them lost their goods-character since their complementary good, cotton, was unavailable, and the specific labor services could not by themselves, for the most part, be directed to the satisfaction of any human need. But these labor services immediately became goods again when their complementary good again became available as the result of increased cotton imports, partly from other sources of supply, and partly, after the end of the American Civil War, from the old source.

Conversely, goods often lose their goods-character because men do not have command of the necessary labor services, complementary to them. In sparsely populated countries, particularly in countries raising one predominant crop such as wheat, a very serious shortage of labor services frequently occurs after especially good harvests, both because agricultural workers, few in numbers and living separately, find few incentives for hard work in times of abundance, and because the harvesting work, as a result of the exclusive cultivation of wheat, is concentrated into a very brief period of time. Under such conditions (on the fertile plains of Hungary, for instance), where the requirements for labor services, within a short interval of time, are very great but where the available labor services are not sufficient, large quantities of grain often spoil on the fields. The reason for this is that the goods complementary to the crops standing on the fields (the labor services necessary for harvesting them) are missing, with the result that the crops themselves lose their goods-character.

When the economy of a people is highly developed, the various complementary goods are generally in the hands of different persons. The producers of each individual article usually carry on their business in a mechanical way, while the producers of the complementary goods realize just as little that the goods-character of the things they produce or manufacture depends on the existence of other goods that are not in their possession. The error that goods of higher order possess goods-character by themselves, and without regard to the availability of complementary goods, arises most easily in countries where, owing to active commerce and a highly developed economy, almost every product comes into existence under the tacit, and as a rule quite unconscious, supposition of the producer that other persons, linked to him by trade, will provide the complementary goods at the right time. Only when this tacit assumption is disappointed by such a change of conditions that the laws governing goods make their operation manifestly apparent, are the usual mechanical business transactions interrupted, and only then does public attention turn to these manifestations and to their underlying causes.

B. *The goods-character of goods of higher order is derived from that of the corresponding goods of lower order.*

Examination of the nature and causal connections of goods as I have presented them in the first two sections leads to the recognition of a further law that goods obey as such—that is, without regard to their economic character.

It has been shown that the existence of human needs is one of the essential prerequisites of goods-character, and that if the human needs with whose satisfaction a thing may be brought into causal connection completely disappear, the goods-character of the thing is immediately lost unless new needs for it arise.

From what has been said about the nature of goods, it is directly evident that goods of first order lose their goods-character immediately if the needs they previously served to satisfy all disappear without new needs arising for them. The problem becomes more complex when we turn to the entire range of goods causally connected with the satisfaction of a human need, and inquire into the effect of the disappearance of this need on the goods-character of the goods of higher order causally connected with its satisfaction.

Suppose that the need for direct human consumption of tobacco should disappear as the result of a change in tastes, and that at the same time all other needs that the tobacco already prepared for human consumption might serve to satisfy should also disappear. In this event, it is certain that all tobacco products already on hand, in the final form suited to human consumption, would immediately lose their goods-character. But what would happen to the corresponding goods of higher order? What would be the situation with respect to raw tobacco leaves, the tools and appliances used for the production of the various kinds of tobacco, the specialized labor services employed in the industry, and in short, with respect to all the goods of second order used for the production of tobacco destined for human consumption? What, furthermore, would be the situation with respect to tobacco seeds, tobacco farms, the labor services and the tools and appliances employed in the production of raw tobacco, and all the other goods that may be regarded as goods of third order in relation to the need for tobacco? What, finally, would be the situation with respect to the corresponding goods of fourth, fifth, and higher orders?

The goods-character of a thing is, as we have seen, dependent on its being capable of being placed in a causal connection with the satisfaction of human needs. But we have also seen that a *direct* causal connection between a thing and the satisfaction of a need is by no means a necessary prerequisite of its goods-character. On the contrary, a large number of things derive their goods-character from the fact that they stand only in a more or less *indirect* causal relationship to the satisfaction of human needs.

If it is established that the existence of human needs capable of satisfaction is a prerequisite of goods-character in all cases, the principle that the goods-character of things is immediately lost upon the disappearance of the needs they previously served to satisfy is, at the same time, also proven. This principle is valid whether the goods can be placed in *direct* causal connection with the satisfaction of human needs, or derive their goods-character from a more or less *indirect* causal connection with the satisfaction of human needs. It is clear that with the disappearance of the corresponding needs the entire foundation of the relationship we have seen to be responsible for the goods-character of things ceases to exist.

Thus quinine would cease to be a good if the diseases it serves to cure should disappear, since the only need with the satisfaction of which it is causally connected would no longer exist. But the disappearance of the usefulness of quinine would have the further consequence that a large part of the corresponding goods of higher order would also be deprived of their goods-character. The inhabitants of quinine-producing countries, who currently earn their livings by cutting and peeling cinchona trees, would suddenly find that not only their stocks of cinchona bark, but also, in consequence, their cinchona trees, the tools and appliances applicable only to the production of quinine, and above all the specialized labor services, by means of which they previously earned their livings, would at once lose their goods-character, since all these things would, under the changed circumstances, no longer have any causal relationship with the satisfaction of human needs.

If, as the result of a change in tastes, the need for tobacco should diasppear completely, the first consequence would be that all stocks of finished tobacco products on hand would be deprived of their goods-character. A further consequence would be that the raw tobacco leaves, the machines, tools, and implements applicable exclusively to the processing of tobacco, the specialized labor services employed in the production of tobacco products, the available stocks of tobacco seeds, etc., would lose their goods-character. The services, presently so well paid, of the agents who have so much skill in the grading and merchandising of tobaccos in such places as Cuba, Manila, Puerto Rico, and Havana, as well as the specialized labor services of the many people, both in Europe and in those distant countries, who are employed in the manufacture of cigars, would cease to be goods. Even tobacco boxes, humidors, all kinds of tobacco pipes, pipe stems, etc., would lose their goods-character. This apparently very complex phenomenon is explained by the fact that all the goods enumerated above derive their goods-char-

acter from their causal connection with the satisfaction of the
human need for tobacco. With the disappearance of this need,
one of the foundations underlying their goods-character is
destroyed.

But goods of first order frequently, and goods of higher order
as a rule, derive their goods-character not merely from a single
but from more or less numerous causal connections with the
satisfaction of human needs. Goods of higher order thus do not
lose their goods-character if but one, or if, in general, but a part
of these needs ceases to be present. On the contrary, it is evident
that this effect will take place only if *all* the needs with the satisfaction of which goods of higher order are causally related
disappear, since otherwise their goods-character would, *in strict
accordance with economic law,* continue to exist with respect to
needs with the satisfaction of which they have continued to be
causally related even under the changed conditions. But even
in this case, their goods-character continues to exist only to the
extent to which they continue to maintain a causal relationship
with the satisfaction of human needs, and would disappear immediately if the remaining needs should also cease to exist.

To continue the previous example, should the need of people for the consumption of tobacco cease completely to exist,
the tobacco already manufactured into products suited to human
consumption, and probably also the stocks of raw tobacco
leaves, tobacco seeds, and many other goods of higher order having a causal connection with the satisfaction of the need for tobacco, would be completely deprived of their goods-character.
But not all the goods of higher order used by the tobacco industry would necessarily meet this fate. The land and agricultural implements used in the cultivation of tobacco, for instance,
and perhaps also many tools and machines used in the manufacture of tobacco products, would retain their goods-character
with respect to other human needs since they can be placed in
causal connection with these other needs even after the disappearance of the need for tobacco.

The law that the goods-character of goods of higher order is
derived from the goods-character of the corresponding goods of
lower order in whose production they serve must not be regarded as a modification affecting the substance of the primary

principle, but merely as a restatement of that principle in a more concrete form.

In what has preceded we have considered in general terms all the goods that are causally connected both with one another and with the satisfaction of human needs. The object of our investigation was the whole causal chain up to the last link, the satisfaction of human needs. Having stated the principle of the present section, we may now, in the section following, turn our attention to a few links of the chain at a time—by disregarding the causal connection between goods of third order for instance, and the satisfaction of human needs for the time being, and by observing only the causal connection of goods of that order with the corresponding goods of any higher order of our choice.

4. TIME AND ERROR

The process by which goods of higher order are progressively transformed into goods of lower order and by which these are directed finally to the satisfaction of human needs is, as we have seen in the preceding sections, not irregular but subject, like all other processes of change, to the law of causality. The idea of causality, however, is inseparable from the idea of time. A process of change involves a beginning and a becoming, and these are only conceivable as processes in time. Hence it is certain that we can never fully understand the causal interconnections of the various occurrences in a process, or the process itself, unless we view it in time and apply the measure of time to it. Thus, in the process of change by which goods of higher order are gradually transformed into goods of first order, until the latter finally bring about the state called the satisfaction of human needs, time is an essential feature of our observations.

When we have the complementary goods of some particular higher order at our command, we must transform them first into goods of the next lower order, and then by stages into goods of successively still lower orders until they have been fashioned into goods of first order, which alone can be utilized directly for the satisfaction of our needs. However short the time periods lying between the various phases of this process may often appear (and progress in technology and in the means of transport tend continually to shorten them), their complete disappearance is nevertheless inconceivable. It is impossible to transform goods of any given order into the corresponding goods of lower order by a mere wave of the hand. On the contrary, nothing is more certain than that a person having goods of higher order at his disposal will be in the actual position of having command of goods of the next lower order only after an appreciable period of time, which may, according to the particular circumstances involved, sometimes be shorter and sometimes longer. But what has been said here of a single link of the causal chain is even more valid with respect to the whole process.

The period of time this process requires in particular instances differs considerably according to the nature of the case. An individual, having at his disposal all the land, labor services, tools, and seed required for the production of an oak forest, will be compelled to wait almost a hundred years before the timber is ready for the axe, and in most cases actual possession of timber in this condition will come only to his heirs or other assigns. On the other hand, in some cases a person who has at his disposal the ingredients and the necessary tools, labor services, etc., required for the production of foods or beverages, will be in a position to use the foods or beverages themselves in only a few moments. Yet however great the difference between the various cases, one thing is certain: the time period lying between command of goods of higher order and possession of the corresponding goods of lower order can never be completely eliminated. Goods of higher order acquire and maintain their goods-character, therefore, not with respect to needs of the immediate present, but as a result of human foresight, only with respect to needs that will be experienced when the process of production has been completed.

After what has been said, it is evident that command of goods of higher order and command of the corresponding goods of first order differ, with respect to a particular kind of consumption, in that the latter can be consumed *immediately* whereas the former represent an earlier stage in the formation of consumption goods and hence can be utilized for direct consumption only after the passage of an appreciable period of time, which is longer or shorter according to the nature of the case. But another exceedingly important difference between immediate command of a consumption good and indirect command of it (through possession of goods of higher order) demands our consideration.

A person with consumption goods directly at his disposal is certain of their quantity and quality. But a person who has only indirect command of them, through possession of the corresponding goods of higher order, cannot determine with the same certainty the quantity and quality of the goods of first order that will be at his disposal at the end of the production process.

A person who has a hundred bushels [9] of grain can plan his disposition of this good with that certainty, as to quantity and quality, which the immediate possession of any good is generally able to offer. But a person who has command of such quantities of land, seed, fertilizer, labor services, agricultural implements, etc., as are normally required for the production of a hundred bushels of grain, faces the chance of harvesting more than that quantity of grain, but also the chance of harvesting less. Nor can the possibility of a complete harvest failure be excluded. He is exposed, moreover, to an appreciable uncertainty with respect to the quality of the product.

This uncertainty with respect to the quantity and quality of product one has at one's disposal through possession of the corresponding goods of higher order is greater in some branches of production than it is in others. An individual who has at his disposal the materials, tools, and labor services necessary for the production of shoes, will be able, from the quantity and quality of goods of higher order on hand, to draw conclusions with a considerable degree of precision about the quantity and quality of shoes he will have at the end of the production process. But

9. *"Metzen."* One *Metze* is equal to 3.44 liters, or approximately 3 quarts. But here as elsewhere in the translation we have chosen approximate modern equivalents since the old Austrian units of weight and measure are unfamiliar not only to English and American but even to present-day German-speaking readers. In any case, the units are used only for illustrative purposes.—TR.

a person with command of a field suitable for growing flax, the
corresponding agricultural implements, as well as the necessary
labor services, flaxseed, fertilizer, etc., will be unable to form a
perfectly certain judgment about the quantity and quality of
oilseed he will harvest at the end of the production process. Yet
he will be exposed to less uncertainty with respect to the quantity and quality of his product than a grower of hops, a hunter,
or even a pearl-fisher. However great these differences between
the various branches of production may be, and even though
the progress of civilization tends to diminish the uncertainty
involved, it is certain that an appreciable degree of uncertainty
regarding the quantity and quality of a product finally to be
obtained will always be present, although sometimes to a greater
and sometimes to a less extent, according to the nature of the
case.

The final reason for this phenomenon is found in the peculiar
position of man in relation to the causal process called production of goods. Goods of higher order are transformed, in accordance with the laws of causality, into goods of the next lower
order; these are further transformed until they become goods of
first order, and finally bring about the state we call satisfaction
of human needs. Goods of higher order are the most important
elements of this causal process, but they are by no means the
only ones. There are other elements, apart from those belong-
ing to the world of goods, that affect the quantity and quality of
the outcome of the causal process called production of goods.
These other elements are either of such a kind that we have not
recognized their causal connection with our well-being, or they
are elements whose influence on the product we well know but
which are, for some reason, beyond our control.

Thus, until a short time ago, men did not know the influence
of the different types of soils, chemicals, and fertilizers, on the
growth of various plants, and hence did not know that these
factors sometimes have a more and sometimes a less favorable
(or even an unfavorable) effect on the outcome of the production process, with respect to both its quantity and its quality.
As a result of discoveries in the field of agricultural chemistry,
a certain portion of the uncertainties of agriculture has already
been eliminated, and man is in a position, to the extent per-

mitted by the discoveries themselves, to induce the favorable effects of the known factors in each case and to avoid those that are detrimental.

Changes in weather offer an example from the second category. Farmers are usually quite clear about the kind of weather most favorable for the growth of plants. But since they do not have the power to create favorable weather or to prevent weather injurious to seedlings, they are dependent to no small extent on its influence upon the quantity and quality of their harvested product. Although weather, like all other natural forces, makes itself felt in accordance with inexorable causal laws, it appears to economizing men as a series of accidents, since it is outside their sphere of control.

The greater or less degree of certainty in predicting the quality and quantity of a product that men will have at their disposal due to their possession of the goods of higher order required for its production, depends upon the greater or less degree of completeness of their knowledge of the elements of the causal process of production, and upon the greater or less degree of control they can exercise over these elements. The degree of uncertainty in predicting both the quantity and quality of a product is determined by opposite relationships. Human uncertainty about the quantity and quality of the product (corresponding goods of first order) of the whole causal process is greater the larger the number of elements involved in any way in the production of consumption goods which we either do not understand or over which, even understanding them, we have no control—that is, the larger the number of elements that do not have goods-character.

This uncertainty is one of the most important factors in the economic uncertainty of men, and, as we shall see in what follows, is of the greatest practical significance in human economy.

5. THE CAUSES OF PROGRESS IN HUMAN WELFARE

"The greatest improvement in the productive powers of labour," says Adam Smith, "and the greater part of the skill, dexterity, and judgment with which it is anywhere directed, or applied, seem to have been the effects of the division of labour." [10] And: "It is the great multiplication of the productions of all the different arts, in consequence of the division of labour, which occasions, in a well-governed society, that universal opulence which extends itself to the lowest ranks of the people." [11]

In such a manner Adam Smith has made the progressive division of labor the central factor in the economic progress of mankind—in harmony with the overwhelming importance he attributes to labor as an element in human economy. I believe, however, that the distinguished author I have just quoted has cast light, in his chapter on the division of labor, on but a single cause of progress in human welfare while other, no less efficient, causes have escaped his attention.

We may assume that the tasks in the collecting economy of an Australian tribe are, for the most part, divided in the most efficient way among the various members of the tribe. Some are hunters; others are fishermen; and still others are occupied exclusively with collecting wild vegetable foods. Some of the women are wholly engaged in the preparation of food, and others in the fabrication of clothes. We may imagine the division of labor of the tribe to be carried still further, so that each distinct task comes to be performed by a particular specialized member of the tribe. Let us now ask whether a division of labor carried so far, would have such an effect on the increase of the quantity of consumable goods available to the members of the tribe as that regarded by Adam Smith as being the consequence of the progressive division of labor. Evidently, as the result of such a change, this tribe (or any other people) will achieve either the same result from their labor with less effort or, with the same effort, a greater result than before. It will thus improve its condition, insofar as this is at all possible, by means of a more appropriate and efficient allocation of occupational tasks. But this improvement is very different from that

10. Adam Smith, *An Inquiry into the Nature and Causes of the Wealth of Nations*, Modern Library Edition, New York, 1937, p. 3.
11. *Ibid.*, p. 11.

which we can observe in actual cases of economically progressive peoples.

Let us compare this last case with another. Assume a people which extends its attention to goods of third, fourth, and higher orders, instead of confining its activity merely to the tasks of a primitive collecting economy—that is, to the acquisition of naturally available goods of lowest order (ordinarily goods of first, and possibly second, order). If such a people progressively directs goods of ever higher orders to the satisfaction of its needs, and especially if each step in this direction is accompanied by an appropriate division of labor, we shall doubtless observe that progress in welfare which Adam Smith was disposed to attribute exclusively to the latter factor. We shall see the hunter, who initially pursues game with a club, turning to hunting with bow and hunting net, to stock farming of the simplest kind, and in sequence, to ever more intensive forms of stock farming. We shall see men, living initially on wild plants, turning to ever more intensive forms of agriculture. We shall see the rise of manufactures, and their improvement by means of tools and machines. And in the closest connection with these developments, we shall see the welfare of this people increase.

The further mankind progresses in this direction, the more varied become the kinds of goods, the more varied consequently the occupations, and the more necessary and economic also the progressive division of labor. But it is evident that the increase in the consumption goods at human disposal is not the exclusive effect of the division of labor. Indeed, the division of labor cannot even be designated as the most important cause of the economic progress of mankind. Correctly, it should be regarded only as one factor among the great influences that lead mankind from barbarism and misery to civilization and wealth.

The explanation of the effect of the increasing employment of goods of higher order upon the growing quantity of goods available for human consumption (goods of first order) is a matter of little difficulty.

In its most primitive form, a collecting economy is confined to gathering those goods of lowest order that happen to be offered by nature. Since economizing individuals exert no influence on the production of these goods, their origin is independent of the wishes and needs of men, and hence, so far as they are concerned, accidental. But if men abandon this most primitive form of economy, investigate the ways in which things may be combined in a causal process for the production of consumption goods, take possession of things capable of being so combined, and treat them as goods of higher order, they will obtain consumption goods that are as truly the results of natural processes as the consumption goods of a primitive collecting economy, but the available quantities of these goods will no longer be independent of the wishes and needs of men. Instead, the quantities of consumption goods will be determined by a process that is in the power of men and is regulated by human purposes within the limits set by natural laws. Consumption goods, which before were the product of an accidental concurrence of the circumstances of their origin, become products of human will, within the limits set by natural laws, as soon as men have recognized these circumstances and have achieved control of them. The quantities of consumption goods at human disposal are limited only by the extent of human knowledge of the causal connections between things, and by the extent of human control over these things. Increasing understanding of the causal connections between things and human welfare, and increasing control of the less proximate conditions responsible for human welfare, have led mankind, therefore, from a state of barbarism and the deepest misery to its present stage of civilization and well-being, and have changed vast regions inhabited by a few miserable, excessively poor, men into densely populated civilized countries. Nothing is more certain than that the degree of economic progress of mankind will still, in future epochs, be commensurate with the degree of progress of human knowledge.

6. PROPERTY

The needs of men are manifold, and their lives and welfare are not assured if they have at their disposal only the means, however ample, for the satisfaction of but one of these needs. Although the manner, and the degree of completeness, of satisfaction of the needs of men can display an almost unlimited variety, a certain harmony in the satisfaction of their needs is nevertheless, up to a certain point, indispensable for the preservation of their lives and welfare. One man may live in a palace, consume the choicest foods, and dress in the most costly garments. Another may find his resting place in the dark corner of a miserable hut, feed on leftovers, and cover himself with rags. But each of them must try to satisfy his needs for shelter and clothing as well as his need for food. It is clear that even the most complete satisfaction of a single need cannot maintain life and welfare.

In this sense, it is not improper to say that all the goods an economizing individual has at his command are mutually interdependent with respect to their goods-character, since each particular good can achieve the end they all serve, the preservation of life and well-being, not by itself, but only in combination with the other goods.

In an isolated household economy, and even when but little trade exists between men, this joint purpose of the goods necessary for the preservation of human life and welfare is apparent, since all of them are at the disposal of a single economizing individual. The harmony of the needs that the individual households attempt to satisfy is reflected in their property.[12] At a higher stage of civilization, and particularly in our highly developed exchange economy, where possession of a substantial quantity of any one economic good gives command of corresponding quantities of all other goods, the interdependence of goods is seen less clearly in the economy of the individual members of society, but appears much more distinctly if the economic system as a whole is considered.

We see everywhere that not single goods but combinations of goods of different kinds serve the purposes of economizing men. These combinations of goods are at the command of individuals either directly, as is the case in the isolated household economy, or in part directly and in part indirectly, as is the case in our developed exchange economy. Only in their entirety do these goods bring about the effect that we call the satisfaction of our requirements, and in consequence, the assurance of our lives and welfare.

12. Lorenz v. Stein, *Lehrbuch der Volkswirthschaft*, Wien, 1858, pp. 36 ff.

The entire sum of goods at an economizing individual's command for the satisfaction of his needs, we call his *property*. His property is not, however, an arbitrarily combined quantity of goods, but a direct reflection of his needs, an integrated whole, no essential part of which can be diminished or increased without affecting realization of the end it serves.

CHAPTER II | ECONOMY AND ECONOMIC GOODS

NEEDS ARISE from our drives and the drives are imbedded in our nature. An imperfect satisfaction of needs leads to the stunting of our nature. Failure to satisfy them brings about our destruction. But to satisfy our needs is to live and prosper. Thus the attempt to provide for the satisfaction of our needs is synonymous with the attempt to provide for our lives and well-being. It is the most important of all human endeavors, since it is the prerequisite and foundation of all others.

In practice, the concern of men for the satisfaction of their needs is expressed as an attempt to attain command of all the things on which the satisfaction of their needs depends. If a person has command of all the consumption goods necessary to satisfy his needs, their actual satisfaction depends only on his

will. We may thus consider his objective as having been attained when he is in possession of these goods, since his life
and well-being are then in his own hands. The quantities of
consumption goods a person must have to satisfy his needs may
be termed his *requirements*.[1] The concern of men for the maintenance of their lives and well-being becomes, therefore, an attempt to provide themselves with their requirements.

But if men were concerned about providing themselves with
their requirements for goods only when they experienced an
immediate need of them, the satisfaction of their needs, and
hence their lives and well-being, would be very inadequately
assured.

If we suppose the inhabitants of a country to be entirely
without stocks of foodstuffs and clothing at the beginning of
winter, there can be no doubt that the majority of them would
be unable to save themselves from destruction, even by the most
desperate efforts directed to the satisfaction of their needs. But
the further civilization advances, and the more men come to
depend upon procuring the goods necessary for the satisfaction
of their needs by a long process of production (pp. 67 ff.), the
more compelling becomes the necessity of arranging in advance
for the satisfaction of their needs—that is, of providing their
requirements for future time periods.

Even an Australian savage does not postpone hunting until
he actually experiences hunger. Nor does he postpone building
his shelter until inclement weather has begun and he is already
exposed to its harmful effects.[2] But men in civilized societies
alone among economizing individuals plan for the satisfaction
of their needs, not for a short period only, but for much longer
periods of time. Civilized men strive to ensure the satisfaction
of their needs for many years to come. Indeed, they not only
plan for their entire lives, but as a rule, extend their plans still

1. *"Bedarf."* The reader is first referred to Menger's own note on this
   term (note 3 of this Chapter). Since Menger uses the term *Bedarf* in
   both of the senses mentioned in his note, and since he uses the term
   "Nachfrage" (demand) at several points, even if infrequently, we feel
   it best to translate *"Bedarf"* as "requirements" throughout to preserve
   as exactly as possible Menger's own terminology.—TR.
2. Even some animals lay by stores and thus ensure in advance that they
   will not lack food and a warm abode in winter.

further in their concern that even their descendants shall not lack means for the satisfaction of their needs.

Wherever we turn among civilized peoples we find a system of large-scale advance provision for the satisfaction of human needs. When we are still wearing our heavy clothes for protection against the cold of winter, not only are ready-made spring clothes already on the way to retail stores, but in factories light cloths are being woven which we will wear next summer, while yarns are being spun for the heavy clothing we will use the following winter. When we fall ill we need the services of a physician. In legal disputes we require the advice of a lawyer. But it would be much too late, for a person in either contingency to meet his need, if he should only then attempt to acquire the medical or legal knowledge and skills himself, or attempt to arrange the special training of other persons for his service, even though he might possess the necessary means. In civilized countries, the needs of society for these and similar services are provided for in good time, since experienced and proven men, having prepared themselves for their professions many years ago, and having since collected rich experiences from their practices, place their services at the disposal of society. And while we enjoy the fruits of the foresight of past times in this way, many men are being trained in our universities to meet the needs of society for similar services in the future.

The concern of men for the satisfaction of theirs needs thus becomes an attempt to *provide in advance* for meeting their requirements in the future, and we shall therefore call a person's requirements those quantities of goods that are necessary to satisfy his needs within the time period covered by his plans.[3]

3. The word "requirements" (*Bedarf*) has a double meaning in our language. It is used on the one hand to designate the quantities of goods that are necessary to satisfy a person's needs completely, and on the other to designate the quantities that a person intends to consume. In the latter meaning, a man receiving a rent of 20,000 Thalers and accustomed to using it all for consumption has very great requirements, whereas a rural laborer whose income amounts to 100 Thalers has very small requirements, and a beggar in the depths of extreme poverty no requirements whatsoever. In the former meaning, the requirements of men also differ greatly due to differences in their education and habits. But even a person devoid of all means has require-

There are two kinds of knowledge that men must possess as a prerequisite for any successful attempt to provide in advance for the satisfaction of their needs. They must become clear: (a) about their requirements—that is, about the quantities of goods they will need to satisfy their needs during the time period over which their plans extend, and (b) about the quantities of goods at their disposal for the purpose of meeting these requirements.

All provident activity directed to the satisfaction of human needs is based on knowledge of these two classes of quantities. Lacking knowledge of the first, the activity of men would be conducted blindly, for they would be ignorant of their objective. Lacking knowledge of the second, their activity would be planless, for they would have no conception of the available means.

In what follows, it will first be shown how men arrive at a knowledge of their requirements for future time periods; it will then be shown how they estimate the quantities of goods that will be at their disposal during these time periods; and finally a description will be given of the activity by which men endeavor to direct the quantities of goods (consumption goods and means of production) at their disposal to the most effective satisfaction of their needs.

1. HUMAN REQUIREMENTS

A. *Requirements for goods of first order (consumption goods).*

Human beings experience directly and immediately only needs for goods of first order—that is, for goods that can be used directly for the satisfaction of their needs (p. 56). If no requirements for these goods existed, none for goods of higher order could arise. Requirements for goods of higher order are thus dependent upon requirements for goods of first order, and an investigation of the latter constitutes the necessary foundation

---

ments equal to the quantities of goods that would be necessary to satisfy his needs. Merchants and industrialists generally employ the term "requirements" in the narrower sense of the word, and often mean by it the "expected demand" for a good. In this sense also, one says that there are requirements for a commodity "at a given price" but not at another price, etc.

for the investigation of human requirements in general. We shall first, accordingly, be occupied with human requirements for goods of first order, and then with an exposition of the principles according to which human requirements for goods of higher order are regulated.

The quantity of a good of first order necessary to satisfy a concrete human need [4] (and hence also the quantity necessary to satisfy all the needs for a good of first order arising in a certain period of time) is determined directly by the need itself (by the needs themselves) and bears a direct quantitative relationship to it (them). If, therefore, men were always correctly and completely informed, as a result of previous experience, about the concrete needs they will have, and about the intensity with which these needs will be experienced during the time period for which they plan, they could never be in doubt about the quantities of goods necessary for the satisfaction of their needs—that is, about the magnitude of their requirements for goods of first order.

But experience tells us that we are often more or less in doubt whether certain needs will be felt in the future at all. We are aware, of course, that we will need food, drink, clothing, shelter, etc., during a given time period. But the same certainty does not exist with respect to many other goods, such as medical services, medicines, etc., since whether we shall experience a need for these goods or not often depends upon influences that we cannot foresee with certainty.

Even with needs that we know in advance will be experienced in the time period for which we plan, we may be uncertain about the quantities involved. We are well aware that these needs will make themselves felt, but we do not know before-

4. The term "concrete human need" recurs from time to time in the text. Menger uses the term to refer to a need (or rather a portion of a need) that is satisfied by consumption of a single unit of a good. When an individual consumes successive units of a good, Menger pictures him as satisfying successive "concrete needs" of diminishing psychological importance. At some points he adopts a different terminology, and speaks of the consumption of successive units of a commodity as successive "acts of satisfaction." See also note 3 of Chapter III and Appendix D for some suggestions regarding the meaning of "concrete."—TR.

hand in exactly what degree—that is, we do not know the exact quantities of goods that will be necessary for their satisfaction. But these are the very quantities here in question.

In the case of needs about which there is uncertainty as to whether they will arise at all in the time periods for which men make their plans, experience teaches us that, in spite of their deficient foresight, men by no means fail to provide for their eventual satisfaction. Even healthy persons living in the country are, to the extent permitted by their means, in possession of a medicine chest, or at least of a few drugs for unforeseen emergencies. Careful householders have fire extinguishers to preserve their property in case of fire, weapons to protect it if necessary, probably also fire- and burglar-proof safes, and many similar goods. Indeed, even among the goods of the poorest people I believe that some goods will be found that are expected to be utilized only in unforeseen contingencies.

The circumstance that it is uncertain whether a need for a good will be felt during the period of our plans does not, therefore, exclude the possibility that we will provide for its eventual satisfaction, and hence does not cause the reality of our requirements for goods necessary to satisfy such needs to be in question. On the contrary, men provide in advance, and as far as their means permit, for the eventual satisfaction of these needs also, and include the goods necessary for their satisfaction in their calculations whenever they determine their requirements as a whole.[5]

But what has been said here of needs whose appearance is altogether uncertain is fully as true where there is no doubt that a need for a good will arise but only uncertainty as to the intensity with which it will be felt, since in this case also men correctly consider their requirements to be fully met when they are able to have at their disposal quantities of goods sufficient for all anticipated eventualities.

A further point that must be taken into consideration here is the *capacity* of human needs *to grow*. If human needs are capable of growth and, as is sometimes maintained, capable of infinite growth, it could appear as if this growth would extend

5. See E. B. de Condillac, *Le commerce et le gouvernement*, in E. Daire (ed.), *Mélanges d'économie politique*, Paris, 1847, p. 248.

the limits of the quantities of goods necessary for the satisfaction of human needs continually, indeed even to complete infinitely, and that therefore any advance provision by men with respect to their requirements would be made utterly impossible.

On this subject of the capacity of human needs for infinite growth, it appears to me, first of all, that the concept of infinity is applicable only to unlimited progress in the development of human needs, but not to the quantities of goods necessary for the satisfaction of these needs during a given period of time. Although it is granted that the series is infinite, each individual element of the series is nevertheless finite. Even if human needs can be considered unlimited in their development into the most distant periods of the future, they are nevertheless capable of quantitative determination for all given, and especially for all economically significant, time periods. Thus, even under the assumption of uninterrupted progress in the development of human needs, we have to deal with finite and never with infinite, and thus completely indeterminate, magnitudes if we concern ourselves only with definite time periods.

If we observe people in provident activity directed to the satisfaction of their future needs, we can easily see that they are far from letting the capacity of their needs to grow escape their attention. On the contrary, they are most diligently concerned to take account of it. A person expecting an increase in his family or a higher social position will pay due attention to his increased future needs in the construction and furnishing of dwellings and in the purchase of carriages and similar durable goods. As a rule, and as far as his means will permit, he will attempt to take account of the higher claims of the future, not in a single connection only, but with respect to his holdings of goods as a whole. We can observe an analogous phenomenon in the activities of municipal governments. We see municipalities constructing waterworks, public buildings (schools, hospitals, etc.), parks, streets, and so on, with attention not only to the needs of the present, but with due consideration to the increased needs of the future. Naturally this tendency to give attention to future needs is even more distinctly evident in the activities of national governments.

To summarize what has been said, it appears that human requirements for consumption goods are magnitudes whose quantitative determination with respect to future time periods poses no fundamental difficulties. They are magnitudes about which, in activities directed to the satisfaction of their needs, men actually endeavor to attain clarity within feasible limits and insofar as a practical necessity compels them—that is, their attempts to determine these magnitudes are limited, on the one hand, to those time periods for which, at any time, they plan to make provision and, on the other hand, to a degree of exactness that is sufficient for the practical success of their activity.

B. *Requirements for goods of higher order (means of production)*.

If our requirements for goods of first order for a coming time period are already directly met by existing quantities of these goods, there can be no question of a further provision for these same requirements by means of goods of higher order. But if these requirements are not met, or are not completely met, by existing goods of first order (that is, if they are not met directly), requirements for goods of higher order for the time period in question do arise. These requirements are the quantities of goods of higher order that are necessary, in the existing state of technology of the relevant branches of production, for supplying our full requirements for goods of first order.

The simple relationship just presented with respect to our requirements for the means of production is to be observed, however, as we shall see in what follows, only in rare cases. An important modification of this principle arises from the causal interrelationships between goods.

It was demonstrated earlier (pp. 58 ff.) that it is impossible for men to employ any one good of higher order for the production of corresponding goods of lower order unless they are able, at the same time, to have the complementary goods at their disposal. Now what was said earlier of goods in general becomes more sharply precise here when we take into account the available quantities of goods. It was shown earlier that we can change goods of higher order into goods of lower order, and thus use them for the satisfaction of human needs, only if we have the complementary goods simultaneously at our disposal. This principle can now be restated in the following terms: *We can bring quantities of goods of higher order to the production of given quantities of goods of lower order, and thus finally to the meeting of our requirements, only if we are in the position of having the complementary quantities of the other goods of higher order simultaneously at our disposal.* Thus, for instance, even the largest quantity of land cannot be employed for the production of a quantity of grain, however small, unless we have at our disposal the (complementary) quantities of seed, labor services, etc., that are necessary for the production of this small quantity of grain.

Hence requirements for a single good of higher order are never encountered. On the contrary, we often observe that, whenever the requirements for a good of lower order are not at all or are only incompletely met, requirements for each of the corresponding goods of higher order are experienced only jointly with quantitatively corresponding requirements for the other complementary goods of higher order.

Suppose, for example, that with still unfilled requirements for 10,000 pairs of shoes for a given time period, we can command the quantities of tools, labor services, etc., necessary for the production of this quantity of shoes but only enough leather for the production of 5,000 pairs. Or else suppose that we are in a position to command all the other goods of higher order necessary for the production of 10,000 pairs of shoes but only enough labor services for the production of 5,000 pairs. In both instances, there can be no doubt that our *full requirements,* with respect to the given time period, would extend to such quantities of the various goods of higher order necessary for the production of shoes as would suffice for the production of 10,000 pairs. Our *effective requirements,* however, with respect to the other complementary goods, would, in each case, extend to such quantities only as are needed for the production of 5,000 pairs. The remaining requirements would be *latent,* and would only become *effective* if the other, lacking, complementary quantities should also become available.

From what has been said, we derive the principle that, *with respect to given future time periods, our effective requirements for particular goods of higher order are dependent upon the availability of complementary quantities of the corresponding goods of higher order.*

When cotton imports to Europe declined considerably because of the American Civil War, requirements for cotton piece goods remained evidently quite unaffected since that war could not change the needs for these goods significantly. To the extent to which there were future requirements for cotton piece goods that were not already met by finished manufactured products, there were also, as a result, requirements for the corresponding quantities of goods of *higher* order necessary for the production of cotton cloth. Hence these requirements also could not, on the whole, be altered significantly in any way by the civil war. But since the available quantity of one of the necessary goods of higher order, namely raw cotton, declined considerably, the natural consequence was that a part of the previous requirements for goods complementary to raw cotton with respect to the production of cotton cloth (labor services, machines, etc.) became *latent*, and the *effective* requirements for them diminished to such quantities as were necessary for processing the available quantities of raw cotton. As soon, however, as imports of raw cotton revived again, the effective requirements for these goods also experienced an increase—to the exact extent, of course, that the *latent* requirements diminished.

Immigrants, bringing with them viewpoints acquired in highly developed mother countries, often fall into the error of striving from the outset for an extended landed property to the neglect of more important considerations, and even without regard to whether the corresponding quantities of the other goods, complementary to the land, are available in their settlements. Yet nothing is more certain than that they can progress in using the land for the satisfaction of their needs only to the extent that they are able to acquire the corresponding complementary quantities of seed grain, cattle, agricultural instruments, etc. Their course of action betrays an ignorance of the above principle, which makes itself so inexorably felt that men must either submit to its validity or bear the injurious consequences of its neglect.

The further civilization progresses with a highly developed

division of labor, the more accustomed do people in various lines become to producing quantities of goods of higher order under the implicit and as a rule correct assumption that other persons will produce the corresponding quantities of the complementary goods. Manufacturers of opera glasses very seldom produce the glass lenses, the ivory or tortoise-shell cases, and the bronze parts, used in assembling the opera glasses. On the contrary, it is known that the producers of these glasses generally obtain the separate parts from specialized manufacturers or artisans and only assemble these parts, adding perhaps a few finishing touches. The glass-cutter who makes the lenses, the fancy-goods worker who makes the ivory or tortoise-shell cases, and the bronze-worker who makes the bronze castings, all operate under the implicit assumption that requirements for their products do exist. And yet nothing is more certain than that the effective requirements for the products of each one of them are dependent upon the production of the complementary quantities in such a fashion that, if the production of glass lenses were to suffer an interruption, the effective requirements for the other goods of higher order necessary for the production of telescopes, opera-glasses, and similar goods, would become latent. At this point, economic disturbances would appear that laymen usually consider completely abnormal, but which are, in reality, entirely in accordance with economic laws.

C. *The time limits within which human needs are felt.*

In our present investigation, the only topic still remaining to be taken into consideration is the problem of time, and we must demonstrate for what time periods men actually plan their requirements.

On this question, it is clear, in the first place, that our requirements for goods of first order appear to be met, with reference to a given future time period, if, within this time period, we will be in the position of having *directly* at our disposal the quantities of goods of first order that we require. It is different if we must meet our requirements for goods of first or, in general, of lower order indirectly (that is, by means of quantities of the corresponding goods of higher order), because of the lapse of time that is inevitable in any production process. Let us designate as Period I the time period that begins now and extends to the point in time when a good of first order can be produced from the corresponding goods of second order now at our disposal. Let us call Period II the time period following Period I and extending to the point in time when a good of first order can be produced from the goods of third order now available to us. And similarly, let us designate the following time periods III, IV, and so on. A sequence of time periods is thus defined for each particular kind of good. For each of these time periods we have immediate and direct requirements for the good of first order, and these requirements are actually met since, during these time periods, we come to have direct command of the necessary quantities of the good of first order.

Suppose, however, that we should try to meet our requirements for a good of first order during Period II by means of goods of fourth order. It is clear that this would be physically impossible, and that an actual provision of our requirements for the good of first order within the posited time period could result only from the use of goods of first or second order.

The same observation can be made not only with respect to our requirements for goods of first order, but with respect to our requirements for all goods of lower order in relation to the available goods of higher order. We cannot, for example, provide our requirements for goods of third order during Period V by obtaining command, during that time period, of the corresponding quantities of goods of sixth order. On the contrary, it is clear that for this purpose we would already have had to obtain command of the latter goods during Period II.[6]

If the requirements of a people for grain for the current year were not directly covered in late autumn by the then existing stocks of grain, it would be much too late to attempt to employ the available land, agricultural implements, labor services, etc., for that purpose. But autumn would be the proper time to provide for the grain requirements of the following year by utilizing the above-mentioned goods of higher order. Similarly, to

6. In this paragraph Menger implicitly assumes his time periods to be of equal duration. Reference to the definitions of the second paragraph preceding will confirm that this need not be the case.—TR.

meet our requirements for the labor services of competent teachers a decade from now, we must already, at the present time, educate capable persons for this purpose.

Human requirements for goods of higher order, like those for goods of lower order, are not only magnitudes that are quantitatively determined in strict accordance with definite laws, and that can be estimated beforehand by men where a practical necessity exists, but they are magnitudes also which, within certain time limits, men do calculate with an exactness sufficient for their practical affairs. Moreover, the record of the past demonstrates that, on the basis of previous experience as to their needs and as to the processes of production, men continually improve their ability to estimate more exactly the quantities of the various goods that will be needed to satisfy their needs, as well as the particular time periods within which these requirements for the various goods will arise.

2. THE AVAILABLE QUANTITIES

If it is generally correct that clarity about the objective of their endeavors is an essential factor in the success of every activity of men, it is also certain that knowledge of requirements for goods in future time periods is the first prerequisite for the planning of all human activity directed to the satisfaction of needs. Whatever may be the external conditions, therefore, under which this activity of men develops, its success will be dependent principally upon correct foresight of the quantities of goods they will find necessary in future time periods—that is, upon correct advance formulation of their requirements. It is clear also that a complete lack of foresight would make any planning of activity directed to the satisfaction of human needs completely impossible.

The second factor that determines the success of human activity is the knowledge gained by men of the means available to them for the attainment of the desired ends. Wherever, therefore, men may be observed in activities directed to the satisfaction of their needs, they are seen to be seriously concerned to obtain as exact a knowledge as possible of the quantities of goods available to them for this purpose. How they proceed to do so is the subject that will occupy us in this section.

The quantities of goods available, at any time, to the various members of a society are set by existing circumstances, and in determining these quantities the only problems they have are to measure and take inventory of the goods at their disposal. The ideal result of these two varieties of provident human activity is the complete enumeration of the goods available to them at a given point in time, their classification into perfectly homogeneous categories, and the exact determination of the number of items in each category. In practical life, however, far from pursuing this ideal, men customarily do not even attempt to obtain results as fully exact as is possible in the existing state of the arts of measuring and taking inventory, but are satisfied with just the degree of exactness that is necessary for practical purposes. Yet it is significant evidence of the great practical importance that exact knowledge of the existing quantities of goods available to them has for many people that we find a quite exceptional degree of exactness of this knowledge among merchants, industrialists, and such persons generally as have developed a high degree of provident activity. But even at the lowest levels of civilization we encounter a certain amount of knowledge of the available quantities of goods, since it is evident that a complete lack of this knowledge would make impossible any provident activity of men directed to the satisfaction of their needs.

To the degree to which men engage in planning activity directed to the satisfaction of their needs, they endeavor to attain clarity as to the quantities of goods available to them at any time. Wherever a considerable trade in goods already exists, therefore, we will find men attempting to form a judgment about the quantities of goods currently available to the other members of the society with whom they maintain trading connections.

As long as men have no considerable trade with one another, each man obviously has but a small interest in knowing what quantities of goods are in the hands of other persons. As soon, however, as an extensive trade develops, chiefly as a result of division of labor, and men find themselves dependent in large

part upon exchange in meeting their requirements, they naturally acquire a very obvious interest in being informed not only
about all the goods in their own possession but also about the
goods of all the other persons with whom they maintain trading relations, since part of the possessions of these other persons
is then accessible to them, if not directly, yet indirectly (by way
of trade).

As soon as a society reaches a certain level of civilization, the
growing division of labor causes the development of a special
professional class which operates as an intermediary in exchanges and performs for the other members of society not only
the mechanical part of trading operations (shipping, distribution, the storing of goods, etc.), but also the task of keeping records of the available quantities. Thus we observe that a specific
class of people has a special professional interest in compiling
data about the quantities of goods, so-called *stocks* in the widest
sense of the word, currently at the disposal of the various peoples and nations whose trade they mediate. The data they com-
pile cover trading regions that are smaller or larger (single
counties, provinces, or even entire countries or continents) according to the position the intermediaries in question occupy in
commercial life. They have, moreover, an interest in many
other general kinds of information, but we will have occasion
to discuss this at a later point.

The keeping of such statistical records, insofar as they relate
to the quantities of goods currently at the disposal of sizeable
groups of individuals, or even at the disposal of whole nations
or groups of nations, meets, however, with not inconsiderable
difficulties, since the exact determination of these stocks can be
made only by means of a census. The procedure of a census
presupposes a complicated apparatus of public officials, covering an entire trading area and equipped with the necessary
powers. Such an apparatus can be supplied only by national
governments, and by these only within their own territories.
Moreover, a census fails to be efficient even within these limits,
as is known to every expert, when it deals with goods whose
available quantities are not easily accessible to official enumeration.

Censuses, too, can be undertaken conveniently only from

time to time. Indeed, it is ordinarily possible to undertake them only at considerable intervals of time. Hence the data obtained at a certain point in time for all goods whose available quantities are subject to severe fluctuations will not infrequently already have lost practical value, even though the figures may lay claim to reliability.

Government activity directed to the determination of the quantities of goods available at any time to a given people or nation is, therefore, naturally confined: (1) to goods whose quantities are subject only to slight changes, as is the case with land, buildings, domestic animals, transportation facilities, etc., since a census of such items, taken at a particular point in time, maintains its validity for later points in time as well, and (2) to goods whose available quantities are subject to such a degree of public control that the correctness of the figures obtained is thereby guaranteed, at least in some degree.

With the signal interest that the business world, under the circumstances just described, has in as exact a knowledge as possible of the quantities of goods available in certain trading areas, it is understandable that it is not satisfied with the incomplete results of this activity of governments, performed, as it is for the most part, with little commercial understanding and always covering only particular countries or parts of countries rather than entire trading areas. On the contrary, the business world itself attempts to provide independently, and not infrequently at considerable financial sacrifice, as inclusive and as exact information as is possible of the quantities in question. This need has produced many organs serving the special interests of the business world, whose task consists, in considerable part, of informing the members of each branch of production about the current state of stocks in the various trading areas.[7]

Among these organs are the correspondents who are maintained by large business houses at the major markets for each of their commodities. One of the chief duties of these correspondents is to keep their employers continuously informed about the condition of commodity stocks. For every important commodity there is also a considerable number of periodically published business reports that serve the same purpose. Anyone

7. The next paragraph appears here as a footnote in the original.—TR.

who carefully follows the grain reports of Bell in London or
Meyer in Berlin, the sugar reports of Licht in Magdeburg, the
cotton reports of Ellison and Haywood in Liverpool, etc., will
find reliable information in them about the current state of
commodity stocks (and many other data of importance to the
business world, which I will discuss later) based on investigations of various kinds and on ingenious calculation where investigation is not feasible. These estimates of commodity stocks
have a very definite influence, as we shall see, on economic
phenomena, notably price formation. The cotton reports of
Ellison and Haywood, for example, contain periodical information about current stocks of the different grades of cotton in
Liverpool, in England in general, on the continent, and in
America, India, Egypt and the other producing regions; they
inform us regularly about the quantities of cotton in process of
shipment on the high seas (floating cargo), about the ports to
which they are consigned, and whether the quantities in England are still in the hands of the wholesalers, already in the
warehouses of spinners or other buyers, or assigned for export,
etc.

These reports are based on public censuses of all kinds, which
the business world immediately strives to make serviceable if
they prove at all trustworthy, on information gathered by expert correspondents in various places, and in part also on the
estimates of experienced businessmen of proven reliability.
They cover not only the stocks available at any given time but
also the quantities of goods expected to be at the disposal of
men in future time periods.[8] In the above-mentioned reports of
Licht, for example, one finds not only news of the fluctuations
of sugar stocks in all the trading areas in contact with Germany,
but also a comprehensive collection of facts concerning raw material and manufacturing production. In particular, one finds
current reports on the area of land planted in sugar cane and
sugar beets, on the present condition of the cane and beet crops,
on the expected influence of the weather on the time and quantitative and qualitative results of the harvest, on the harvest
itself, on the capacities of sugar factories and refineries, on the

8. The remainder of this paragraph appears here as a footnote in the
    original.—TR.

number of these plants that are active and the number that are idle, on the amount of foreign and domestic output that is expected to reach the German market and the times of expected arrival, on technical progress in methods of sugar production, on disturbances in the distributive apparatus, etc. Similar data on other commodities are contained in the other business reports mentioned in the previous paragraph.

Such reports are usually sufficient to inform the business world about the available quantities of certain commodities in the more or less extensive trading areas relevant to each commodity, and to provide it with a basis for judging prospective changes in stocks. Where actual uncertainties exist, the reports serve to draw attention to this circumstance, so that, in all cases where the outcome of a particular transaction depends upon the larger or smaller available quantity of a good, its risky character is brought to the attention of the business world.

3. THE ORIGIN OF HUMAN
ECONOMY AND ECONOMIC GOODS

A. *Economic goods.*

In the two preceding sections we have seen how separate individuals, as well as the inhabitants of whole countries and groups of countries united by trade, attempt to form a judgment on the one hand about their requirements for future time periods and, on the other, about the quantities of goods available to them for meeting these requirements, in order to gain in this way the indispensable foundation for activity directed to the satisfaction of their needs. The task to which we now turn is to show how men, on the basis of this knowledge, direct the available quantities of goods (consumption goods and means of production) to the greatest possible satisfaction of their needs.

An investigation of the requirements for, and available quantities of, a good may establish the existence of any one of the three following relationships:

(a) that requirements are larger than the available quantity.
(b) that requirements are smaller than the available quantity.
(c) that requirements and the available quantity are equal.

We can regularly observe the first of these relationships—where a part of the needs for a good must necessarily remain unsatisfied—with by far the greater number of goods. I do not refer here to articles of luxury since, with them, this relationship seems self-evident. But even the coarsest pieces of clothing, the most ordinary living accommodations and furnishings, the most common foods, etc., are goods of this kind. Even earth, stones, and the most insignificant kinds of scrap are, as a rule, not available to us in such great quantities that we could not employ still greater quantities of them.

Wherever this relationship appears with respect to a given time period—that is, wherever men recognize that the requirements for a good are greater than its available quantity—they achieve the further insight that no part of the available quantity, in any way practically significant, may lose its useful properties or be removed from human control without causing some concrete human needs, previously provided for, to remain unsatisfied, or without causing these needs now to be satisfied less completely than before.

The first effects of this insight upon the activity of men intent to satisfy their needs as completely as possible are that they strive: (1) to maintain at their disposal every unit of a good standing in this quantitative relationship, and (2) to conserve its useful properties.

A further effect of knowledge of this relationship between requirements and available quantities is that men become aware, on the one hand, that under all circumstances a part of their needs for the good in question will remain unsatisfied and, on the other hand, that any inappropriate employment of partial quantities of this good must necessarily result in part of the needs that would be provided for by appropriate employment of the available quantity remaining unsatisfied.

Accordingly, with respect to a good subject to the relationship under discussion, men endeavor, in provident activity directed to the satisfaction of their needs: (3) to make a choice between their more important needs, which they will satisfy with the available quantity of the good in question, and needs that they must leave unsatisfied, and (4) to obtain the greatest possible result with a given quantity of the good or a given

result with the smallest possible quantity—or in other words, to
direct the quantities of consumers' goods available to them, and
particularly the available quantities of the means of production,
to the satisfaction of their needs in the most appropriate manner.

The complex of human activities directed to these four objectives is called economizing, and goods standing in the quantitative relationship involved in the preceding discussion are
the exclusive objects of it. These goods are *economic* goods in
contrast to such goods as men find no practical necessity of economizing—for reasons which, as we shall see later, can be traced
to quantitative relationships accessible to exact measurement,
just as this has been shown to be possible in the case of economic goods.[9]

But before we proceed to demonstrate these relationships and
the phenomena of life ultimately determined by them, we will
consider a phenomenon of social life which has assumed im-
measurable significance for human welfare and which, in its
ultimate causes, springs from the same quantitative relationship
that we became acquainted with earlier in this section.

So far we have presented the phenomena of life that result
from the fact that the requirements of men for many goods are
greater than the quantities available to them in a very general
way, and without special regard to the social organization of
men. What has been said to this point therefore applies equally
to an isolated individual and to a whole society, however it may
be organized. But the social life of men, pursuing their individual interests even as members of society, brings to view a
special phenomenon in the case of all goods whose available
quantities are less than the requirements for them. An account
of this phenomenon may find its place here.

If the quantitative relationship under discussion occurs in
a society (that is, if the requirements of a society for a good are
larger than its available quantity), it is impossible, in accordance with what was said earlier, for the respective needs of all
individuals composing the society to be completely satisfied. On
the contrary, nothing is more certain than that the needs of

    9. See the first five paragraphs of Appendix B (p. 288) for the material
       originally appearing here as a footnote.—TR.

some members of this society will be satisfied either not at all or, at any rate, only in an incomplete fashion. Here human self-interest finds an incentive to make itself felt, and where the available quantity does not suffice for all, every individual will attempt to secure his own requirements as completely as possible to the exclusion of others.

In this struggle, the various individuals will attain very different degrees of success. But whatever the manner in which goods subject to this quantitative relationship are divided, the requirements of some members of the society will not be met at all, or will be met only incompletely. These persons will therefore have interests opposed to those of the present possessors with respect to each portion of the available quantity of goods. But with this opposition of interest, it becomes necessary for society to protect the various individuals in the possession of goods subject to this relationship against all possible acts of force. In this way, then, we arrive at the economic origin of our present legal order, and especially of the so-called *protection of ownership*, the basis of property.

Thus human economy and property have a joint economic origin since both have, as the ultimate reason for their existence, the fact that goods exist whose available quantities are smaller than the requirements of men. Property, therefore, like human economy, is not an arbitrary invention but rather the only practically possible solution of the problem that is, in the nature of things, imposed upon us by the disparity between requirements for, and available quantities of, all economic goods.

As a result, it is impossible to abolish the institution of property without removing the causes that of necessity bring it about —that is, without simultaneously increasing the available quantities of all economic goods to such an extent that the requirements of all members of society can be met completely, or without reducing the needs of men far enough to make the available goods suffice for the complete satisfaction of their needs. Without establishing such an equilibrium between requirements and available amounts, a new social order could indeed ensure that the available quantities of economic goods would be used for the satisfaction of the needs of different persons than at present. But by such a redistribution it could never surmount the fact that there would be persons whose requirements for economic goods would either not be met at all, or met only incompletely, and against whose potential acts of force, the possessors of economic goods would have to be protected. Property, in this sense, is therefore inseparable from human economy in its social form, and all plans of social reform can reasonably be directed only toward an appropriate distribution of economic goods but never to the abolition of the institution of property itself.

B. *Non-economic goods.*

In the preceding section I have described the every-day phenomena that result from the fact that requirements for certain goods are larger than their available quantities. I shall now demonstrate the phenomena arising from the opposite relationship—that is, as a consequence of a relationship in which the requirements of men for a good are smaller than the quantity of it available to them.

The first result of this relationship is that men not only know that the satisfaction of all their needs for such goods is completely assured, but know also that they will be incapable of exhausting the whole available quantity of such goods for the satisfaction of these needs.

Suppose that a village is dependent for water on a mountain stream with a normal flow of 200,000 pails of water a day. When there are rainstorms, however, and in the spring, when the snow melts on the mountains, the flow rises to 300,000 pails. In times of greatest drought it falls to but 100,000 pails of water daily. Suppose further that the inhabitants of the village, for drinking and other uses, usually need 200, and at the most 300, pails daily for the complete satisfaction of their needs. Their highest requirement of 300 pails is in contrast with an available minimum of at least 100,000 pails per day. In this and in every other case where a quantitative relationship of this kind is found, it is clear not only that the satisfaction of all needs for the good in question is assured, but also that the economizing individuals will be able to utilize the available quantity only *partially* for the satisfaction of their needs. It is evident also that partial quantities of these goods may be removed from their disposal, or may lose their useful properties, without any resultant diminution in the satisfaction of their needs, provided only that the aforementioned quantitative relationship is not thereby reversed. As a result, economizing men are under no practical necessity of either preserving every unit of such goods at their command or conserving its useful properties.

Nor can the third and fourth of the above-described phenomena of human economic activity be observed in the case of goods whose available quantities exceed requirements for them. If such a relationship should exist, what sense would there be in any attempt to make a choice between needs that men should satisfy with the available quantity and needs that they will resign themselves to leaving unsatisfied, when they are unable to exhaust the whole quantity available to them even with the most complete satisfaction of all their needs? And what could move men to achieve the greatest possible result with each quantity of such goods, and any given result with the least possible quantity?

It is clear, accordingly, that all the various forms in which human economic activity expresses itself are absent in the case of goods whose available quantities are larger than the requirements for them, just as naturally as they will necessarily be present in the case of goods subject to the opposite quantitative relationship. Hence they are not objects of human economy, and for this reason we call them *non-economic* goods.

To this point we have considered the relationship underlying the non-economic character of goods in a general way—that is, without regard to the present social organization of men. There remains only the task of indicating the special social phenomena that result from this quantitative relationship.

As we have seen, the effort of individual members of a society to attain command of quantities of goods adequate for their needs to the exclusion of all other members has its origin in the fact that the quantity of certain goods available to society is smaller than the requirements for them. Since it is therefore impossible, when such a relationship exists, to meet the requirements of all individuals completely, each individual feels prompted to meet his own requirements to the exclusion of all

other economizing individuals. Thus, when all the members of
a society compete for a given quantity of goods that is insufficient, under any circumstances, to satisfy completely all the
needs of the various individuals, a practical solution to this conflict of interests is, as we have seen, only conceivable if the various portions of the whole amount at the disposal of society pass
into the possession of some of the economizing individuals, and
if these individuals are protected by society in their possession
to the exclusion of all other individuals in the economy.

The situation with respect to goods that do not have economic character is profoundly different. Here the quantities of
goods at the disposal of society are larger than its requirements,
with the result that all individuals are able to satisfy their respective needs completely, and portions of the available amount
of goods remain unused because they are useless for the satisfaction of human needs. Under such circumstances, there is no
practical necessity for any individual to secure a part of the
whole sufficient to meet his requirements, since the mere recognition of the quantitative relationship responsible for the non-
economic character of the goods in question gives him sufficient
assurance that, even if all other members of society completely
meet their requirements for these goods, more than sufficient
quantities will still remain for him to satisfy his needs.

As experience teaches, the efforts of single individuals in society are therefore not directed to securing possession of quantities of non-economic goods for the satisfaction of their own
individual needs to the exclusion of other individuals. These
goods are therefore neither objects of economy nor objects of
the human desire for property. On the contrary, we can actually observe a picture of communism with respect to all goods
standing in the relationship causing non-economic character;
for men are communists whenever possible under existing natural conditions. In towns situated on rivers with more water
than is wanted by the inhabitants for the satisfaction of their
needs, everyone goes to the river to draw any desired quantity
of water. In virgin forests, everyone fetches unhindered the
quantity of timber he needs. And everyone admits as much light
and air into his house as he thinks proper. This communism is

as naturally founded upon a non-economic relationship as property is founded upon one that is economic.

C. *The relationship between economic and non-economic goods.*

In the two preceding sections we examined the nature and origin of human economy, and demonstrated that the difference between economic and non-economic goods is ultimately founded on a difference, capable of exact determination, in the relationship between requirements for and available quantities of these goods.

But if this has been established, it is also evident that the economic or non-economic character of goods is nothing inherent in them nor any property of them, and that therefore every good, without regard to its internal properties or its external attributes, attains economic character when it enters into the quantitative relationship explained above, and loses it when this relationship is reversed.[10]

Economic character is by no means restricted to goods that are the objects of human economy in a social context. If an isolated individual's requirements for a good are greater than the quantity of the good available to him, we will observe him retaining possession of every unit at his command, conserving it for employment in the manner best suited to the satisfaction of his needs, and making a choice between needs that he will satisfy with the quantity available to him and needs that he will leave unsatisfied. We will also find that the same individual has no reason to engage in this activity with respect to goods that are available to him in quantities exceeding his requirements. Hence economic and non-economic goods also exist for an isolated individual. The cause of the economic character of a good cannot therefore be the fact that it is either an "object of exchange" or an "object of property." Nor can the fact that some goods are products of labor while others are given us by nature without labor be represented with any greater justice as the criterion for distinguishing economic from non-economic character, in spite of the fact that a great deal of clever reasoning has been devoted to attempting to interpret actual phe-

10. The next paragraph originally appears here as a footnote.—TR.

nomena that contradict this view in a sense that does not. For experience tells us that many goods on which no labor was expended (alluvial land, water power, etc.) display economic character whenever they are available in quantities that do not meet our requirements. Nor does the fact that a thing is a product of labor by itself necessarily result in its having goods-character, let alone economic character. Hence the labor expended in the production of a good cannot be the criterion of economic character. On the contrary, it is evident that this criterion must be sought exclusively in the relationship between requirements for and available quantities of goods.

Experience, moreover, teaches us that goods of the same kind do not show economic character in some places but are economic goods in other places, and that goods of the same kind and in the same place attain and lose their economic character with changing circumstances.

While quantities of fresh drinking water in regions abounding in springs, raw timber in virgin forests, and in some countries even land, do not have economic character, these same goods exhibit economic character in other places at the same time. Examples are no less numerous of goods that do not have economic character at a particular time and place but which, at this same place, attain economic character at another time. These differences between goods and their changeability cannot, therefore, be based on the properties of the goods. On the contrary, one can, if in doubt, convince oneself in all cases, by an exact and careful examination of these relationships, that when goods of the same kind have a different character in two different places at the same time, the relationship between requirements and available quantities is different in these two places, and that wherever, in one place, goods that originally had non-economic character become economic goods, or where the opposite takes place, a change has occurred in this quantitative relationship.

According to our analysis, there can be only two kinds of reasons why a non-economic good becomes an economic good: an increase in human requirements or a diminution of the available quantity.

The chief causes of an increase in requirements are: (1)

growth of population, especially if it occurs in a limited area, (2) growth of human needs, as the result of which the requirements of any given population increase, and (3) advances in the knowledge men have of the causal connection between things and their welfare, as the result of which new useful purposes for goods arise.

I need hardly point out that all these phenomena accompany the transition of mankind from lower to higher levels of civilization. From this it follows, as a natural consequence, that with advancing civilization non-economic goods show a tendency to take on economic character, chiefly because one of the factors involved is the magnitude of human requirements, which increase with the progressive development of civilization. If to this is added a diminution of the available quantities of goods that previously did not exhibit economic character (timber, for instance, through the clearance or devastation of forests associated with certain phases of cultural development), nothing is more natural than that goods, whose available quantities on an earlier level of civilization by far outstripped requirements, and which therefore did not show economic character, should become economic goods with the passage of time. In many places, especially in the new world, this transition from non-economic to economic character can be proven historically for many goods, especially timber and land. Indeed the transition can be observed even at the present time. Despite the fact that information in this field is only fragmentary, I believe that in Germany, once so densely forested, but few places are to be found where the inhabitants have not, at some time, experienced this transition—in the case of firewood, for example.

From what has been said, it is clear that all changes by which economic goods become non-economic goods, and conversely, by which the latter become economic goods can be reduced simply to a change in the relationship between requirements and available quantities.

Goods that occupy an intermediate position between economic and non-economic goods with respect to the characteristics they exhibit may lay claim to a special scientific interest.

In this class must be counted, above all, such goods in highly civilized countries as are produced by the government and offered for public use in such large quantities that any desired amount of them is at the disposal of even the poorest member of society, with the result that they do not attain economic character for the consumers.

Public school education, for instance, in a highly developed society is usually such a good. Pure healthy drinking water also is considered a good of such importance by the inhabitants of many cities that, wherever nature does not make it abundantly available, it is brought by aquaducts to the public fountains in such large quantities that not only are the requirements of the inhabitants for drinking water completely met but also, as a rule, considerable quantities above these requirements are available. While instruction by a teacher is an economic good for those in need of such instruction in societies at a low level of civilization, this same good becomes a non-economic good in more highly developed societies, since it is provided by the state. Similarly, in many large cities pure and healthy drinking water, which previously had economic character for consumers, becomes a non-economic good.

Conversely, goods that are naturally available in quantities exceeding requirements may attain economic character for their consumers if a powerful individual excludes the other members of the economy from freely acquiring and using them. In densely wooded countries, there are many villages surrounded by natural forests abounding in timber. In such places, the available quantity of timber by far exceeds the requirements of the inhabitants, and uncut wood would not have economic character in the natural course of events. But when a powerful person seizes the whole forest, or the greater part of it, he can regulate the quantities of timber actually available to the inhabitants of his village in such a way that timber nevertheless acquires economic character for them. In the heavily wooded Carpathians, for instance, there are numerous places where peasants (the former villeins) must buy the timber they need from large landholders, even while the latter let many thousands of logs rot every year in the forest because the quantities available to them far exceed their present requirements. This, however, is a case in which goods that would not possess economic character in the natural course of events artificially become economic goods for the consumers. In such circumstances, these goods actually manifest all the phenomena of economic life that are characteristic of economic goods.[11]

Finally, goods belong in this category that do not exhibit economic character at the present time but which, in view of future developments, are already considered by economizing men as economic goods in many respects. More precisely, if the available quantity of a non-economic good is continually diminishing, or if the requirements for it are continually increasing, and the relationship between requirements and available quantity is such that the final transition of the good in question from non-economic to economic status can be foreseen, economizing individuals will usually make portions of the available quantity objects of their economic activity. They will do this even when the quantitative relationship responsible for the non-economic character of the good still actually prevails, and will, when living as members of a society, usually guarantee themselves their individual requirements by taking possession of quantities corresponding to these requirements. The same reasoning applies to non-economic goods whose available quantities are subject to such violent fluctuations that only command of a certain surplus in normal times assures command of requirements in times of scarcity. It applies also to all non-economic goods with respect to which the boundary between requirements and available quantities is already so close (the third case mentioned on p. 94, above all, belongs in this category) that any misuse or ignorance on the part of some members of the economy may easily become injurious to the others, or when special considerations (considerations of comfort or cleanliness for example) apparently make expedient the seizure of partial quantities of the non-economic goods. For these and similar reasons the phenomenon of property can also be observed in the case of goods that appear to us still, with respect to other aspects of economic life, as non-economic goods.

Finally, I would like to direct the attention of my readers to a circumstance that is of great importance in judging the eco-

11. Using a mode of expression already current in our science, we could, by analogy, call the latter *quasi-economic* goods (as opposed to true economic goods), and the former *quasi-non-economic* goods.

nomic character of goods. I refer to differences in the quality of goods. If the total available quantity of a good is not sufficient to meet the requirements for it, every appreciable part of the total quantity becomes an object of human economy and thus an economic good whatever its quality. And if the available quantities of a good are greater than the requirements for it, and there are therefore portions of the total stock that are utilized for the satisfaction of no need whatever, all units of the good must, in accordance with what has already been said about the nature of non-economic goods, have non-economic character if they are all of exactly the same quality. But if some portions of the available stock of a good have certain advantages over the other portions, and these advantages are of such a kind that various human needs can be better satisfied or, in general, more completely satisfied by using these rather than the other, less useful, portions, it may happen that the goods of better quality will attain economic character while the other (inferior) goods still exhibit non-economic character. Thus, in a country with a superabundance of land, for instance, land that is preferable because of the composition of the soil or by reason of its location may already have attained economic character while poorer lands still exhibit non-economic character. And in a city situated on a river with drinking water of inferior quality, quantities of spring water may already be objects of individual economy when the river water does not, as yet, show economic character.

Thus, if we sometimes find that different portions of the whole supply of a good differ in character at the same time, the reason, in this case too, always lies solely in the fact that the available quantities of the goods of better grade are smaller than requirements while the poorer goods are available in quantities exceeding requirements (requirements not covered by the goods of better grade). Such instances do not, therefore, constitute exceptions, but are, on the contrary, a confirmation of the principles stated in this chapter.

D. *The laws governing the economic character of goods.*

In our investigation of the laws governing human requirements, we have reached the result that the existence of requirements for goods of higher order is dependent: (1) on our having requirements for the corresponding goods of lower order, and also (2) on these requirements for goods of lower order being not already provided for, or at least not completely provided for. We have defined an economic good as a good whose available quantity does not meet requirements completely, and thus we have the principle that *the existence of requirements for goods of higher order is dependent upon the corresponding goods of lower order having economic character.*

In places where pure and healthy drinking water is present in quantities exceeding the requirements of the population, and where this good therefore does not exhibit economic character, requirements for the various implements or means of transportation serving exclusively for carrying or piping and filtering drinking water cannot arise. And in regions in which there is a natural superabundance of firewood (trees, to be exact), and in which, as a result, this good has non-economic character, obviously all requirements for goods of higher order suitable exclusively for the production of firewood are absent from the very beginning. In regions, on the other hand, where firewood or drinking water have economic character, requirements for the corresponding goods of higher order will certainly exist.

But if it has now been established that human requirements for goods of higher order are determined by the economic character of the corresponding goods of lower order, and that requirements for goods of higher order cannot arise at all if they are not applicable to the production of economic goods, it follows that requirements for goods of higher order can never, in this event, become larger than their available quantities, however small, and hence that it is impossible from the very beginning for them to attain economic character.

From this we derive the general principle that the *economic character of goods of higher order depends upon the economic character of the goods of lower order for whose production they serve.* In other words, no good of higher order can attain economic character or maintain it unless it is suitable for the production of some economic good of lower order.

If, therefore, goods of lower order displaying economic character are under consideration, and if the question arises as to the ultimate causes of their economic character, it would be a complete reversal of the true relationship, if one were to assume that they are economic goods because the goods employed in producing them displayed economic character before the production process was undertaken. Such a supposition would contradict, in the first place, all experience, which teaches us that, from goods of higher order whose economic character is beyond all doubt, completely useless things may be produced, and in consequence of economic ignorance, actually are produced—things that do not even have goods-character let alone economic character. Moreover, cases can be conceived where, from economic goods of higher order, things can be produced that have goods-character but not economic character. By way of illustration, one need only imagine persons using costly economic goods to produce timber in virgin forests, to store up drinking water in regions abounding in freshwater springs, or to make air, etc.!

The economic character of a good thus cannot be a consequence of the circumstance that it has been produced from economic goods of higher order, and this explanation would have to be rejected in any case, even if it were not involved in a further internal contradiction. The explanation of the economic character of goods of lower order by that of goods of higher order is only a pseudo-explanation, and apart from being incorrect and in contradiction with all experience, it does not even fulfill the formal conditions for the explanation of a phenomenon. If we explain the economic character of goods of first order by that of goods of second order, the latter by the economic character of goods of third order, this again by the economic character of goods of fourth order, and so on, the solution of the problem is not advanced fundamentally by a single step, since the question as to the last and true cause of the economic character of goods always still remains unanswered.

Our previous explanation, however, demonstrates that man, with his needs and his command of the means to satisfy them, is himself the point at which human economic life both begins and ends. Initially, man experiences needs for goods of first order, and makes those whose available quantities are smaller than his requirements the objects of his economic activity (that is, he treats them as economic goods) while he finds no practical inducement to bring the other goods into the sphere of his economic activity.

Later, thought and experience lead men to ever deeper insights into the causal connections between things, and especially into the relations between things and their welfare. They learn to use goods of second, third, and higher orders. But with these goods, as with goods of first order, they find that some are available in quantities exceeding their requirements while the opposite relationship prevails with others. Hence they divide goods of higher order also into one group that they include in the sphere of their economic activity, and another group that they do not feel any practical necessity to treat in this way. This is the origin of the economic character of goods of higher order.

4. WEALTH

Earlier (p. 76) we called "the entire sum of goods at a person's command" his *property*. The entire sum of *economic* goods at an economizing individual's command [12] we will, on the other hand, call his *wealth*.[13, 14] The non-economic goods at an economizing individual's command are not objects of his economy, and hence must not be regarded as parts of his wealth. We saw that economic goods are goods whose available quantities are smaller than the requirements for them. Wealth can therefore also be defined as *the entire sum of goods at an economizing individual's command, the quantities of which are smaller than the requirements for them.* Hence, if there were a society where all goods were available in amounts exceeding the requirements for them, there would be no economic goods nor

12. A good is at a person's "command" in the economic sense of the term if he is in a position to employ it for the satisfaction of his needs. Either physical or legal obstacles can prevent a good from being at one's command. A minor's wealth, for example, is not at his guardian's command in this sense of the word.

13. F. B. W. von Hermann, *Staatswirthschaftliche Untersuchungen,* München, 1874, p. 21.

14. See the last two paragraphs of Appendix B (p. 291) for the material originally appearing here as a footnote.—TR.

any "wealth." Although wealth is thus a measure of the degree
of completeness with which one person can satisfy his needs in
comparison with other persons who engage in economic activity
under the same conditions, it is never an absolute measure of
his welfare,[15] for the highest welfare of all individuals and of
society would be attained if the quantities of goods at the disposal of society were so large that no one would be in need of
wealth.

These remarks are intended to introduce the solution of a
problem which, because of the apparent contradictions to which
it leads, is capable of creating distrust as to the accuracy of the
principles of our science. The problem arises from the fact that
a continuous increase in the amounts of economic goods available to economizing individuals would necessarily cause these
goods eventually to lose their economic character, and in this
way cause the components of wealth to suffer a diminution.
Hence we have the queer contradiction that a continuous increase of the objects of wealth would have, as a necessary final
consequence, a diminution of wealth.[16]

Suppose that the quantity of a certain mineral water available to a people is smaller than requirements for it. The various
portions of this good at the command of the several economizing persons, as well as the mineral springs themselves, are there-
for economic goods, and hence constituent parts of wealth.
Suppose now that this medicinal water should suddenly begin
to flow in several brooks in such abundant measure as to lose

15. Since wealth provides only a relative measure of the degree of completeness with which an individual can satisfy his needs, some writers
have defined wealth as a sum of *economic* goods, when applying the
term to the economy of a single individual, and as the sum of *all*
goods when applying it to the social economy. The main reason for
doing this was that they had in mind the relative welfare of the different individuals in the first definition and the absolute welfare of
society in the second. See especially, James Maitland, Earl of Lauderdale, *An Inquiry into the Nature and Origin of Public Wealth*, Edinburgh, 1804, pp. 39 ff., esp. pp. 56 ff. The question recently raised by
Wilhelm Roscher (*System der Volkswirthschaft*, Twentieth edition,
Stuttgart, 1892, I, 16 ff.), about whether or not social wealth is to be
estimated by its use value and private wealth by its exchange value can
be traced to the same distinction.
16. See already Lauderdale, *op. cit.*, p. 43.

its previous economic character. Nothing is more certain, than that the quantities of mineral water that were at the command of economizing individuals before this event, as well as the mineral springs themselves, would now cease to be components of wealth. Thus it would indeed be the case that a progressive increase in the component parts of wealth would finally have caused a diminution of wealth.

This paradox is exceedingly impressive at first sight, but upon more exact consideration, it proves to be only an apparent one. As we saw earlier, economic goods are goods whose available quantities are smaller than the requirements for them. They are goods of which there is a partial deficiency, and the wealth of economizing individuals is nothing but the sum of these goods. If their available quantities are progressively increased until they finally lose their economic character, a deficiency no longer exists, and they move out of the category of goods constituting the wealth of economizing individuals—that is, they leave the class of goods of which there is a partial deficiency. There is certainly no contradiction in the fact that the progressive increase of a good of which there was previously a deficiency finally brings about the result that the good ceases to be in short supply.

On the contrary, that the progressive increase of economic goods must finally lead to a reduction in the number of goods of which there was previously a deficiency is a proposition that is as immediately evident to everyone as the contrary proposition that a long continued diminution of abundantly available (non-economic) goods must finally make them scarce in some degree—and thus components of wealth, which is thereby increased.

The above paradox, which was raised not only with regard to the extent of objects of wealth but in an analogous manner also with regard to the value and price of economic goods,[17] is therefore only an apparent one, and is founded upon a misinterpretation of the nature of wealth and its components.

We have defined wealth as the entire sum of economic goods at the command of an economizing individual. The existence

17. Pierre-Joseph Proudhon, *Système des contradictions économiques*, Third edition, Paris, 1867, I, 59 ff.

of any item of wealth presupposes, therefore, an economizing individual, or at any rate one in whose behalf acts of economizing are performed. Quantities of economic goods destined for a specific purpose are therefore not wealth in the economic sense of the word. The fiction of a legal person may be valid for purposes of legal practice or even for purposes of juridical constructions but not for our science which decidedly rejects all fictions. So-called "trust funds" [18] are therefore quantities of economic goods devoted to specific purposes, but they are not wealth in the economic sense of the word.

This leads to the question of the nature of *public wealth.* States, provinces, communities, and associations generally have quantities of economic goods at their disposal in order to satisfy *their* needs, to realize *their* ends. Here the fiction of a legal person is not necessary for the political economist. Without calling upon any fiction, he can observe an economizing unit, a social organization, whose personnel administer certain economic goods that are available to it for the purpose of satisfying its needs, and direct them to this objective. Hence no-one will hesitate to admit the existence of governmental, provincial, municipal and corporate wealth.

The situation is different with what is designated by the term *"national wealth."* Here we have to deal not with the entire sum of economic goods available to a nation for the satisfaction of *its* needs, administered by government employees, and devoted by them to its purposes, but with the totality of goods at the disposal of the separate economizing individuals and associations of a society for their individual purposes. Thus we have to deal with a concept that deviates in several important respects from what we term wealth.

If we employ the fiction of conceiving of the totality of economizing persons in a society, each striving for the satisfaction of his special needs, and driven not infrequently by interests opposed to the interests of others, as *one* great economizing unit, and if we further assume that the quantities of economic goods at the disposal of the separate economizing individuals are not applied to the satisfaction of their special needs but to the satisfaction of the needs of the totality of individuals com-

18. *"Zweckvermögen."*—TR.

posing the economy, then we do, of course, arrive at the concept of a sum of economic goods at the disposal of an economizing unit (here, at the disposal of society) that are available for the purpose of satisfying its collective needs. Such a concept could correctly be designated by the term national wealth. But under our present social arrangements, the sum of economic goods at the disposal of the individual economizing members of society for the purpose of satisfying their special individual needs obviously does not constitute wealth in the economic sense of the term but rather a complex of wealths linked together by human intercourse and trade.[19]

The need for a scientific designation for the sum of goods just mentioned is, however, so just, and the term "national wealth" for that concept is so generally accepted and sanctioned by usage, that we would serve this need badly if we were to drop the existing term as we become clearer about the correct nature of the so-called national wealth.

It is, then, only necessary that we guard against the error that must arise if we pay no attention to the distinction discussed here. In all questions where the issue is merely the quantitative determination of the so-called national wealth, the sum of the wealths of the individuals of the nation may be designated as national wealth. But when inferences running from the magnitude of the national wealth to the welfare of a people, or when phenomena resulting from contacts between the various economizing individuals, are involved, the concept of national wealth in the literal sense of the term must necessarily lead to frequent errors. In all these cases, the national wealth must be regarded rather as a complex composite of the wealths of the members of society, and we must direct our attention to the different sizes of these individual wealths.

19. See Carl Dietzel, *Die Volkswirthschaft und ihr Verhältniss zu Gesellschaft und Staat,* Frankfurt am Main, 1864, pp. 106 ff.

CHAPTER III | THE THEORY OF VALUE

1. THE NATURE AND ORIGIN OF VALUE

IF THE requirements for a good, in a time period over which the provident activity of men is to extend, are greater than the quantity of it available to them for that time period, and if they endeavor to satisfy their needs for it as completely as possible in the given circumstances, men feel impelled to engage in the activity described earlier and designated *economizing*. But their perception of this relationship gives rise to another phenomenon, the deeper understanding of which is of decisive importance for our science. I refer to the value of goods.

If the requirements for a good are larger than the quantity of it available, and some part of the needs involved must remain unsatisfied in any case, the available quantity of the good can be diminished by no part of the whole amount, in any way practically worthy of notice, without causing some need, previously provided for, to be satisfied either not at all or only less completely than would otherwise have been the case. The satisfaction of some one human need is therefore dependent on the availability of each concrete, practically significant, quantity of all goods subject to this quantitative relationship. If economizing men become aware of this circumstance (that is, if they perceive that the satisfaction of one of their needs, or the greater or less completeness of its satisfaction, is dependent on their command of each portion of a quantity of goods or on each individual good subject to the above quantitative relationship) these goods attain for them the significance we call *value*. Value is thus the importance that individual goods or quantities of goods attain for us because we are conscious of being dependent on command of them for the satisfaction of our needs.[1]

The value of goods, accordingly, is a phenomenon that springs from the same source as the economic character of goods—that is, from the relationship, explained earlier, between requirements for and available quantities of goods.[2] But there is a difference between the two phenomena. On the one hand, perception of this quantitative relationship stimulates our provident activity, thus causing goods subject to this relationship to become objects of our economizing (i. e. economic goods). On the other hand, perception of the same relationship makes us aware

1. See Appendix C (p. 292) for the material originally appearing here as a footnote.—TR.
2. In the preceding chapter we were occupied with an evaluation of the attempts that have been made to trace the differences between economic and non-economic goods back to economic goods being products of labor and objects of exchange and to non-economic goods being "free gifts of nature" and not objects of exchange. We reached the conclusion that the economic character of goods is not dependent on either of these two factors. The same thing is true of value. Like the economic character of goods, value is the result of the relationship between requirements and available quantities of goods to which reference has already been made several times. The same reasons that argue against defining economic goods as "products of labor" or "objects of exchange," also rule out these criteria whenever it is a question of distinguishing between goods that do and goods that do not have value for us.

of the significance that command of each concrete unit [3] of the available quantities of these goods has for our lives and well-being, thus causing it to attain *value* for us.[4] Just as a penetrating investigation of mental processes makes the cognition of external things appear to be merely our consciousness of the impressions made by the external things upon our persons, and thus, in the final analysis, merely the cognition of states of our own persons, so too, in the final analysis, is the importance that we attribute to things of the external world only an outflow of the importance to us of our continued existence and development (life and well-being). Value is therefore nothing inherent in goods, no property of them, but merely the importance that we first attribute to the satisfaction of our needs, that is, to our lives and well-being, and in consequence carry over to economic goods as the exclusive causes of the satisfaction of our needs.

From this, it is also clear why only economic goods have value to us, while goods subject to the quantitative relationship responsible for non-economic character cannot attain value at all. The relationship responsible for the non-economic character of goods consists in requirements for goods being smaller than their available quantities. Thus there are always portions of the whole supply of non-economic goods that are related to no unsatisfied human need, and which can therefore lose their goods-character without impinging in any way on the satisfaction of human needs. Hence no satisfaction [5] depends on our control of any one of the units of a good having non-economic

3. The confusion of "use value" with "utility," with "degree of utility," or with "estimated utility," arises from the doctrine of the *abstract* value of goods (see Karl Heinrich Rau, *Grundsätze der Volkswirthschaftslehre*, Heidelberg, 1847, pp. 79 ff.). A species can have useful properties that make its concrete units suitable for the satisfaction of human needs. Different species can have different degrees of utility in a given use (beechwood and willow wood as fuel, etc.). But neither the utility of a species nor the varying degree of utility of different species or subspecies can be called "value." Not species as such, but only concrete things are *available* to economizing individuals. Only the latter, therefore, are *goods*, and only goods are *objects of our economizing* and of our *valuation*. See O. Michaelis, "Das Kapital vom Werthe", *Vierteljahrschrift für Volkswirthschaft*, I (1863), 16 ff.

4. The remainder of this paragraph is a footnote in the original.—TR.

5. *"Bedürfnissbefriedigung,"* literally "need-satisfaction," has been translated throughout by the word "satisfaction."—TR.

character, and from this it follows that definite quantities of goods subject to this quantitative relationship (non-economic goods) also have no value to us.

If an inhabitant of a virgin forest has several hundred thousand trees at his disposal while he needs only some twenty a year for the full provision of his requirements for timber, he will not consider himself injured in any way, in the satisfaction of his needs, if a forest fire destroys a thousand or so of the trees, provided he is still in a position to satisfy his needs as completely as before with the rest. In such circumstances, therefore, the satisfaction of none of his needs depends upon his command of any single tree, and for this reason a tree also has no value to him.

But suppose there are also in the forest ten wild fruit trees whose fruit is consumed by the same individual. Suppose too, that the amount of fruit available to him is not larger than his requirements. Certainly then, not a single one of these fruit trees can be burned in the fire without causing him to suffer hunger as a result, or without at least causing him to be unable to satisfy his need for fruit as completely as before. For this reason each one of the fruit trees has value to him.

If the inhabitants of a village need a thousand pails of water daily to meet their requirements completely, and a brook is at their disposal with a daily flow of a hundred thousand pails, a concrete portion of this quantity of water, one pail for instance, will have no value to them, since they could satisfy their needs for water just as completely if this partial amount were removed from their command, or if it were altogether to lose its goods-character. Indeed, they will let many thousands of pails of this good flow to the sea every day without in any way impairing satisfaction of their need for water. As long as the relationship responsible for the non-economic character of water continues, therefore, the satisfaction of none of their needs will depend upon their command of any one pail of water in such a way that the satisfaction of this need would not take place if they were not in a position to use that particular pail. For this reason a pail of water has no value to them.

If, on the other hand, the daily flow of the brook were to fall to five hundred pails daily due to an unusual drought or other act of nature, and the inhabitants of the village had no other source of supply, the result would be that the total quantity then available would be insufficient to satisfy their full needs for water, and they could not venture to lose any part of that quantity, one pail for instance, without impairing the satisfaction of their needs. Each concrete portion of the quantity at their disposal would certainly then have value to them.

Non-economic goods, therefore, not only do not have exchange value, as has previously been supposed in the literature of our subject, but no value at all, and hence no use value. I shall attempt to explain the relationship between exchange value and use value in greater detail later, when I have dealt with some of the principles relevant to their consideration. For the time being, let it be observed that exchange value and use value are two concepts subordinate to the general concept of value, and hence coordinate in their relations to each other. All that I have already said about value in general is accordingly as valid for use value as it is for exchange value.

If then, a large number of economists attribute use value (though not exchange value) to non-economic goods, and if some recent English and French economists even wish to banish the concept use value entirely from our science and see it replaced with the concept utility,[6] their desire rests on a mis-

6. Menger's use of the term "utility" may prove confusing to modern readers unless the meaning he attaches to it is kept constantly in mind. This meaning does not permit him to use the term in designating the concept now called "marginal utility." A thing has "utility" (in Menger's sense of the term) if all the available units of the thing together yield a total utility (in our sense of the term) greater than zero even if the thing's marginal utility (in our sense) is zero. In general, he contends that the concept "utility" is entirely objective and lacking in psychological content. He pictures it as an abstract relation between a species f goods and a human need (in a general sense as distinguished from the "concrete needs" of an individual—see note 4 of Chapter II). Utility is therefore, according to Menger, merely a prerequisite of goods-character (and hence of economic character), but has no quantitative relationship to value. For this reason, he repudiates any identification of "utility" with "use value" (see also note 3 of this chapter and Appendices C, D, and G). It is of course obvious that his lack of the term "marginal utility" was no barrier to his expression and elaboration of the concept.—TR.

understanding of the important difference between the two concepts and the actual phenomena underlying them.

Utility is the capacity of a thing to serve for the satisfaction of human needs, and hence (provided the utility is *recognized*) it is a general prerequisite of goods-character. Non-economic goods have utility as well as economic goods, since they are just as capable of satisfying our needs. With these goods also, their capacity to satisfy needs must be *recognized* by men, since they could not otherwise acquire goods-character. But what distinguishes a non-economic good from a good subject to the quantitative relationship responsible for economic character is the circumstance that the satisfaction of human needs does not depend upon the availability of concrete quantities of the former but does depend upon the availability of concrete quantities of the latter. For this reason the former possesses utility, but only the latter, in addition to utility, possesses also that significance for us that we call value.

Of course the error underlying the confusion of utility and use value has had no influence on the practical activity of men. At no time has an economizing individual attributed value under ordinary circumstances to a cubic foot of air or, in regions abounding in springs, to a pint of water. The practical man distinguishes very well the capacity of an object to satisfy one of his needs from its value. But this confusion has become an enormous obstacle to the development of the more general theories of our science.[7]

The circumstance that a good has value to us is attributable, as we have seen, to the fact that command of it has for us the significance of satisfying a need that would not be provided for if we did not have command of the good. Our needs, at any rate in part, at least as concerns their origin, depend upon our wills or on our habits. Once the needs have come into existence, however, there is *no further arbitrary element* in the value goods have for us, for their value is then the necessary consequence of our knowledge of their importance for our lives or well-being. It would be impossible, therefore, for us to regard a

7. It was this error that misled Proudhon, *op. cit.*, pp. 59 ff., into stating that there is an irreconcilable contradiction between use value and exchange value.

good as valueless when we know that the satisfaction of one of our needs depends on having it at our disposal. It would also be impossible for us to attribute value to goods when we know that we are not dependent upon them for the satisfaction of our needs. The value of goods is therefore nothing arbitrary, but always the necessary consequence of human knowledge that the maintenance of life, of well-being, or of some ever so insignificant part of them, depends upon control of a good or a quantity of goods.

Regarding this *knowledge,* however, men can be in error about the value of goods just as they can be in error with respect to all other objects of human knowledge. Hence they may attribute value to things that do not, according to economic considerations, possess it in reality, if they mistakenly assume that the more or less complete satisfaction of their needs depends on a good, or quantity of goods, when this relationship is really non-existent. In cases of this sort we observe the phenomenon of *imaginary* value.

The value of goods arises from their relationship to our needs, and is not inherent in the goods themselves. With changes in this relationship, value arises and disappears. For the inhabitants of an oasis, who have command of a spring that abundantly meets their requirements for water, a certain quantity of water at the spring itself will have no value. But if the spring, as the result of an earthquake, should suddenly decrease its yield of water to such an extent that the satisfaction of the needs of the inhabitants of the oasis would no longer be fully provided for, each of their concrete needs for water would become dependent upon the availability of a definite quantity of it, and such a quantity would immediately attain value for each inhabitant. This value would, however, suddenly disappear if the old relationship were reëstablished and the spring regained its former yield of water. A similar result would ensue if the population of the oasis should increase to such an extent that the water of the spring would no longer suffice for the satisfaction of all needs. Such a change, due to the increase of consumers, might even take place with a certain regularity at such times as the oasis was visited by numerous caravans.

Value is thus nothing inherent in goods, no property of them, nor an independent thing existing by itself. It is a judgment economizing men make about the importance of the goods at their disposal for the maintenance of their lives and well-being. Hence value does not exist outside the consciousness of men. It is, therefore, also quite erroneous to call a good that has value to economizing individuals a "value," or for economists to speak of "values" as of independent real things, and to objectify value in this way. For the entities that exist objectively are always only particular things or quantities of things, and their value is something fundamentally different from the things themselves; it is a judgment made by economizing individuals about the importance their command of the things has for the maintenance of their lives and well-being. Objectification of the value of goods, which is entirely *subjective* in nature, has nevertheless contributed very greatly to confusion about the basic principles of our science.

2. THE ORIGINAL MEASURE OF VALUE

In what has preceded, we have directed our attention to the nature and ultimate causes of value—that is, to the factors common to value in all cases. But in actual life, we find that the values of different goods are very different in magnitude, and that the value of a given good frequently changes. An investigation of the causes of differences in the value of goods and an investigation of the measure of value are the subjects that will occupy us in this section. The course of our investigation is determined by the following consideration.

The goods at our disposal have no value to us for their own sakes. On the contrary, we have seen that only the satisfaction of our needs has importance to us directly, since our lives and well-being are dependent on it. But I have also explained that men attribute this importance to the goods at their disposal if the goods ensure them the satisfaction of needs that would not be provided for if they did not have command of them—that is, they attribute this importance to economic goods. In the value of goods, therefore, we always encounter merely the significance we assign to the satisfaction of our needs—that is, to our lives

and well-being. If I have adequately described the nature of
the value of goods, if it has been established that in the final
analysis only the satisfaction of our needs has importance to us,
and if it has been established too that the value of all goods is
merely an imputation of this importance to economic goods,
then the *differences* we observe in the magnitude of value of
different goods in actual life can only be founded on differences
in the magnitude of importance of the satisfactions that depend
on our command of these goods. To reduce the differences that
we observe in the magnitude of value of different goods in actual life to their ultimate causes, we must therefore perform a
double task. We must investigate: (1) to what extent different
satisfactions have different degrees of importance to us (subjective factor), and (2) which satisfactions of concrete needs depend, in each individual case, on our command of a particular
good (objective factor). If this investigation shows that separate
satisfactions of concrete needs have different degrees of importance to us, and that these satisfactions, of such different degrees
of importance, depend on our command of particular economic
goods, we shall have solved our problem. For we shall have reduced the economic phenomenon whose explanation we stated
to be the central problem of this investigation to its ultimate
causes. I mean differences in the magnitude of value of goods.

With an answer to the question as to the ultimate causes of
differences in the value of goods, a solution is also provided to
the problem of how it comes about that the value of each of the
various goods is itself subject to change. All change consists of
nothing but differences through time. Hence, with a knowledge
of the ultimate causes of the differences between the members
of a set of magnitudes in general, we also obtain a deeper insight into their changes.

A. *Differences in the magnitude of importance of different satisfactions (subjective factor).*

As concerns the differences in the importance that different
satisfactions have for us, it is above all a fact of the most common experience that the satisfactions of greatest importance to
men are usually those on which the maintenance of life de-

pends, and that other satisfactions are graduated in magnitude of importance according to the degree (duration and intensity) of pleasure dependent upon them. Thus if economizing men must choose between the satisfaction of a need on which the maintenance of their lives depends and another on which merely a greater or less degree of well-being is dependent, they will usually prefer the former. Similarly, they will usually prefer satisfactions on which a higher degree of their well-being depends. With the same intensity, they will prefer pleasures of longer duration to pleasures of shorter duration, and with the same duration, pleasures of greater intensity to pleasures of less intensity.

The maintenance of our lives depends on the satisfaction of our need for food, and also, in our climate, on clothing our bodies and having shelter at our disposal. But merely a higher degree of well-being depends on our having a coach, a chessboard, etc. Thus we observe that men fear the lack of food, clothing, and shelter much more than the lack of a coach, a chessboard, etc. They also attribute a substantially higher importance to securing satisfaction of the former needs than they attribute to the satisfaction of needs on which, as in the cases just mentioned, only a passing enjoyment or increased comfort (that is, merely a higher degree of their well-being) depends. But these satisfactions also have very different degrees of importance. The maintenance of life depends neither on having a comfortable bed nor on having a chessboard, but the use of these goods contributes, and certainly in very different degrees, to the increase of our well-being. Hence there can also be no doubt that, when men have a choice between doing without a comfortable bed or doing without a chessboard, they will forgo the latter much more readily than the former.

We have thus seen that different satisfactions are very unequal in importance, since some are satisfactions that have the full importance to men of maintaining their lives, others are satisfactions that determine their well-being in a higher degree, still others in a less degree, and so on down to satisfactions on which some insignificant passing enjoyment depends. But careful examination of the phenomena of life shows that these differences in the importance of different satisfactions can be observed not only with the satisfaction of needs of *different kinds* but also with the *more or less complete* satisfaction of one and the same need.

The lives of men depend on satisfaction of their need for food in general. But it would be entirely erroneous to regard all the foods they consume as being necessary for the maintenance of their lives or even their health (that is, for their continuing well-being). Everyone knows how easy it is to skip one of the usual meals without endangering life or health. Indeed, experience shows that the quantities of food necessary to maintain life are only a small part of what well-to-do persons as a rule consume, and that men even take much more food and drink than is necessary for the full preservation of health. Men consume food for several reasons: above all, they take food to maintain life; beyond this, they take further quantities to preserve health, since a diet sufficient merely to maintain life is too sparing, as experience shows, to avoid organic disorders; finally, having already consumed quantities sufficient to maintain life and preserve health, men further partake of foods simply for the pleasure derived from their consumption.

The separate concrete acts of satisfying the need for food accordingly have very different degrees of importance. The satisfaction of every man's need for food up to the point where his life is thereby assured has the full importance of the maintenance of his life. Consumption exceeding this amount, again up to a certain point, has the importance of preserving his health (that is, his continuing well-being). Consumption extending beyond even this point has merely the importance—as observation shows—of a progressively weaker pleasure, until it finally reaches a certain limit at which satisfaction of the need for food is so complete that every further intake of food contributes neither to the maintenance of life nor to the preservation of health—nor does it even give pleasure to the consumer, becoming first a matter of indifference to him, eventually a cause of pain, a danger to health, and finally a danger to life itself.

Similar observations can be made with respect to the more or less complete satisfaction of all other human needs. A room, or at least some place to sleep protected from the weather, is necessary in our climate for the maintenance of life, and reasonably spacious quarters for the preservation of health. In addition, however, men usually possess further accommodations, if they have the means, merely for purposes of pleasure (drawing rooms, ballrooms, playrooms, pavilions, hunting lodges, etc.). Thus it is not difficult to recognize that the separate concrete acts of satisfying the need for shelter have very different degrees of importance. Up to a certain point, our lives depend on satisfying our need for shelter. Beyond this, our health depends on a more complete satisfaction. And still further attempts to satisfy the same need will bring at first a greater and then a smaller enjoyment, until eventually a point can be conceived, for each person, at which the further *employment* of available accommodations would become a matter of complete indifference to him, and finally even burdensome.

It is possible, therefore, with respect to the more or less complete satisfaction of one and the same need, to make an observation similar to the one made earlier with respect to the different needs of men. We saw earlier that the different needs of men are very unequal in importance of satisfaction, being graduated from the importance of their lives down to the importance they attribute to a small passing enjoyment. We see now, in addition, that the satisfaction of any one specific need has, up to a certain degree of completeness, relatively the highest importance, and that further satisfaction has a progressively smaller importance, until eventually a stage is reached at which a more complete satisfaction of that particular need is a matter of indifference. Ultimately a stage occurs at which every act having the external appearance of a satisfaction of this need not only has no further importance to the consumer but is rather a burden and a pain.

In order to restate the preceding argument numerically, to facilitate comprehension of the subsequent difficult investigation, I shall designate the importance of satisfactions on which life depends with 10, and the smaller importance of the other satisfactions successively with 9, 8, 7, 6, etc. In this way we obtain a scale of the importance of *different* satisfactions that begins with 10 and ends with 1.

Let us now, for each of these different satisfactions, give numerical expression to the additional importance, diminishing by degrees from the figure indicating the extent to which the particular need is already satisfied, of further acts of satisfaction of that particular need. For satisfactions on which, up to a certain point, our lives depend, and on which, beyond this point, a well-being is dependent that steadily decreases with the degree of completeness of the satisfaction already achieved, we obtain a scale that begins with 10 and ends with 0. Similarly, for satisfactions whose highest importance is 9, we obtain a scale that begins with this figure and also ends with 0, and so on.

The ten scales obtained in this way are given in the following table: [8]

8. The Roman numerals in the top line of the table are symbols designating the different commodities (or classes of commodities) consumed by a single individual. The successive figures down each vertical column represent successive additions to total satisfaction resulting from increased consumption of the designated commodity.

Menger does not, however, explicitly name his independent variable at the outset, and the reader is left to find it for himself in the discussion that follows. At times, Menger states vaguely that the successive additions to total satisfaction are the result of successive "acts of satisfaction," but later (p. 130) he makes it clear that they are the result of successive equal additions to the quantity of the commodity consumed. This is not the end of the matter, however. In the paragraph following the table, Menger compares the figures of one column with those of another column when he argues that, after a fifth unit (?) of food has been consumed, the individual of the table faces the fact that a sixth unit of food will give him less additional satisfaction than would be given by a first unit of tobacco, and that he must therefore bring his consumption of the two commodities into equilibrium. Such a comparison is not valid unless a unit of tobacco and a unit of food are so defined that both are to be obtained with an equal expenditure of some other resource (such as labor or money), since otherwise the two units would not constitute alternatives between which the individual must choose.

A minimum model meeting Menger's discussion requires, therefore, the following assumptions:

(1) The economizing individual of the table is able not only to rank his satisfactions but also to assign cardinal indices to their relative degrees of importance. In other words, he is able to compare different satisfactions in terms of a homogeneous unit of satisfaction. (See also the summary of principles on p. 139 and the discussion in Ch. IV, Sec. 2.)

I	II	III	IV	V	VI	VII	VIII	IX	X
10	9	8	7	6	5	4	3	2	1
9	8	7	6	5	4	3	2	1	0
8	7	6	5	4	3	2	1	0	
7	6	5	4	3	2	1	0		
6	5	4	3	2	1	0			
5	4	3	2	1	0				
4	3	2	1	0					
3	2	1	0						
2	1	0							
1	0								
0									

Suppose that the scale in column I expresses the importance to some one individual of satisfaction of his need for food, this importance diminishing according to the degree of satisfaction already attained, and that the scale in column V expresses similarly the importance of his need for tobacco. It is evident that satisfaction of his need for food, up to a certain degree of completeness, has a decidedly higher importance to this individual than satisfaction of his need for tobacco. But if his need for food is already satisfied up to a certain degree of completeness (if, for example, a further satisfaction of his need for food has only the importance to him that we designated numerically by the figure 6), consumption of tobacco begins to have the same importance to him as further satisfaction of his need for food. The individual will therefore endeavor, from this point on, to bring the satisfaction of his need for tobacco into equilibrium with satisfaction of his need for food. Although satisfaction of his need for food in general has a substantially higher importance to the individual in question than satisfaction of his need for tobacco, with the progressive satisfaction of the former a stage nevertheless comes (as is illustrated in the table) at which further acts of satisfaction of his need for food have a smaller

---

(2) The satisfaction from the consumption of each commodity is independent of the amount of consumption of other commodities.

(3) Successive additions to total satisfaction in each vertical column are the result of successive equal additions to the amount of the commodity consumed.

(4) Additional amounts of the different commodities are all to be obtained by the individual with an equal expenditure of some other resource.—TR.

importance to him than the first acts of satisfying his need for tobacco, which although less important in general is at this stage still wholly unsatisfied.

By this reference to an ordinary phenomenon of life, I believe I have clarified satisfactorily the meaning of the numbers in the table, which were chosen merely to facilitate demonstration of a difficult and previously unexplored field of psychology.

The varying importance that satisfaction of separate concrete needs has for men is not foreign to the consciousness of any economizing man, however little attention has hitherto been paid by scholars to the phenomena here treated. Wherever men live, and whatever level of civilization they occupy, we can observe how economizing individuals weigh the relative importance of satisfaction of their various needs in general, how they weigh especially the relative importance of the separate acts leading to the more or less complete satisfaction of each need, and how they are finally guided by the results of this comparison into activities directed to the fullest possible satisfaction of their needs (economizing). Indeed, this weighing of the relative importance of needs—this choosing between needs that are to remain unsatisfied and needs that are, in accordance with the available means, to attain satisfaction, and determining the degree to which the latter are to be satisfied—is the very part of the economic activity of men that fills their minds more than any other, that has the most far-reaching influence on their economic efforts, and that is exercised almost continually by every economizing individual. But human knowledge of the different degrees of importance of satisfaction of different needs and of separate acts of satisfaction is also the first cause of differences in the value of goods.

B. *The dependence of separate satisfactions on particular goods (objective factor).*

If, opposite each particular concrete need of men, there was but a single available good, and that good was suitable exclusively for the satisfaction of the one need (so that, on the one side, satisfaction of the need would not take place if the particular good were not at our disposal, and on the other side, the

good would be capable of serving for the satisfaction of that
concrete need and no other) the determination of the value of
the good would be very easy; it would be equal to the importance we attribute to satisfaction of that need. For it is evident
that whenever we are dependent, in satisfying a given need, on
the availability of a certain good (that is, whenever this satisfaction would not take place if we did not have the good at our
disposal) and when that good is, at the same time, not suitable
for any other useful purpose, it can attain the full but never
any other importance than that which the given satisfaction has
for us. Hence, according to whether the importance of the given
satisfaction to us, in a case such as this, is greater or smaller, the
value of the particular good to us will be greater or smaller. If,
for instance, a myopic individual were cast away on a lonely
island and found among the goods he had salvaged just *one*
pair of glasses correcting his myopia but no second pair, there
is no doubt that these glasses would have the full importance
to him that he attributes to corrected eye-sight, and just as certainly no greater importance, since the glasses would hardly be
suitable for the satisfaction of other needs.

But in ordinary life the relationship between available goods
and our needs is generally much more complicated. Usually not
a single good but a *quantity* of goods stands opposite not a single concrete need but a *complex* of such needs. Sometimes a
larger and sometimes a smaller number of satisfactions, of very
different degrees of importance, depends on our command of a
given quantity of goods, and each one of the goods has the
ability to produce these satisfactions differing so greatly in
importance.

An isolated farmer, after a rich harvest, has more than two
hundred bushels of wheat at his disposal. A portion of this secures him the maintenance of his own and his family's lives
until the next harvest, and another portion the preservation of
health; a third portion assures him seed-grain for the next seeding; a fourth portion may be employed for the production of
beer, whiskey, and other luxuries; and a fifth portion may be
used for the fattening of his cattle. Several remaining bushels,
which he cannot use further for these more important satisfac-

tions, he allots to the feeding of pets in order to make the balance of his grain in some way useful.

The farmer is, therefore, dependent upon the grain in his possession for satisfactions of very different degrees of importance. At first he secures with it his own and his family's lives, and then his own and his family's health. Beyond this, he secures with it the uninterrupted operation of his farm, an important foundation of his continuing welfare. Finally, he employs a portion of his grain for purposes of pleasure, and in so doing is again employing his grain for purposes that are of very different degrees of importance to him.

We are thus considering a case—one that is typical of ordinary life—in which satisfactions of very different degrees of importance depend on the availability of a quantity of goods that we shall assume, for the sake of greater simplicity, to be composed of completely homogeneous units. The question that now arises is: what, under the given conditions, is the value of a certain portion of the grain to our farmer? Will the bushels of grain that secure his own and his family's lives have a higher value to him than the bushels that enable him to seed his fields? And will the latter bushels have a greater value to him than the bushels of grain he employs for purposes of pleasure?

No one will deny that the satisfactions that seem assured by the various portions of the available supply of grain are very unequal in importance, ranging from an importance of 10 to an importance of 1 in terms of our earlier designations. Yet no one will be able to maintain that some bushels of grain (those, for instance, with which the farmer will nourish himself and his family till the next harvest) will have a higher value to him than other bushels of the same quality (those, for instance, from which he will make luxury beverages).

In this and in every other case where satisfactions of different degrees of importance depend on command of a given quantity of goods, we are, above all, faced with the difficult question: which particular satisfaction is dependent on a particular portion of the quantity of goods in question?

The solution of this most important question of the theory of value follows from reflection upon human economy and the nature of value.

We have seen that the efforts of men are directed toward fully satisfying their needs, and where this is impossible, toward satisfying them *as completely as possible*. If a quantity of goods stands opposite needs of varying importance to men, they will first satisfy, or provide for, those needs whose satisfaction has the greatest importance to them. If there are any goods remaining, they will direct them to the satisfaction of needs that are next in degree of importance to those already satisfied. Any further remainder will be applied consecutively to the satisfaction of needs that come next in degree of importance.[9]

If a good can be used for the satisfaction of several different kinds of needs, and if, with respect to each kind of need, successive single acts of satisfaction each have diminishing importance according to the degree of completeness with which the need in question has already been satisfied, economizing men will first employ the quantities of the good that are available to them to secure those acts of satisfaction, without regard to the kind of need, which have the highest importance for them. They will employ any remaining quantities to secure satisfactions of concrete needs that are next in importance, and any further remainder to secure successively less important satisfactions. The end result of this procedure is that the most important of the satisfactions that cannot be achieved have the same importance for every kind of need, and hence that all needs are being satisfied up to an equal degree of importance of the separate acts of satisfaction.

We have been asking what value a given unit of a quantity of goods possessed by an economizing individual has for him. Our question can be more precisely stated with respect to the nature of value if it is stated in this form: which satisfaction would not be attained if the economizing individual did not have the given unit at his disposal—that is, if he were to have command of a total amount smaller by that one unit? The answer, which follows from the previous exposition of the nature of human economy, is that every economizing individual would in this case, with the quantity of goods yet remaining to him, by all means satisfy his more important needs and forgo satisfaction of the less important ones. Thus, of all the satisfac-

9. The next paragraph appears here as a footnote in the original.—TR.

tions previously obtained, only the one that has the smallest importance to him would now be unattained.

Accordingly, in every concrete case, of all the satisfactions secured by means of the whole quantity of a good at the disposal of an economizing individual, only those that have the least importance to him are dependent on the availability of a given portion of the whole quantity. Hence the value to this person of any portion of the whole available quantity of the good is equal to the importance to him of the satisfactions of least importance among those assured by the whole quantity and achieved with an equal portion.[10]

Suppose that an individual needs 10 discrete units (or 10 measures) of a good for the full satisfaction of all his needs for that good, that these needs vary in importance from 10 to 1, but that he has only 7 units (or only 7 measures) of the good at his command. From what has been said about the nature of human economy it is directly evident that this individual will satisfy only those of his needs for the good that range in importance from 10 to 4 with the quantity at his command (7 units), and that the other needs, ranging in importance from 3 to 1, will remain unsatisfied. What is the value to the economizing individual in question of one of his 7 units (or measures) in this case? According to what we have learned about the nature of the value of goods, this question is equivalent to the question: what is the importance of the satisfactions that would be unattained if the individual concerned were to have only 6 instead of 7 units (or measures) at his command. If some accident were to deprive him of one of his seven goods (or measures), it is clear that the person in question would use the remaining 6 units to satisfy the more important needs and would neglect the least important one. Hence the result of losing one good (or one measure) would be that only the least of all the satisfactions assured by the whole available quantity of seven units (i.e. the satisfaction whose importance was designated as 4) would be lost, while those satisfactions (or acts of satisfying needs) whose importance ranges from 10 to 5 would take place as before. In this case, therefore, only a satisfaction whose importance was designated by 4 will depend on command of a sin-

10. The next paragraph appears here as a footnote in the original.—TR.

gle unit (or measure), and as long as the individual in question continues to have command of 7 units (or measures) of the good, the value of each unit (or measure) will be equal to the importance of this satisfaction. For it is only this satisfaction with an importance of 4 that depends on one unit (or measure) of the available quantity of the good. Other things being equal, if only 5 units (or measures) of the good were available to the economizing individual in question, it is evident that—as long as this economic situation persisted—each discrete unit or partial quantity of the good would have an importance to him expressed numerically by the figure 6. If he had 3 units, each one would have an importance to him expressed numerically by the figure 8. Finally, if he had but a single good, its importance would be equal to 10.

Examination of a number of particular cases will fully elucidate the principles here set forth, and I do not wish to shirk this important task, even though I know that I shall appear tiresome to some readers. Following in the path of Adam Smith, I will risk some tediousness to gain clarity of exposition.

To begin with the simplest case, suppose that an isolated economizing individual inhabits a rocky island in the sea, that he finds only a single spring on the island, and that he is exclusively dependent upon it for satisfaction of his need for fresh water. Assume that this isolated individual needs: (a) one unit of water daily for the maintenance of his life, (b) nineteen units for the animals whose milk and meat provide him with the most necessary means of subsistence, (c) forty units, partly so that he may consume the full quantity necessary to the maintenance not only of his life but also his health; partly, to the extent necessary for the continuance of his health and general well-being, to clean his body, his clothes, and his implements; and partly for the support of some additional animals whose milk and meat he finds needful, and finally (d) forty additional units of water daily, partly for his flower garden, and partly for some animals, which he keeps, not for the maintenance of his life and health, but simply for the purpose of a more varied diet, or for mere companionship. Assume too that he does not know how to employ more than this total of one hundred units of water.

As long as the spring provides water so copiously that he
can not only satisfy all his needs for water but let several thousand pails flow into the sea every day, and thus as long as the
satisfaction of none of his needs depends upon whether he has
one unit more or one unit less (e.g. one pailful) at his disposal,
a unit of water will, as we have seen, have neither economic
character nor value to him, and thus there can be no question
of the magnitude of its value. But if some natural event should
now suddenly cause the spring to become partially exhausted,
and if our island dweller should, as a result, have only 90 units
of water at his disposal while he continues to require 100 units
for the full satisfaction of his needs, it is clear that some satisfaction would then be dependent on the availability of each
portion of the whole supply of water, and hence that each particular unit of water would attain that significance for him that
we call value.

If we now, however, ask which of his satisfactions is, in this
case, dependent on a given portion of the 90 units of water
available to him, on 10 units for instance, our question takes
the following form: which satisfactions of our isolated individual would not be attained if he did not have this given portion
of the supply at his disposal—that is, if he should have only 80
instead of 90 units?

Nothing is more certain than that our economizing individual would continue, even if he had only 80 units of water available daily, to consume the quantity necessary for the preservation of his life, and as much more as will maintain as many animals as are indispensable for keeping him alive. Since these
purposes require only 20 units of water daily, he would apply
the remaining 60 units first to the satisfaction of all the needs
on which his health and his continuing general well-being depend. Since for this purpose he requires a total of only 40 pails
of water daily, he would have 20 units left, which could be employed for purposes of mere enjoyment. The last 20 units could
thus maintain either his flower garden or the animals he owns
purely for pleasure. He would certainly choose, from the two
satisfactions, the one appearing to him to be the more important, and would neglect the less important one.

When our Crusoe has 90 units of water available to him

daily, the question whether he will continue to have this quantity or 10 units less at his disposal is, for him, equivalent to the question whether or not he will be in a position to continue to satisfy the least important needs that are being satisfied with 10 units of water daily. As long, therefore, as a total quantity of 90 units continues at his disposal, 10 units of water will have only the importance of these least important satisfactions—that is, only the importance of relatively insignificant enjoyments.

Suppose now that the spring supplying the individual of the isolated economy with water is even further exhausted, to such an extent indeed, that only forty units of water are available to him daily. Now again, just as before, the maintenance of his life and well-being will depend on the availability of this whole quantity of water. But the situation has changed in an important respect. If earlier some one of his pleasures or comforts depended on the availability of each, in any way practically significant, part of the whole supply (one unit, for instance), now the question of a unit more or a unit less of water being available per day is, for our Crusoe, already a question of the more or less complete maintenance of his health or general well-being. In other words, if he should lose one unit, the effect would be that he could no longer satisfy one of the needs on whose satisfaction the preservation of his health and his continuing general well-being depend. If a single pail of water had no value whatsoever to our Crusoe as long as he had several hundred pails at his disposal daily, and if later, when he had only 90 units daily, each unit had only the importance of some particular enjoyment dependent upon it, now each part of the forty units still available has the importance to him of much more important satisfactions. For now the satisfaction of needs whose non-satisfaction impairs his health and continuing well-being depends on each one of the forty units. But the value of each quantity of goods is equal to the importance of the satisfactions that depend on it. If the value of one unit of water to our Crusoe was at first equal to zero, and in the second case equal to one, it would now already be expressed numerically by something like the figure six.

Suppose, with continued drought, the spring should become more and more exhausted, and finally yield just the amount of water daily that is required barely to support the life of this isolated individual (hence in our case approximately 20 units, since he requires that much for himself and for those animals of his herd without whose milk and meat he cannot keep alive). In such a case, it is clear that each practically significant quantity of water available to him would have the full importance of the maintenance of his life. Hence a unit of water would have a still higher value than before, a value expressed numerically by the figure 10.

Thus, in the first of our cases, we saw that as long as the individual had several thousand pails of water at his disposal daily, a small portion of this quantity, one pail for instance, had no value to him at all because no kind of satisfaction depended on any single pail. In the second case, we saw that a concrete unit of the 90 units available to him already had the importance of certain minor enjoyments, since the least important satisfactions that depended on 90 units were these enjoyments. In the third case, when only 40 units of water a day were at his disposal, we saw that more important satisfactions were dependent on each concrete unit. In the fourth case, still more important satisfactions became dependent on each concrete unit. In each succeeding case, we saw the value of the remaining units rising successively as more important satisfactions became dependent on them.

To pass on to more complicated (social) relationships, suppose that a sailing ship still has 20 days of sailing to reach land, that by some accident its stores of food are almost completely lost, and that only such a quantity of some one variety of food, biscuits for instance, is left for each of the shipmates as is just sufficient for the preservation of his life for the 20 days. This is a case in which given needs of the persons on the sailing ship stand opposite command of just the precise quantity of a given good that makes the satisfaction of these needs wholly dependent on the available quantity of the good. If it is assumed that the lives of the voyagers can be maintained only if each of them consumes a half pound of biscuits daily, and that each voyager has actual possession of 10 pounds of biscuits, then this quantity of food will have for each voyager the full importance of maintaining his life. Under such conditions, no one who prizes his own life at all could be prevailed upon to surrender this quantity of goods, or even any appreciable part of it, for any goods other than foodstuffs, even for the most valuable goods of ordinary life. If, for example, a rich man travelling on the boat should offer a pound of gold for the same weight of biscuits to alleviate the pangs of hunger inevitable with such scant rations, he would find none of his shipmates ready to accept such a bargain.

Suppose next that the voyagers on the ship have command of another five pounds of ship's biscuits each, in addition to the 10 pounds already mentioned. In this case their lives would no longer depend on their command of a single pound of biscuits, since one pound could be withdrawn from their control, or exchanged by them for goods other than foodstuffs, without endangering their lives. Even though their very lives would no longer depend on one pound of the food, a pound of it would nevertheless constitute a protection against the pangs of hunger, as well as a means to the preservation of their health, since such scanty nourishment, continued for twenty days, as would be the fare of all persons having only ten pounds of biscuits at their disposal, would unquestionably have an injurious effect on their well-being. Under such circumstances, although a single pound of biscuits would no longer have the importance to them of maintaining their lives, it would nevertheless have the importance everyone attaches to the preservation of his health and well-being, insofar as these depend on a single pound of biscuits.

Let us assume, finally, that the galley of the ship has been completely denuded of all its food stores; that the voyagers are also without any food of their own; that the ship is laden with a cargo of several thousand hundred-weight of biscuits; and that the captain of the ship, in consideration of the unfortunate situation of the voyagers as a result of this calamity, authorizes everyone to nourish himself at will with biscuits. The voyagers will, of course, take the biscuits to still their hunger. But no one will doubt that a palatable piece of meat would, in such a case, have considerable value to a voyager whose entire fare for twenty days would otherwise consist of biscuits alone, while a pound of biscuits would have an extraordinarily small value, and perhaps no value at all.

Why did command of a pound of biscuits have the full importance of maintaining his life to each voyager in the first of these cases, still a very great importance in the second case, but no importance whatsoever, or at any rate only an exceedingly slight importance, in the third case?

The needs of the voyagers remained the same in all three cases, since neither their personalities nor their requirements changed. What did change, however, was the quantity of food standing opposite these requirements in each case. Opposite identical requirements for food on the part of the voyagers, there were ten pounds of food per person in the first case, a larger quantity in the second case, and a still larger quantity in the third case. Hence, from one case to the next, the importance of the satisfactions that were dependent on single units of the food declined progressively.

But what we have been able to observe here, at first with an isolated individual, and then in a small group temporarily isolated from the rest of humanity, is equally valid for the more complex interrelationships of a people and of human society in general. The situation of the inhabitants of a country after a crop failure, after an average crop, and finally, in a year following a bumper crop, presents relationships analogous in nature to those described above. Here also, opposite certain definite requirements, there is a smaller available quantity of food in the first case than in the second, and a smaller one in the second case than in the third. Hence, in these cases also, the importance of the satisfactions that depend on single units of the whole supply varies considerably.

If an elevator with 100,000 bushels of wheat burns down in a country that has just had a bumper crop, the effect of the calamity will at most be that less alcohol will be produced, or that the poorer part of the population will at worst be fed somewhat more scantily, without suffering deprivation; if the calamity occurs after an average crop, many people will already have to forgo more important satisfactions; and if the misfortune coincides with a famine, a great many people will die of hunger. In each of the three cases, satisfactions of very different degrees of

importance depend on each concrete unit of the grain available to the people concerned, and for this reason the value of a
unit of grain varies greatly in the three cases.

If we summarize what has been said, we obtain the following
principles as the result of our investigation thus far:

(1) The importance that goods have for us and which we call
value is merely imputed. Basically, only satisfactions have
importance for us, because the maintenance of our lives
and well-being depend on them. But we logically impute
this importance to the goods on whose availability we are
conscious of being dependent for these satisfactions.

(2) The magnitudes of importance that different satisfactions
of concrete needs (the separate acts of satisfaction that can
be realized by means of individual goods) have for us are
unequal, and their measure lies in the degree of their importance for the maintenance of our lives and welfare.

(3) The magnitudes of the importance of our satisfactions that
are imputed to goods—that is, the magnitudes of their values—are therefore also unequal, and their measure lies in
the degree of importance that the satisfactions dependent
on the goods in question have for us.

(4) In each particular case, of all the satisfactions assured by the
whole available quantity of a good, only those that have the
least importance to an economizing individual are dependent on command of a given portion of the whole quantity.

(5) The value of a particular good or of a given portion of the
whole quantity of a good at the disposal of an economizing
individual is thus for him equal to the importance of the
least important of the satisfactions assured by the whole
available quantity and achieved with any equal portion.
For it is with respect to these least important satisfactions
that the economizing individual concerned is dependent
on the availability of the particular good, or given quantity
of a good.[11]

11. See Appendix D (p. 295) for the material originally appearing here as
a footnote.—TR.

Thus, in our investigation to this point, we have traced the differences in the value of goods back to their ultimate causes, and have also, at the same time, found the ultimate, and original, measure by which the values of all goods are judged by men.

If what has been said is correctly understood, there can be no difficulty in solving any problem involving the explanation of the causes determining the differences between the values of two or more concrete goods or quantities of goods.

If we ask, for example, why a pound of drinking water has no value whatsoever to us under ordinary circumstances, while a minute fraction of a pound of gold or diamonds generally exhibits a very high value, the answer is as follows: Diamonds and gold are so rare that all the diamonds available to mankind could be kept in a chest and all the gold in a single large room, as a simple calculation will show. Drinking water, on the other hand, is found in such large quantities on the earth that a reservoir can hardly be imagined large enough to hold it all. Accordingly, men are able to satisfy only the most important needs that gold and diamonds serve to satisfy, while they are usually in a position not only to satisfy their needs for drinking water fully but, in addition, also to let large quantities of it escape unused, since they are unable to use up the whole available quantity. Under ordinary circumstances, therefore, no human need would have to remain unsatisfied if men were unable to command some particular quantity of drinking water. With gold and diamonds, on the other hand, even the least significant satisfactions assured by the total quantity available still have a relatively high importance to economizing men. Thus concrete quantities of drinking water usually have *no* value to economizing men but concrete quantities of gold and diamonds a *high* value.

All this holds only for the ordinary circumstances of life, when drinking water is available to us in copious quantities and gold and diamonds in very small quantities. In the desert, however, where the life of a traveller is often dependent on a drink of water, it can by all means be imagined that more important satisfactions depend, for an individual, on a pound of water than on even a pound of gold. In such a case, the value of a pound of water would consequently be greater, for the individual concerned, than the value of a pound of gold. And experience teaches us that such a relationship, or one that is similar, actually develops where the economic situation is as I have just described.

C. *The influence of differences in the quality of goods on their value.*

Human needs can often be satisfied by goods of different types and still more frequently by goods that differ, not as to type, but as to kind. Where we deal with given complexes of human needs, on the one side, and with the quantities of goods available for their satisfaction, on the other side (p. 129), the needs do not, therefore, always stand opposite quantities of homogeneous goods, but often opposite goods of different types, and still more frequently opposite goods of different kinds.

For greater simplicity of exposition I have, until now, omitted consideration of the differences between goods, and have, in the preceding sections, considered only cases in which quantities of completely homogeneous goods stand opposite needs of a specific type (stressing particularly the way in which their importance decreases in accordance with the degree of completeness of the satisfaction already attained). In this way, I was able to give greater emphasis to the influence that differences in the available quantities exercise on the value of goods.

The cases that now remain to be taken into consideration are those in which given human needs may be satisfied by goods of different types or kinds and in which, therefore, given human requirements stand opposite available quantities of goods of which separate portions are qualitatively different.

In this connection, it should first be noted that differences between goods, whether they be differences of type or of kind, cannot affect the value of the different units of a given supply if the satisfaction of human needs is in no way affected by these differences. Goods that satisfy human needs in an identical fashion are for this very reason regarded as completely homogeneous from an economic point of view, even though they may belong to different types or kinds on the basis of external appearance.

If the differences, as to type or kind, between two goods are to be responsible for differences in their value, it is necessary that they also have different capacities to satisfy human needs. In other words, it is necessary that they have what we call, from an economic point of view, differences in *quality*. An examination of the influence that differences in quality exercise on the value of particular goods is therefore the subject of the following investigation.

From an economic standpoint, the qualitative differences between goods may be of two kinds. Human needs may be satisfied either in a *quantitatively* or in a *qualitatively* different manner by means of equal quantities of qualitatively different goods. With a given quantity of beech-wood, for instance, the human need for warmth may be satisfied in a *quantitatively* more intensive manner than with the same quantity of fir. But two equal quantities of foodstuffs of equal food value may satisfy the need for food in *qualitatively* different fashions, since the consumption of one dish may, for example, provide enjoyment while the other may provide either no enjoyment or only an inferior one. With goods of the first category, the inferior quality can be fully compensated for by a larger quantity, but with goods of the second category this is not possible. Fir, alder, or pine can replace beech-wood for heating purposes, and if coal of inferior carbon content, oak bark of inferior tannin content, and the ordinary labor services of tardy or less efficient day-laborers are only available to economizing men in sufficiently large quantities, they can generally replace the more highly qualified goods perfectly. But even if unpalatable foods or beverages, dark and wet rooms, the services of mediocre physicians, etc., are available in the largest quantities, they can never satisfy our needs as well, *qualitatively,* as the corresponding more highly qualified goods.

When economizing individuals appraise the value of a good, it is purely a question, as we have seen, of estimating the importance of satisfaction of those needs with respect to which they are dependent on command of the good (p. 122). The quantity of a good that will bring about a given satisfaction is, however, only a secondary factor in valuation. For if smaller quantities of a more highly qualified good will satisfy a human need in the same (that is, in a quantitatively and qualitatively identical) manner as larger quantities of a less qualified good, it is evident that the smaller quantities of the more highly qualified good will have the same value to economizing men as the larger quantities of the less qualified good. Thus equal quantities of goods having different qualities of the first kind will display values that are unequal in the proportion indicated. If, for example, in determining the value of oak bark we take account exclusively of its tannin content, and seven hundredweight of one grade has the same effectiveness as eight hundredweight of another grade, it will also have the same value as the latter quantity to the artisans using the bark. Merely reducing these goods to quantities of equal economic effectiveness (a procedure actually employed in the economic activities of men in all such cases) thus completely removes the difficulty in determining the value of given quantities of different qualities (so far as their effectiveness is merely quantitatively different). In this way, the more complicated case under consideration is reduced to the simple relationship explained earlier (pp. 123 ff).

The question of the influence of different qualities on the values of particular goods is more complicated when the qualitative differences between the goods cause needs to be satisfied in qualitatively different ways. There can be no doubt, after what has been said about the general principle of value determination (p. 122), that it is the importance of the needs that would remain unsatisfied if we did not have command of a particular good of not only the general type but also the specific quality corresponding to these needs that is, in this case too, the factor determining its value. The difficulty I am discussing here does not, therefore, lie in the general principle of value determination being inapplicable to these goods, but rather in the determination of the particular satisfaction that depends on a particular concrete good when a whole group of needs stands opposite goods whose various units are capable of satisfying these needs in qualitatively different ways. In other words, it lies in the practical application of the general principle of value determination to human economic activity. The solution to this problem arises from the following considerations.

Economizing individuals do not use the quantities of goods available to them without regard to differences in quality when these exist. A farmer who has grain of different grades at his disposal does not, for example, use the worst grade for seeding, grain of medium quality as cattle feed, and the best for food and the production of beverages. Nor does he use the grains of different grades indiscriminately for one purpose or another. Rather, with a view to his requirements, he employs the best grade for seeding, the best that remains for food and beverages, and the grain of poorest quality for fattening cattle.

With goods whose units are homogeneous, the total available quantity of a good stands opposite the whole set of concrete needs that can be satisfied by means of it. But in cases where the different units of a good satisfy human needs in qualitatively different ways, the total available quantity of a good no longer stands opposite the whole set of needs; each available quantity of specific quality instead stands opposite corresponding specific needs of the economizing individuals.

If, with respect to a given consumption purpose, a good of a certain quality cannot be replaced at all by goods of any other quality, the principle of value determination previously demonstrated (p. 132) applies fully and directly to particular quantities of that good. Thus the value of any particular unit of such a good is equal to the importance of the least important satisfaction that is provided for by the total available quantity of this precise quality of good, since it is with respect to this satisfaction that we are actually dependent on command of the particular unit of this quality.

But human needs can be satisfied by means of goods of different qualifications, although in qualitatively different ways. If goods of one quality can be replaced by goods of another quality, though not with the same effectiveness, the value of a unit of the goods of superior quality is equal to the importance of the least important satisfaction that is provided for by the goods of superior quality minus a value quota [12] that is greater: (1)

12. *"Werthquote."* Menger presents the argument underlying this proposition at length on pages 163 to 165. But an explanatory note may

the smaller the value of the goods of inferior quality by which the particular need in question can also be satisfied, and (2) the smaller the difference to men between the importance of satisfying the particular need with the superior good and the importance of satisfying it with the inferior one.

Thus we arrive at the result that, even in cases in which a complex of needs stands opposite a quantity of goods of different qualities, satisfactions of given intensities always depend on each partial quantity or on each concrete unit of these goods. Hence, in all the cases discussed, the principle of value determination that I formulated above maintains its full applicability.

D. *The subjective character of the measure of value. Labor and value. Error.*

When I discussed the nature of value, I observed that value is nothing inherent in goods and that it is not a property of

---

perhaps be helpful due to the brevity and peculiar form of the present passage.

Assume that the least important satisfaction rendered by a unit of the superior good has an importance of 5 in Use A, that the least important satisfaction rendered by a unit of the inferior good in Use B has an importance of 2, and that a unit of the inferior good would render a satisfaction with an importance of 3 if it were to replace a unit of the superior good in Use A. Menger contends that the use-value of a unit of a superior good that can be replaced by an inferior good is equal, not to the importance of the least important satisfaction actually rendered by a unit of the superior good, but to the importance of the satisfactions dependent on continued command of that unit. In the present instance, if command of a unit of the superior good is lost and a unit of the inferior good is moved from Use B to Use A to take its place, the satisfactions lost to the consumer are: (1) a satisfaction in Use B with an importance of 2, which is lost because one less unit of the inferior good is employed in Use B, and (2) a satisfaction in Use A with an importance of 2 (the difference between the 5 units lost because one unit less of the superior good is employed in Use A and the 3 units gained because of the employment of a unit of the inferior good in its place). The use-value of a unit of the superior good is therefore 4, the sum of these two items. The "value quota" mentioned by Menger in the text is the difference between the least important satisfaction that the superior good would render in Use A and its use-value calculated in this way. The "value-quota" in this example is thus 5 minus 4, or 1.—TR.

goods. But neither is value an independent thing. There is no reason why a good may not have value to one economizing individual but no value to another individual under different circumstances. The *measure* of value is entirely subjective in nature, and for this reason a good can have great value to one economizing individual, little value to another, and no value at all to a third, depending upon the differences in their requirements and available amounts. What one person disdains or values lightly is appreciated by another, and what one person abandons is often picked up by another. While one economizing individual esteems equally a given amount of one good and a greater amount of another good, we frequently observe just the opposite evaluations with another economizing individual.

Hence not only the *nature* but also the *measure* of value is subjective. Goods always have value *to* certain economizing individuals and this value is also *determined* only by these individuals.

The value an economizing individual attributes to a good is equal to the importance of the particular satisfaction that depends on his command of the good. There is no necessary and direct connection between the value of a good and whether, or in what quantities, labor and other goods of higher order were applied to its production. A non-economic good (a quantity of timber in a virgin forest, for example) does not attain value for men if large quantities of labor or other economic goods were applied to its production. Whether a diamond was found accidentally or was obtained from a diamond pit with the employment of a thousand days of labor is completely irrelevant for its value. In general, no one in practical life asks for the history of the origin of a good in estimating its value, but considers solely the services that the good will render him and which he would have to forgo if he did not have it at his command. Goods on which much labor has been expended often have no value, while others, on which little or no labor was expended, have a very high value. Goods on which much labor was expended and others on which little or no labor was expended are often of equal value to economizing men. The quantities of labor or of other means of production applied to its production cannot, therefore, be the determining factor in the value of a good. Comparison of the value of a good with the value of the means of production employed in its production does, of course, show whether and to what extent its production, an act of *past* human activity, was appropriate or economic. But the quantities of goods employed in the production of a good have neither a necessary nor a directly determining influence on its value.

Equally untenable is the opinion that the determining factor in the value of goods is the quantity of labor or other means of production that are necessary for their *reproduction*. A large number of goods cannot be reproduced (antiques, and paintings by old masters, for instance) and thus, in a number of cases, we can observe value but no possibility of reproduction. For this reason, any factor connected with reproduction cannot be the determining principle of value in general. Experience, moreover, shows that the value of the means of production necessary for the reproduction of many goods (old-fashioned clothes and obsolete machines, for instance) is sometimes considerably higher and sometimes lower than the value of the products themselves.

The determining factor in the value of a good, then, is neither the quantity of labor or other goods necessary for its production nor the quantity necessary for its reproduction, but rather the magnitude of importance of those satisfactions with respect to which we are conscious of being dependent on command of the good. This principle of value determination is universally valid, and no exception to it can be found in human economy.

The importance of a satisfaction to us is not the result of an arbitrary decision, but rather is measured by the importance, which is not arbitrary, that the satisfaction has for our lives or for our well-being. The relative degrees of importance of different satisfactions and of successive acts of satisfaction are nevertheless matters of judgment on the part of economizing men, and for this reason, their knowledge of these degrees of importance is, in some instances, subject to error.

We saw earlier that the satisfactions on which their lives depend have the highest importance to men, that the satisfactions following next in importance are those on which their well-being depends, and that satisfactions on which a higher degree of well-being depends (with equal intensity a longer enduring satisfaction, and with the same duration a more intensive one) have a higher importance to men than those on which a lower degree of their well-being is dependent.

But what has been said by no means excludes the possibility that stupid men may, as a result of their defective knowledge, sometimes estimate the importance of various satisfactions in a manner contrary to their real importance. Even individuals whose economic activity is conducted rationally, and who therefore certainly endeavor to recognize the true importance of satisfactions in order to gain an accurate foundation for their economic activity, are subject to error. Error is inseparable from all human knowledge.

Men are especially prone to let themselves be misled into overestimating the importance of satisfactions that give intense momentary pleasure but contribute only fleetingly to their well-being, and so into underestimating the importance of satisfactions on which a less intensive but longer enduring well-being depends. In other words, men often esteem passing, intense enjoyments more highly than their permanent welfare, and sometimes even more than their lives.

If men are thus already often in error with respect to their knowledge of the subjective factor of value determination, when it is merely a question of appraising their own states of mind, they are even more likely to err when it is a question of their perception of the objective factor of value determination, especially when it is a question of their knowledge of the magnitudes of the quantities available to them and of the different qualities of goods.

For these reasons alone it is clear why the determination of the value of particular goods is beset with manifold errors in economic life. But in addition to value fluctuations that arise from changes in human needs, from changes in the quantities of goods available to men, and from changes in the physical properties of goods, we can also observe fluctuations in the values of goods that are caused simply by *changes in* the *knowledge* men have of the importance of goods for their lives and welfare.

3. THE LAWS GOVERNING THE VALUE
OF GOODS OF HIGHER ORDER

A. *The principle determining the value of goods of higher order.*

Among the most egregious of the fundamental errors that have had the most far-reaching consequences in the previous development of our science is the argument that goods attain value for us because goods were employed in their production that had value to us. Later, when I come to the discussion of the prices of goods of higher order, I shall show the specific causes that were responsible for this error and for its becoming the foundation of the accepted theory of prices (in a form hedged about with all sorts of special provisions, of course). Here I want to state, above all, that this argument is so strictly opposed to all experience (p. 146) that it would have to be rejected even if it provided a *formally* correct solution to the problem of establishing a principle explaining the value of goods.

But even this last purpose cannot be achieved by the argument in question, since it offers an explanation only for the value of goods we may designate as "products" but not for the value of all other goods, which appear as original factors of production. It does not explain the value of goods directly provided by nature, especially the services of land. It does not explain the value of labor services. Nor does it even, as we shall see later, explain the value of the services of capital. For the value of all these goods cannot be explained by the argument that goods derive their value from the value of the goods expended in their production. Indeed, it makes their value completely incomprehensible.

This argument, therefore, provides neither a formally correct solution nor one that conforms with the facts of reality, to the problem of discovering a universally valid explanation of the value of goods. On the one hand, it is in contradiction with experience; and on the other hand, it is patently inapplicable wherever we have to deal with goods that are not the product of the combination of goods of higher order. The value of goods of lower order cannot, therefore, be determined by the value of the goods of higher order that were employed in their production. On the contrary, it is evident that the value of goods of higher order is always and without exception determined by the prospective value of the goods of lower order in whose production they serve.[13] The existence of our *requirements* for goods of higher order is dependent upon the goods they serve to produce having expected economic character (p. 107) and hence expected *value*. In securing our requirements for the satisfaction of our needs, we do not need command of goods that are suitable for the production of goods of lower order that have no expected value (since we have no requirements for them). We therefore have the principle that the value of goods of higher order is dependent upon the expected value of the goods of lower order they serve to produce. Hence goods of higher order can attain value, or retain it once they have it, only if, or as long as, they serve to produce goods that we expect to have value for us. If this fact is established, it is clear also that the value of goods of higher order cannot be the *determining* factor in the prospective value of the corresponding goods of lower order. Nor can the value of the goods of higher order already expended in producing a good of lower order be the determining factor in its present value. On the contrary, the value of goods of higher order is, in all cases, regulated by the prospective value of the goods of lower order to whose production they have been or will be assigned by economizing men.

The prospective value of goods of lower order is often—and this must be carefully observed—very different from the value that similar goods have in the present. For this reason, the value of the goods of higher order by means of which we shall have command of goods of lower order at some future time (pp. 67 ff.) is by no means measured by the current value of similar goods of lower order, but rather by the prospective value of the goods of lower order in whose production they serve.

Suppose, for example, that we have the saltpetre, sulphur, charcoal, specialized labor services, appliances, etc., necessary for the production of a certain quantity of gunpowder, and that thus, by means of these goods, we shall have this quantity of

13. The remainder of this paragraph is a footnote in the original.—TR.

gunpowder at our command in three months time. It is clear that the value this gunpowder is expected to have for us in three months time need not necessarily be equal to, but may be greater or less than, the value of an identical quantity of gunpowder at the present time. Hence also, the magnitude of the value of the above goods of higher order is measured, not by the value of gunpowder at present, but by the prospective value of their product at the end of the production period. Cases can even be imagined in which a good of lower or first order is completely valueless at present (ice in winter, for example), while simultaneously available corresponding goods of higher order that assure quantities of the good of lower order for a future time period (all the materials and implements necessary for the production of artificial ice, for example) have value with respect to this future time period—and vice versa.

Hence there is no necessary connection between the value of goods of lower or first order in the present and the value of currently available goods of higher order serving for the production of such goods. On the contrary, it is evident that the former derive their value from the relationship between requirements and available quantities in the present, while the latter derive their value from the prospective relationship between the requirements and the quantities that will be available at the future points in time when the products created by means of the goods of higher order will become available. If the prospective future value of a good of lower order rises, other things remaining equal, the value of the goods of higher order whose possession assures us future command of the good of lower order rises also. But the rise or fall of the value of a good of lower order available in the present has no necessary causal connection with the rise or fall of the value of currently available corresponding goods of higher order.

Hence the principle that the value of goods of higher order is governed, not by the value of corresponding goods of lower order of the present, but rather by the prospective value of the product, is the universally valid principle of the determination of the value of goods of higher order.[14]

Only the satisfaction of our needs has direct and immediate

14. The next paragraph appears here as a footnote in the original.—TR.

significance to us. In each concrete instance, this significance is measured by the importance of the various satisfactions for our lives and well-being. We next attribute the exact quantitative magnitude of this importance to the specific goods on which we are conscious of being directly dependent for the satisfactions in question—that is, we attribute it to economic goods of first order, as explained in the principles of the previous section. In cases in which our requirements are not met or are only incompletely met by goods of first order, and in which goods of first order therefore attain value for us, we turn to the corresponding goods of the next higher order in our efforts to satisfy our needs as completely as possible, and attribute the value that we attributed to goods of first order in turn to goods of second, third, and still higher orders whenever these goods of higher order have economic character. The value of goods of *higher order* is therefore, in the final analysis, nothing but a special form of the importance we attribute to our lives and well-being. Thus, as with goods of first order, the factor that is ultimately responsible for the value of goods of higher order is merely the importance that we attribute to those satisfactions with respect to which we are aware of being dependent on the availability of the goods of higher order whose value is under consideration. But due to the causal connections between goods, the value of goods of higher order is not measured directly by the expected importance of the final satisfaction, but rather by the expected value of the corresponding goods of lower order.

B. *The productivity of capital.*

The transformation of goods of higher order into goods of lower order takes place, as does every other process of change, in time. The times at which men will obtain command of goods of first order from the goods of higher order in their present possession will be more distant the higher the order of these goods. While it is true, as we saw earlier (pp. 71 ff.), that the more extensive employment of goods of higher order for the satisfaction of human needs brings about a continuous expansion in the quantities of available consumption goods, this extension is only possible if the provident activities of men are extended

to ever more distant time periods. A primitive Indian is occupied incessantly with the task of meeting his requirements
for a few days at a time. A nomad who does not consume the
domestic animals at his command but decides to breed them
for their young is already producing goods that will become
available to him only after a few months. But among civilized
peoples, a considerable proportion of the members of society
is occupied with the production of goods that will contribute
only after years, and often only after decades, to the direct satisfaction of human needs.

Thus by relinquishing their collecting economy, and by making progress in the employment of goods of higher orders for
the satisfaction of their needs, economizing men can most as-
suredly increase the consumption goods available to them accordingly—but only on condition that they lengthen the periods
of time over which their provident activity is to extend in the
same degree that they progress to goods of higher order.

There is, in this circumstance, an important restraint upon
economic progress. The most anxious care of men is always
directed to assuring themselves the consumption goods necessary for the maintenance of their lives and well-being in the
present or in the immediate future, but their anxiety diminishes as the time period over which it is extended becomes
longer. This phenomenon is not accidental but deeply imbedded in human nature. To the extent that the maintenance
of our lives depends on the satisfaction of our needs, guaran-
teeing the satisfaction of earlier needs must necessarily precede
attention to later ones. And even where not our lives but
merely our continuing well-being (above all our health) is dependent on command of a quantity of goods, the attainment of
well-being in a nearer period is, as a rule, a prerequisite of well-
being in a later period. Command of the means for the maintenance of our well-being at some distant time avails us little
if poverty and distress have already undermined our health or
stunted our development in an earlier period. Similar considerations are involved even with satisfactions having merely the
importance of enjoyments. All experience teaches that a present
enjoyment or one in the near future usually appears more im-

portant to men than one of equal intensity at a more remote time in the future.

Human life is a process in which the course of future development is always influenced by previous development. It is a process that cannot be continued once it has been interrupted, and that cannot be completely rehabilitated once it has become seriously disordered. A necessary prerequisite of our provision for the maintenance of our lives and for our development in future periods is a concern for the preceding periods of our lives. Setting aside the irregularities of economic activity, we can conclude that economizing men generally endeavor to ensure the satisfaction of needs of the immediate future first, and that only after this has been done, do they attempt to ensure the satisfaction of needs of more distant periods, in accordance with their remoteness in time.

The circumstance that places a restraint upon the efforts of economizing men to progress in the employment of goods of higher orders is thus the necessity of first making provision, with the goods at present available to them, for the satisfaction of their needs in the immediate future; for only when this has been done can they make provision for more distant time periods. In other words, the economic gain men can obtain from more extensive employment of goods of higher orders for the satisfaction of their needs is dependent on the condition that they *still have further quantities of goods available for more distant time periods* after they have met their requirements for the immediate future.

In the early stages and at the beginning of every new phase of cultural development, when a few individuals (the first discoverers, inventors, and enterprisers) are first making the transition to the use of goods of the next higher order, the portion of these goods that had existed previously but which until then had had no application of any sort in human economy, and for which there were therefore no requirements, naturally have non-economic character. When a hunting people is passing over to sedentary agriculture, land and materials that were not previously used and are now employed for the first time for the satisfaction of human needs (lime, sand, timber, and stones for building, for example) usually maintain their non-economic character for some time after the transition has begun. It is therefore not the limited quantities of these goods that prevents economizing men in the first stages of civilization from making progress in the employment of goods of higher orders for the satisfaction of their needs.

But there is, as a rule, another portion of the complementary goods of higher order, which has already been serving for the satisfaction of human needs in some branch or other of production before the transition to the employment of a new order of goods, and which therefore previously exhibited economic character. The seed grain and labor services needed by an individual passing from the stage of collecting economy to agriculture are examples of this kind.

These goods, which the individual making the transition previously used as goods of lower order, and which he might continue to use as goods of lower order, must now be employed as goods of higher order if he wishes to take advantage of the economic gain mentioned earlier. In other words, he can procure this gain only by employing goods, which are available to him, if he so chooses, for the *present* or for the *near future*, for the satisfaction of the needs of a *more distant time period*.

Meanwhile, with the continuous development of civilization and with progress in the employment of further quantities of goods of higher order by economizing men, a large part of the other, previously non-economic, goods of higher order (land, limestone, sand, timber, etc., for example) attains economic character (p. 103). When this occurs, each individual can participate in the economic gains connected with employment of goods of higher order in contrast to purely collecting activity (and, at higher levels of civilization, with the employment of goods of higher order in contrast to the limitations of means of production of lower order) only if he already has command of quantities of economic goods of higher order (or quantities of economic goods of any kind, when a brisk commerce has already developed and goods of all kinds may be exchanged for one another) in the present for future periods of time—in other words, only if he possesses *capital*.[15]

15. See Appendix E (p. 303) for the material originally appearing here as a footnote.—TR.

With this proposition, however, we have reached one of the most important truths of our science, the "productivity of capital." The proposition must not be understood to mean that command of quantities of economic goods in an earlier period for a later time can contribute anything by itself *during* this period to the increase of the consumption goods available to men. It merely means that command of quantities of economic goods for a certain period of time is *for economizing individuals* a means to the better and more complete satisfaction of their needs, and therefore a *good*—or rather, an *economic good,* whenever the available quantities of capital services are smaller than the requirements for them.

The more or less complete satisfaction of our needs is therefore no less dependent on command of quantities of economic goods for certain periods of time (on capital services) than it is on command of other economic goods. For this reason, capital services are objects to which men attribute value, and as we shall see later, they are also objects of commerce.[16]

Some economists represent the payment of interest as a reimbursement for the abstinence of the owner of capital. Against this doctrine, I must point out that the abstinence of a person cannot, by itself, attain goods-character and thus value. Moreover, capital by no means always originates from abstinence, but in many cases as a result of mere seizure (whenever formerly non-economic goods of higher order attain economic character because of society's increasing requirements, for example). Thus the payment of interest must not be regarded as a compensation of the owner of capital for his abstinence, but as the exchange of one economic good (the use of capital) for another (money, for instance). Carey [17] falls into the opposite error, however, when he assigns to parsimony a tendency directly inimical to the creation of capital.

16. The next paragraph appears here as a footnote in the original.—TR.
17. Henry C. Carey, *Principles of Social Science,* Philadelphia, 1859, III, 60-61.

C. *The value of complementary quantities of goods of higher order.*

In order to transform goods of higher order [18] into goods of lower order, the passage of a certain period of time is necessary. Hence, whenever economic goods are to be produced, *command of the services of capital is necessary for a certain period of time.* The length of this period varies according to the nature of the production process. In any given branch of production, it is longer the higher the order of the goods to be directed to the satisfaction of human needs. But some passage of time is inseparable from any process of production.

During these time periods, the quantity of economic goods of which I am speaking (capital) is *fixed,*[19] and not available for other productive purposes. In order to have a good or a quantity of goods of lower order at our command at a future time, it is not sufficient to have fleeting possession of the corresponding goods of higher order at some single point in time, but instead necessary that we retain command of these goods of higher order for a period of time that varies in length according to the nature of the particular process of production, and that we *fix* them in this production process for the duration of that period.

In the preceding section, we saw that command of quantities of economic goods for given periods of time has value to economizing men, just as other economic goods have value to them. From this it follows that the aggregate present value of all the goods of higher order necessary for the production of a good of lower order can be set equal to the prospective value of the

18. It is not just the technical means of production that must be regarded as goods of higher order, but in general, all goods that can be used for the satisfaction of human needs only by being combined with other goods of higher order. The commodities that a wholesale merchant can pass on to the retailer only by employing capital, incurring costs of shipping, and using various specific labor services, must be regarded as goods of higher order. The same is true of the commodities in the hands of a grocer. Even the speculator adds to the objects of his speculation at least his entrepreneurial activities and his capital services, and often storage services, warehousing, etc., as well (see Hermann, *op. cit.,* p. 65).

19. *"gebunden."*—TR.

product to economizing men only if the value of the services of
capital during the production period is included.

Suppose, for example, we wish to determine the value of the
goods of higher order that assure us command of a given quantity of grain a year hence. The value of the seed grain, the services of land, the specialized agricultural labor services, and all
the other goods of higher order necessary for the production of
the given quantity of grain will indeed be equal to the *prospective* value of the grain at the end of the year (p. 150), but only
on condition that the value of a year's command of these economic goods to the economizing individuals concerned is
included in the sum. The *present* value of these goods of higher
order by themselves is therefore equal to the value of the prospective product minus the value of the services of the capital
employed.

To express what has been said numerically, suppose that the
prospective value of the product that will be available at the
end of the year is 100, and that the value of a year's command of
the necessary quantities of economic goods of higher order (the
value of the services of capital) is 10. It is clear that the aggregate value of all the complementary goods of higher order
required for the production of the product, excluding the services of capital, is equal not to 100, but only to 90. If the value
of the services of capital were 15, the present value of the other
goods of higher order would be only 85.

The value of goods to the economizing individuals concerned
is, as I have already stated several times, the most important
foundation of price formation. Now if, in ordinary life, we see
that buyers of goods of higher order never pay the full prospective price of a good of lower order for the complementary
means of production technically necessary for its production,[20]
that they are always only in a position to grant, and actually do
grant, prices for them that are somewhat lower than the price
of the product, and that the sale of goods of higher order thus
has a certain similarity to discounting, the prospective price of

20. Leopold v. Hasner, *System der politischen Oekonomie*, Prag, 1860, I,
    29.

the product forming the basis of the computation,[21] these facts are explained by the preceding argument.[22]

A person who has at his disposal the goods of higher order required for the production of goods of lower order does not, by virtue of this fact, have command of the goods of lower order immediately and directly, but only after the passage of a period of time that is longer or shorter according to the nature of the production process. If he wishes to exchange his goods of higher order immediately for the corresponding goods of lower order, or for what is the same thing under developed trade relations, a corresponding sum of money, he is evidently in a position similar to that of a person who is to receive a certain sum of money at a future point in time (after 6 months, for example) but who wants to obtain command of it immediately. If the owner of goods of higher order intends to transfer them to a third person and is willing to receive payment only after the end of the production process, naturally no "discounting" takes place. In fact, we can observe the prices of goods that are sold on credit rising higher (apart from the risk premium) the further the agreed-upon date of payment lies in the future. All this, however, explains at the same time why the productive activity of a people is greatly promoted by credit. In by far the greater number of cases, credit transactions consist in handing goods of higher order over to persons who transform them into corresponding goods of lower order. Production, or more extensive fabrication at least, is very often only possible through credit; hence the pernicious stoppage and curtailment of the productive activity of a people when credit suddenly ceases to flow.

The process of transforming goods of higher order into goods of lower or first order, provided it is economic in other respects, must also always be planned and conducted, with some eco-

21. Since, other things being equal, the productiveness of a production process and the value of the capital services used are both greater the longer the time period required for the production process, the values of goods of higher order, which can be employed in productive processes of very different duration, and which therefore assure us, at our choice, consumption goods of different values at different points in time, are brought into equilibrium with respect to the present.
22. The next paragraph appears here as a footnote in the original.—TR.

nomic purpose in view, by an economizing individual. This individual must carry through the economic computations of which I have just been speaking, and he must actually bring the goods of higher order, including technical labor services, together (or cause them to be brought together) for the purpose of production.[23] The question as to which functions are included in this so-called *entrepreneurial activity* has already been posed several times. Above all we must bear in mind that an enterpreneur's own *technical* labor services are often among the goods of higher order that he has at his command for purposes of production. When this is the case, he assigns them, just like the services of other persons, their roles in the production process. The owner of a magazine is often a contributor to his own magazine. The industrial entrepreneur often works in his own factory. Each of them is an entrepreneur, however, not because of his technical participation in the production process, but because he makes not only the underlying economic calculations but also the actual decisions to assign goods of higher order to particular productive purposes. Entrepreneurial activity includes: (a) obtaining *information* about the economic situation; (b) economic *calculation*—all the various computations that must be made if a production process is to be efficient (provided that it is economic in other respects); (c) the *act of will* by which goods of higher order (or goods in general —under conditions of developed commerce, where any economic good can be exchanged for any other) are assigned to a particular production process; and finally (d) *supervision* of the execution of the production plan so that it may be carried through as economically as possible. In small firms, these entrepreneurial activities usually occupy but an inconsiderable part of the time of the entrepreneur. In large firms, however, not only the entrepreneur himself, but often several helpers, are fully occupied with these activities. But however extensive the activities of these helpers may be, the four functions listed above can always be observed in the actions of the entrepreneur, even if they are ultimately confined (as in corporations) to determining the allocation of portions of wealth to particular productive purposes only by general categories, and to the

23. The remainder of this paragraph is a footnote in the original.—TR.

selection and control of persons. After what has been said, it will be evident that I cannot agree with Mangoldt,[24] who designates "risk bearing" as the *essential* function of entrepreneurship in a production process, since this "risk" is only incidental and the chance of loss is counterbalanced by the chance of profit.

In the early stages of civilization and even later in the case of small manufactures, entrepreneurial activity is usually performed by the same economizing individual whose technical labor services also constitute one of the factors in the production process. With progressive division of labor and an increase in the size of enterprises, entrepreneurial activity often occupies his full time. For this reason, entrepreneurial activity is just as necessary a factor in the production of goods as technical labor services. It therefore has the character of a good of higher order, and value too, since like other goods of higher order it is also generally an economic good. Hence whenever we wish to determine the present value of complementary quantities of goods of higher order, the prospective value of the product determines the total value of all of them together only if the value of entrepreneurial activity is included in the total.

Let me summarize the results of this section. The aggregate present value of all the complementary quantities of goods of higher order (that is, all the raw materials, labor services, services of land, machines, tools, etc.) necessary for the production of a good of lower or first order is equal to the prospective value of the product. But it is necessary to include in the sum not only the goods of higher order technically required for its production but also the services of capital and the activity of the entrepreneur. For these are as unavoidably necessary in every economic production of goods as the technical requisites already mentioned. Hence the *present* value of the technical factors of production by themselves is not equal to the full prospective value of the product, but always behaves in such a way that a margin for the value of the services of capital and entrepreneurial activity remains.

24. H. v. Mangoldt, *Die Lehre vom Unternehmergewinn*, Leipzig, 1855, pp. 36 ff.

D. *The value of individual goods of higher order.*

We have seen that the value of a particular good (or of a given quantity of goods) to the economizing individual who has it at his command is equal to the importance he attaches to the satisfactions he would have to forgo if he did not have command of it. From this we could infer, without difficulty, that the value of each unit of goods of higher order is likewise equal to the importance of the satisfactions assured by command of a unit if we were not impeded by the fact that a good of higher order cannot be employed for the satisfaction of human needs by itself but only in combination with other (the complementary) goods of higher order. Because of this, however, the opinion could arise that we are dependent, for the satisfaction of concrete needs, not on command of an individual concrete good (or concrete quantity of some one kind of good) of higher order, but rather on command of complementary quantities of goods of higher order, and that therefore only aggregates of complementary goods of higher order can independently attain value for an economizing individual.

It is, of course, true that we can obtain quantities of goods of lower order only by means of *complementary* quantities of goods of higher order. But it is equally certain that the various goods of higher order need not always be combined in the production process in fixed proportions (in the manner, perhaps, that is to be observed in the case of chemical reactions, where only a certain weight of one substance combines with an equally fixed weight of another substance to yield a given chemical compound). The most ordinary experience teaches us rather that a given quantity of some one good of lower order can be produced from goods of higher order that stand in very different quantitative relationships with one another. In fact, one or several goods of higher order that are complementary to a group of certain other goods of higher order may often be omitted altogether without destroying the capacity of the remaining complementary goods to produce the good of lower order. The services of land, seed, labor services, fertilizer, the services of agricultural implements, etc., are used to produce grain. But no one will be able to deny that a *given* quantity of grain can also be produced without the use of fertilizer and without employing a large part of the usual agricultural implements, provided only that the other goods of higher order used for the production of grain are available in correspondingly larger quantities.

If experience thus teaches us that some complementary goods of higher order can often be omitted entirely in the production of goods of lower order, we can much more frequently observe, not only that given products can be produced by varying quantities of goods of higher order, but also that there is generally a very wide range within which the proportions of goods applied to their production can be, and actually are, varied. Everyone knows that, even on land of homogeneous quality, a given quantity of grain can be produced on fields of very different sizes if more or less intensively tilled—that is, if larger or smaller quantities of the other complementary goods of higher order are applied to them. In particular, an insufficiency of fertilizer can be compensated for by the employment of a larger amount of land or better machines, or by the more intensive application of agricultural labor services. Similarly, a diminished quantity of almost every good of higher order can be compensated for by a correspondingly greater application of the other complementary goods.

But even where particular goods of higher order cannot be replaced by quantities of other complementary goods, and a diminution of the available quantity of some particular good of higher order causes a corresponding diminution of the product (in the production of some chemical, for instance), the corresponding quantities of the other means of production do not necessarily become valueless when this one production good is lacking. The other means of production can, as a rule, still be applied to the production of other consumption goods, and so in the last analysis to the satisfaction of human needs, even if these needs are usually less important than the needs that could have been satisfied if the missing quantity of the complementary good under consideration had been available.

As a rule, therefore, what depends on a given quantity of a good of higher order is not command of an exactly corresponding quantity of product, but only a portion of the product and often only its higher quality. Accordingly, the value of a given quantity of a particular good of higher order is not equal to the importance of the satisfactions that depend on the whole product it helps to produce, but is equal merely to the importance of the satisfactions provided for by the portion of the product that would remain unproduced if we were not in a position to command the given quantity of the good of higher order. Where the result of a diminution of the available quantity of a good of higher order is not a decrease in the quantity of product but a worsening of its quality, the value of a given quantity of a good of higher order is equal to the difference in importance between the satisfactions that can be achieved with the more highly qualified product and those that can be achieved with the less qualified product. In both cases, therefore, it is not satisfactions provided by the whole product that a given quantity of a particular good of higher order helps to produce that are dependent on command of it, but only satisfactions of the importance here explained.

Even where a diminution of the available quantity of a particular good of higher order causes the product (some chemical compound, for example) to diminish proportionately, the other complementary quantities of goods of higher order do not become valueless. Although their complementary factor of production is now missing, they can still be applied to the production of other goods of lower order, and thus directed to the satisfaction of human needs, even if these needs are, perhaps, somewhat less important than would otherwise have been the case. Thus in this case too, the full value of the product that would be lost to us for lack of a particular good of higher order is not the determining factor in its value. Its value is equal only to the difference in importance between the satisfactions that are assured if we have command of the good of higher order whose value we wish to determine and the satisfactions that would be achieved if we did not have it at our command.

If we summarize these three cases, we obtain a general law of the determination of the value of a concrete quantity of a good of higher order. Assuming in each instance that all available goods of higher order are employed in the most economic fashion, the value of a concrete quantity of a good of higher order is equal to the difference in importance between the satisfactions that can be attained when we have command of the given quantity of the good of higher order whose value we wish to determine and the satisfactions that would be attained if we did not have this quantity at our command.

This law corresponds exactly to the general law of value determination (p. 121), since the difference referred to in the law of the preceding paragraph represents the importance of the satisfactions that depend on our command of a given good of higher order.

If we examine this law with respect to what was said earlier (p. 157) about the value of the complementary quantities of goods of higher order required for the production of a consumption good, we obtain a corollary principle: the value of a good of higher order will be greater (1) the greater the prospective value of the product if the value of the other complementary goods necessary for its production remains equal, and (2) the lower, other things being equal, the value of the complementary goods.

E. *The value of the services of land, capital, and labor, in particular.*[25]

Land occupies no exceptional place among goods. If it is used for consumption purposes (ornamental gardens, hunting grounds, etc.), it is a good of first order. If it is used for the production of other goods, it is, like many others, a good of higher order. Whenever there is a question, therefore, of determining the value of land or the value of the services of land, they are subject to the general laws of the determination of value. If certain pieces of land have the character of goods of higher order, their value is subject also to the laws of value determination of goods of higher order that I have explained in the preceding section.

A widespread school of economists has recognized correctly that the value of land cannot validly be traced back to labor or

25. Menger here appends a lengthy footnote which has been incorporated into the text as the last three paragraphs of this chapter.—TR.

to the services of capital. From this, however, they have deduced the legitimacy of assigning land an exceptional position among goods. But the methodological blunder involved in this procedure is easily recognized. That a large and important group of phenomena cannot be fitted into the general laws of a science dealing with these phenomena is telling evidence of the need for reforming the science. It does not, however, constitute an argument that would justify the most questionable methodological procedure of separating a group of phenomena from all other objects of observation exactly similar in general nature, and elaborating special highest principles for each of the two groups.

Recognition of this mistake has led, therefore, in more recent times to numerous attempts to fit land and the services of land into the framework of a system of economic theory with all other goods, and to trace their values and the prices they fetch back to human labor or to the services of capital, in conformity with the accepted principles.[26]

But the violence done to goods in general, and to land in particular, by such an attempt is obvious. A piece of land may have been wrested from the sea with the greatest expenditure of human labor; or it may be the alluvial deposit of some river and thus have been acquired without any labor at all. It may have been originally overgrown with jungle, covered with stones, and reclaimed later with great effort and economic sacrifice; or it may have been free of trees and fertile from the beginning. Such items of its past history are of interest in judging its *natural* fertility, and certainly also for the question of *whether the application of economic goods to this piece of land* (improvements) *were appropriate and economic.* But its history is of no relevance when its general economic relationships, and especially its *value,* are at issue. For these have to do with the importance goods attain for us solely because they assure us future

26. N. F. Canard, *Principes d'économie politique,* Paris, 1901, pp. 5 ff.; Carey, *op. cit.,* III, 131 ff.; Frédéric Bastiat, *Harmonies économiques,* in *Oeuvres complètes de F. Bastiat,* Paris, 1893, VI, 297 ff.; Max Wirth, *Grundzüge der National-Oekonomie,* Köln, 1871, I, 284 ff.; Hermann Roesler, *Grundsätze der Volkswirthschaftslehre,* Rostock, 1864, pp. 500-513.

satisfactions.[27] From these considerations, it also follows that whenever I refer to the services of land I mean the services, measured over time, of pieces of land as we actually find them in the economy of men, and not the use of the "original powers" of land. For only the former are objects of human economizing, while the latter, in concrete cases, are merely at most the objects of a hopeless historical investigation, and in any case irrelevant for economizing men. When a farmer rents a piece of land for one or several years, he cares little whether its soil derives its fertility from capital investments of all kinds or was fertile from the very beginning. These circumstances have no influence on the price he pays for the use of the soil. A buyer of a piece of land attempts to reckon the "future" but never the "past" of the land he is purchasing.

Thus the newer attempts to explain the value of land or the services of land by reducing them to labor services or to the services of capital must be regarded only as an outcome of the effort to make the accepted theory of ground-rent (a part of our science that stands, relatively, in the least contradiction with the phenomena of real life) consistent with prevalent misconceptions of the highest principles of our science. It must further be protested against the accepted theory of rent, especially in the form in which it was expressed by Ricardo,[28] that it brought to light merely an isolated factor having to do with differences in the value of land but not a principle explaining the value of the services of land to economizing men,[29] and that the isolated factor was mistakenly advanced as the principle.

Differences in the fertility and situation of pieces of land are doubtless among the most important causes of differences in the value of the services of land and of land itself. But beyond these there exist still other causes of differences in the value of these goods. Differences in fertility and situation are not even responsible for these other causes, much less a general principle explaining the value of land and services of land. If all pieces of

27. The remainder of this paragraph is a footnote in the original.—TR.
28. Ricardo, *Principles of Political Economy and Taxation*, ed. by E. C. K. Gonner, London, 1891, pp. 44-61 and 392-420.
29. See Karl Rodbertus, *Zur Beleuchtung der socialen Frage*, Berlin, 1890, I, 89 ff.

land had the same fertility and equally favorable locations, they would yield no rent at all, according to Ricardo. But although a single factor accounting for differences between the rents they yield may then indeed be absent, it is quite certain that neither all the differences between the rents nor rent itself would, of necessity, disappear. It is evident rather that even the most unfavorably situated and least fertile pieces of land in a country where land is scarce would yield a rent, a rent that could find no explanation in the Ricardian theory.

Land and the services of land, in the concrete forms in which we observe them, are objects of our value appraisement like all other goods. Like other goods, they attain value only to the extent that we depend on command of them for the satisfaction of our needs. And the factors determining their value are the same as those we encountered earlier in our investigation of the value of goods in general (pp. 121 and 141).[30] A deeper understanding of the differences in their value can, therefore, also only be attained by approaching land and the services of land from the general points of view of our science and, insofar as they are goods of higher order, relating them to the corresponding goods of lower order and especially to their complementary goods.

In the preceding section we obtained the result that the aggregate value of the goods of higher order necessary for the production of a consumption good (including the services of capital and entrepreneurial activity) is equal to the prospective value of the product. Where services of land are applied to the production of goods of lower order, the value of these services,

30. Rodbertus (op. cit., pp. 117 ff.) argues that our social institutions make it possible for the owners of capital and land to take a part of the product of labor away from the laborers, and thereby live without working. His argument is based on the erroneous assumption that the entire result of a production process must be regarded as the product of labor. Labor services are only one of the factors of the production process, however, and are not economic goods in any higher degree than the other factors of production including the services of land and capital. Capitalists and landowners do not, therefore, live on what they take away from laborers, but upon the services of their land and capital which have value, just as do labor services, both to individuals and to society.

together with the value of the other complementary goods, will be equal to the prospective value of the good of lower or first order to whose production they have been applied. As this prospective value is higher or lower, other things remaining equal, the aggregate value of the complementary goods will be higher or lower. As for the separate value of actual pieces of land or services of land, it is regulated, like the value of other goods of higher order, in accordance with the principle that the value of a good of higher order will, other things being equal, be greater (1) the greater the value of the prospective product, and (2) the smaller the value of the complementary goods of higher order.[31]

The value of services of land is therefore not subject to different laws than the value of the services of machines, tools, houses, factories, or any other kind of economic good.

The existence of the special characteristics that land and the services of land, as well as many other kinds of goods, exhibit is by no means denied. In any country, land is usually available only in quantities that cannot be easily increased; it is fixed as to situation; and it has an extraordinary variety of grades. All the peculiarities of value phenomena we are able to observe in the case of land and the services of land can be traced back to these three factors. Since these factors have bearing only upon the quantities and qualities of land available to economizing men in general and to the inhabitants of certain territories in particular, the peculiarities in question are factors in the determination of value that influence not just the value of land and the services of land but, as we saw, the value of all goods. The value of land thus has no exceptional character.

The fact that the prices of *labor services*, like the prices of

31. The value of a piece of land is determined by the expected value of its services, and not the other way around. The value of a piece of land is nothing but the expected value of all its future services discounted to the present. Hence the higher the expected value of the services of land and the lower the value of the services of capital (rate of interest), the higher will be the value of land. We shall see later that the value of goods is the foundation for their prices. That the price of land can regularly be observed to rise rapidly in periods of a people's economic growth is due to an increase in land rent on the one hand, and to a decrease in the rate of interest on the other.

the services of land, cannot without the greatest violence be traced back to the prices of their costs of production has led to the establishment of special principles for this class of prices as well. It is said that the most common labor must support the laborer and his family, since his labor services could not otherwise be contributed permanently to society; and that his labor cannot provide him with much more than the minimum of subsistence, since otherwise an increase of laborers would take place which would reduce the price of labor services to the former low level. The minimum of subsistence is therefore, in this theory, the principle that governs the price of the most common labor, while the higher prices of other labor services are explained by reducing them to capital investment or to rents for special talents.

But experience teaches us that there are labor services that are completely useless, and even injurious, to economizing men. They are therefore not goods. There are other labor services that have goods-character but not economic character, and hence no value. (In this second category belong all labor services that are available to society, for some reason or other, in such large quantities that they attain non-economic character—the labor services connected with some unpaid office, for example). Hence too (as we shall see later) labor services of these categories cannot have prices. Labor services are therefore not always goods or economic goods simply because they are labor services; they do not have value as a matter of necessity. It is thus not always true that every labor service fetches a price, and still less always a *particular* price.

Experience also informs us that many labor services cannot be exchanged by the laborer even for the most necessary means of subsistence,[32] while a quantity of goods ten, twenty, or even a hundred, times that required for the subsistence of a single person can easily be had for other labor services. Wherever the labor

32. In Berlin, a seamstress working 15 hours a day cannot earn what she needs for her subsistence. Her income covers food, shelter, and firewood, but even with the most strenuous industry she cannot earn enough for clothing (see Carnap, in *Deutsche Vierteljahrschrift*, 1868, part II, p. 165). Similar conditions can be observed in most other large cities.

services of a man actually exchange for his bare means of subsistence, it can only be the result of some fortuitous circumstance that his labor services are exchanged, in conformity with
the general principles of price formation, for that particular
price and no other. Neither the means of subsistence nor the
minimum of subsistence of a laborer, therefore, can be the direct cause or determining principle of the price of labor
services.[33]

In reality, as we shall see, the *prices* of actual labor services
are governed, like the prices of all other goods, by their *values*.
But their values are governed, as was shown, by the magnitude
of importance of the satisfactions that would have to remain
unsatisfied if we were unable to command the labor services.
Where labor services are goods of higher order, their values are
governed (proximately and directly) in accordance with the
principle that the value of a good of higher order to economizing men is greater (1) the greater the prospective value of the
product, provided the value of the complementary goods of
higher order is constant, and (2) the lower, other things being
equal, the value of the complementary goods.[34]

A special characteristic of labor services that affects their
value consists in the fact that some varieties of labor services
have unpleasant associations for the laborer, with the result
that these services will be forthcoming only for compensating
economic advantages. Labor services of this kind cannot, therefore, easily attain a non-economic character for society. But the
value of inactivity to most laborers is much less than is generally believed. The occupations of by far the great majority of
men afford enjoyment, are thus themselves true satisfactions of
needs, and would be practised, although perhaps in smaller
measure or in a modified manner, even if men were not forced
by lack of means to exert their powers. The exercising of his

33. A laborer's standard of living is determined by his income, and not
   his income by his standard of living. In a strange confusion of cause
   and effect, however, the latter relationship has nevertheless often been
   maintained.

34. The next two paragraphs appear in the original as a single footnote
   after *"labor services"* at the beginning of the third paragraph preceding.—TR.

powers is a need for every normal human being. That only a few persons nevertheless work without expecting economic compensation is due not so much to the unpleasantness of labor as such but rather to the fact that the opportunities to engage in *remunerative* labor are fully ample.

Entrepreneurial activity must definitely be counted as a category of labor services. It is an economic good as a rule, and as such has *value* to economizing men. Labor services in this category have two peculiarities: (a) they are by nature not commodities (not intended for exchange) and for this reason have no prices; (b) they have command of the services of capital as a necessary prerequisite since they cannot otherwise be performed. This second factor limits the amount of entrepreneurial activity in general that is available to a people. It especially limits to relatively very small quantities entrepreneurial activity that can only be performed if the economizing individuals in question have at their disposal the services of large amounts of capital. Credit increases, and legal uncertainties diminish, these quantities.

The inadequacy of the theory that explained the prices of goods by the prices of the goods of higher order that served to produce them naturally also made itself felt wherever the price of the *services of capital* came in question. I explained the ultimate causes of the economic character and value of goods of this kind earlier in the present chapter, and pointed out the error in the theory that represents the price of the services of capital as a compensation for the abstinence of the owners of capital. In truth, the price that can be obtained for the services of capital is, as we have seen, no less a consequence of their economic character and of their *value,* than is the case with the prices of other goods. The determining principle of the value of the services of capital is the same as the principle determining the value of goods in general.[35, 36]

35. A special characteristic of *price formation* in the case of the services of capital is due, as we shall see later, to the fact that these services cannot ordinarily be sold without transferring the capital itself into the hands of the buyer of the services of capital. There is a resulting risk for the owner of the capital for which he must be compensated by a premium.

The fact that the *prices* of the services of land, capital, and labor, or, in other words, rent, interest, and wages, cannot be reduced without the greatest violence (as we shall see later) to quantities of labor or costs of production, has made it necessary for the proponents of these theories to develop principles of price formation for these three kinds of goods that are entirely different from the principles that are valid for all other goods. In the preceding sections, I have shown with respect to goods of all kinds that all phenomena of *value* are the same in nature and origin, and that the magnitude of value is *always* governed according to the same principles. Moreover, as we shall see in the next two chapters, the *price* of a good is a consequence of its *value* to economizing men, and the magnitude of its price is always determined by the magnitude of its value. It is also evident, therefore, that rent, interest, and wages are all regulated according to the same general principles. In the present section, however, I have dealt merely with the *value* of the services of land, capital, and labor. On the basis of the results obtained here I shall state the principles according to which the prices of these goods are governed after I have explained the general theory of price.

One of the strangest questions ever made the subject of scientific debate is whether rent and interest are justified from an ethical point of view or whether they are "immoral." Among other things, our science has the task of exploring why and under what conditions the services of land and of capital display economic character, attain value, and can be exchanged for quantities of other economic goods (prices). But it seems to me that the question of the legal or moral character of these facts is beyond the sphere of our science. Wherever the services of land and of capital bear a price, it is always as a consequence of their value, and their value to men is not the result of arbitrary judgments (p. 119), but a necessary consequence of their economic character. The prices of these goods (the services of land and of capital) are therefore the necessary products of the economic situation under which they arise, and will be more

---

36. The next three paragraphs appear in the original as a single long footnote appended to the heading of the present section. TR.

certainly obtained the more developed the legal system of a people and the more upright its public morals.

It may well appear deplorable to a lover of mankind that possession of capital or a piece of land often provides the owner a higher income for a given period of time than the income received by a laborer for the most strenuous activity during the same period. Yet the cause of this is not immoral, but simply that the satisfaction of more impo tant human needs depends upon the services of the given amount of capital or piece of land than upon the services of the laborer. The agitation of those who would like to see society allot a larger share of the available consumption goods to laborers than at present really constitutes, therefore, a demand for nothing else than paying labor above its value. For if the demand for higher wages is not coupled with a program for the more thorough training of workers, or if it is not confined to advocacy of freer competition, it requires that workers be paid not in accordance with the value of their services to society, but rather with a view to providing them with a more comfortable standard of living, and achieving a more equal distribution of consumption goods and of the burdens of life. A solution of the problem on this basis, however, would undoubtedly require a complete transformation of our social order.[37]

37. See Schüz, "Ueber die Renten der Grundeigenthümer und den angeblichen Conflict ihrer Interessen mit denen der übrigen Volksklassen," *Zeitschrift für die gesammte Staatswissenschaft*, XI (1855), 171 ff.

CHAPTER IV | THE THEORY OF EXCHANGE

"W

1. THE FOUNDATIONS
OF ECONOMIC EXCHANGE

HETHER the propensity of men to truck, barter, and exchange one thing for another be one of the original principles in human nature, or whether it be the necessary consequence of the faculties of reason and speech," or what other causes induce men to exchange goods, is a question Adam Smith left unanswered. The eminent thinker remarks only that it is certain that the propensity to barter and exchange is common to all men and is found in no other species of animals.[1]

First, in order to clarify the problem, suppose that two neighboring farmers each have a great abundance of the same kind of barley after a good harvest, and that there are no barriers to an actual exchange of quantities of barley between

1. Adam Smith, *op. cit.*, p. 13.

them. In this case, the two farmers could give free rein to their propensity to trade, and could exchange 100 bushels or any other quantity of barley back and forth between themselves. Although there is no reason why they should desist from trading in this case if the exchange of goods, by itself, affords pleasure to the participants, I believe nothing is more certain than that these two individuals will forgo trade altogether. If they should nevertheless engage in this sort of exchange, they would be in danger, precisely because of their enjoyment of trade under such circumstances, of being regarded as insane by other economizing individuals.

Suppose now that a hunter has a great abundance of furs, and hence of materials for clothing, but only a very small store of foodstuffs. His need for clothing is thus fully provided for but his need for food only inadequately. A nearby farmer is assumed to be in precisely the opposite position. Suppose too that there are no barriers to an exchange of the hunter's foodstuffs for the farmer's clothing materials. It is evident that an exchange of goods is still less likely in this case than in the first one. If the hunter should exchange a portion of his scanty store of food for a portion of the farmer's equally scanty stock of furs, the hunter's surplus clothing materials and the farmer's surplus of foodstuffs would both become even greater than before the exchange. Since satisfaction of the hunter's need for food and satisfaction of the farmer's need for clothing were already insufficiently provided for, the economic position of the traders would be decidedly worsened. No one can maintain, therefore, that these two economizing individuals would experience pleasure from such an exchange. On the contrary, nothing is more certain than that the hunter and farmer will both most firmly resist offers to engage in a trade that would definitely reduce their well-being, or possibly even endanger their lives. If an exchange of this sort had nevertheless taken place, the two men would have nothing more urgent to do than to revoke it.

The propensity of men to trade must accordingly have some other reason than enjoyment of trading as such. If trading were a pleasure in itself, hence an end in itself, and not frequently a laborious activity associated with danger and economic sacrifice, there would be no reason why men should not engage in trade in the cases just considered and in thousands of others. There would, in fact, be no reason why they should not trade back and forth an unlimited number of times. But everywhere in practical life, we can observe that economizing men carefully consider every exchange in advance, and that a limit is finally reached beyond which two individuals will not continue to trade at any given time.

Since it has been established that exchange is not an end in itself, and still less itself a pleasure for men, the problem in what follows will be to explain its nature and origin.

To begin with the simplest case, suppose that two farmers, A and B, have both previously been carrying on isolated household economies. But now, after an unusually good harvest, farmer A has so much grain that he is unable, however profusely he may provide for the satisfaction of his needs, to utilize a portion of it for himself and his household. Farmer B, on the other hand, a neighbor of farmer A, is assumed to have had an excellent vintage in the same year. But his cellar is still filled from previous years, and because he lacks additional containers he is considering pouring out a part of the older wine in storage which dates from an inferior vintage year. Each farmer has a surplus of one good and a serious deficiency of the other. The farmer with a surplus of grain must completely forgo consumption of wine since he has no vineyards at all, and the farmer with a surplus of wine is in want of foodstuffs. Farmer A can permit many bushels of grain to spoil on his fields when a keg of wine would afford him considerable pleasure. Farmer B is about to destroy not merely one but several kegs of wine when he could very well use a few bushels of grain in his household. The first farmer thirsts and the second starves when both could be relieved by the grain A is permitting to spoil on his fields and by the wine B has resolved to pour out. Farmer A could still satisfy his and his family's need for food as completely as before and indulge besides in the enjoyment of drinking wine, and farmer B could continue to enjoy as much wine as he pleases but would not need to starve. It is therefore evident that we have encountered a case in which, *if command of a certain amount of A's goods were transferred to B and if command of a certain amount of B's goods were transferred to A, the needs of both economizing individuals could be better satisfied than would be the case in the absence of this reciprocal transfer.*

The case just presented, in which the needs of two persons could be better satisfied than before by a mutual transfer of goods having no value to either of them prior to the exchange, and hence without economic sacrifice on either side, was especially suitable for impressing upon us in the most enlightening manner the nature of the economic relationship leading to trade. But we would construe this relationship too narrowly if we were to confine our attention to cases in which a person who has command of a quantity of one good larger than even his full requirements suffers a deficiency of a second good, while another person has a comparable surplus of this second good and a deficiency of the first. For the relationship in question can also be observed in less obvious cases in which one person possesses goods of which certain quantities have less value to him than quantities of another good owned by a second person who is in the reverse situation.

As an example, let us suppose that the first of the two isolated farmers has not harvested so much grain that he can allow part of it to spoil on the field without injury to the satisfaction of his needs, and that the second does not have so much wine that he can pour any of it away without similar injury. Instead, each of the two farmers can employ the whole quantity of the good at his command in some fashion useful to himself and his household. The first farmer can employ his whole stock of grain usefully by devoting the quantity remaining after complete provision for the satisfaction of his more important needs to the fattening of his cattle. The second farmer does not have so much wine that he must pour some of it away, but just enough to permit him to distribute a portion to his slaves as a reward for greater effort. Thus, although to the grain farmer a certain portion of his grain (a bushel, for instance) and to the wine grower a certain portion of his wine (a keg, for instance) has only a small value, it nevertheless has some value, since directly or indirectly the satisfaction of certain of his needs depends on that portion. But the fact that a given quantity of grain, a bushel for instance, has a certain value to the first farmer by no means excludes the possibility that a certain

quantity of wine, a keg for instance, may have a higher value to
him, as would be the case if the enjoyment afforded by a keg of
wine has a higher importance to him than the more or less thorough fattening of his cattle. Similarly with the second farmer,
the fact that a keg of wine has a certain value to him by no
means excludes the possibility that a bushel of wheat may have
a higher value to him, as would be the case if it would ensure
a more adequate diet for himself and his family, and perhaps
even avoidance of the pains of hunger.

The most general form of the relationship responsible for
human trade is therefore as follows: an economizing individual,
A, has a certain quantity of a good at his disposal which has a
smaller value to him than a given quantity of another good in
the possession of another economizing individual, B, who estimates the values of the same quantities of goods in reverse fashion, the given quantity of the second good having a smaller
value to him than the given quantity of the first good which is
at the disposal of A.[2] Let the quantity of the first good in A's
possession be 10a, and let the quantity of the second good in
B's possession be 10b. Assume the value of the quantity 1a to A
to be W, the value of 1b to A if he should obtain command of
it to be $W+x$, the value of 1b to B to be w, and the value of 1a
to B if he should obtain command of it to be $w + y$. It is evident that A would gain a value of x and that B would gain a
value of y from a transfer of 1a from A's possession to B's and
1b from B's possession to A's. In other words, after an exchange,
A would find himself in the same position as if a good with a
value to him of x had been added to his wealth, and B would
find himself in the same position as if a good with a value of y
to him had been added to his wealth.

If, in addition, the two economizing individuals (a) recognize
the situation, and (b) have the power actually to perform the
transfer of the goods, a relationship exists that makes it possible
for them, by a mere agreement, to provide better, or more completely, for the satisfaction of their needs than would be the
case if the relationship were not exploited.

The same principle that guides men in their economic activ-

2. The remainder of this paragraph appears here as a footnote in the
original.—TR.

ity in general, that leads them to investigate the useful things
surrounding them in nature and to subject them to their command, and that causes them to be concerned about the better-
ment of their economic positions, *the effort to satisfy their
needs as completely as possible,* leads them also to search most
diligently for this relationship wherever they can find it, and
to exploit it for the sake of better satisfying their needs. In the
situation just described, therefore, the two economizing individuals will make certain that the transfer of goods actually
takes place. The effort to satisfy their needs as completely as
possible is therefore the cause of all the phenomena of economic life which we designate with the word "exchange." It
should be observed that this term is used in our science in a
special sense with a much wider application than in popular
or especially than in legal language. For in the economic sense
it also includes purchase and sale, and all partial transfers of
economic goods (tenancy, rental, lending, etc.) for compensation.

If we summarize what has just been said we obtain the following propositions as the result of our investigation thus far:
The principle that leads men to exchange is the same principle
that guides them in their economic activity as a whole; it is the
endeavor to ensure the fullest possible satisfaction of their
needs. The enjoyment men derive from an *economic* exchange
of goods is the general feeling of pleasure they experience when
some event permits them to make a better provision for the satisfaction of their needs than would otherwise have been possible. But the benefits of a mutual transfer of goods depend, as
we have seen, on three conditions: (a) one economizing individual must have command of quantities of goods which have a
smaller value to him than other quantities of goods at the disposal of another economizing individual who evaluates the
goods in reverse fashion, (b) the two economizing individuals
must have recognized this relationship, and (c) they must have
the power actually to perform the exchange of goods. The absence of but one of these conditions means that an essential
prerequisite for an economic exchange is missing, and that an
exchange of goods between two economizing individuals is
economically impossible.

2. THE LIMITS OF ECONOMIC EXCHANGE

If each economizing individual had but a single good of each kind at his disposal, and if each of these goods were indivisible with respect to its goods-character, there would be no difficulty in investigating the limits to which exchange operations would proceed in each given case to result in the greatest economic gain for each participant. Suppose that A has a glass goblet and B a piece of jewelry made of the same material, and that neither of the two individuals has command of more than the one unit of each article. According to what was said in the preceding section, only two situations are conceivable: either the basis for an economic exchange between the two individuals exists with respect to the two goods, or it does not. If it does not, the question of an exchange cannot arise at all from an economic standpoint. And if it does exist, there can be no doubt that an actual exchange of the two goods will naturally preclude any further exchange of goods of exactly the same kinds between A and B.

But whenever *quantities* of goods are at the command of different persons which can be subdivided into portions of any desired size, or which are composed of *several* discrete pieces, each of which is indivisible by nature or use, the situation is different.

Suppose that A, an American frontiersman, owns several horses but no cow, while B, his neighbor, has a number of cows but no horses. Provided that A has requirements for milk and milk products and B for draft animals, it is easy to see that a basis for exchange operations is present. But no one will maintain that the exchange of *one* of A's horses, for example, for *one* of B's cows would necessarily exhaust the existing basis for economic exchange operations between A and B with respect to these goods. It is equally certain, however, that a basis need not necessarily exist for exchange of the total quantities they possess. A who owns (for example) six horses may be able to satisfy his needs better if he exchanges one, or two, or perhaps even three, of his horses for B's cows. But from this it does not necessarily follow that he would derive an economic gain from the exchange transaction if he were to barter all his horses for all of B's cows. Although the initial economic situation provides a basis for economic exchange operations between A and B, the consequence of carrying the exchange too far might be that the needs of the two contracting parties would be less well provided for than before the exchange.

The relationship we are now considering, in which not merely single goods but quantities of goods are at the disposal of men, can be regularly observed in human economy. An endless number of cases can be observed in which two economizing individuals have command of quantities of different goods, and in which the foundations for economic exchange operations are present, but where the gains to be derived from trade would be exploited only incompletely if the two economizing individuals were to exchange too little, and would be again diminished, reduced to nothing, or even converted to losses, if they should drive their exchange operations too far and exchange too much.

But if we can observe cases where "too little" of an exchange does not yield the full gains to be derived from the exploitation of an existing relationship and where "too much" leads to the same result, indeed often even to a deterioration in the economic positions of the two traders, there must be a limit at which the full economic gains to be obtained from the exploitation of the given relationship are reached, and beyond which any exchange of further portions begins to become uneconomic. The determination of this limit is the object of the subsequent investigation.

I shall present a simple case for this purpose in which we can most carefully observe the relationship we wish to consider, undisturbed by secondary influences.

Suppose that in a virgin forest, far away from other economizing individuals, there live two frontiersmen who maintain friendly intercourse with each other. It is assumed that the compass and intensity of their needs are exactly the same. Each of them requires several horses to work his land. One horse is absolutely necessary if he is to be able to produce the food required for the maintenance of his and his family's lives. A second horse is required to produce the somewhat greater amount of food needed for an adequate diet for himself and his family.

Each of the farmers could use a third horse to transport the timber and firewood he finds necessary from the forest to his log cabin, to draw loads of sand, stones, etc., and to work a field on which he will raise some luxury foods for his and his family's enjoyment. A fourth would be used solely for pleasure, and a fifth horse would have only the importance resulting from its availability as a substitute in case one of the other horses should become incapacitated. But neither of the frontiersmen could use a sixth horse. It is assumed also that each of them would need five cows to meet his full requirements for milk and milk products, that there is the same gradation in the importance of their needs for these products, and that a sixth cow could not be used by either of them.

For greater clarity, let us cast the situation just described in numerical form (pp. 125, ff). We can represent the graduated importance of the satisfactions that are provided for by the possessions of the two frontiersmen with a set of numbers that decrease in arithmetic series, with the series 50, 40, 30, 20, 10, 0, for example.[3]

Assuming that A, the first frontiersman, has 6 horses and only one cow, while B, the other frontiersman, has one horse and 6 cows, the successive degrees of importance of the satisfactions provided for by the possessions of the two persons can be represented in the following table:

A		B	
Horses	Cows	Horses	Cows
50	50	50	50
40			40
30			30
20			20
10			10
0			0

From what was said in the first section of this chapter, it is easily seen that the basis for economic exchange operations is

3. I need hardly point out that the figures in the text are not intended to express numerically the *absolute* but merely the *relative* magnitudes of importance of the satisfactions in question. Thus when I designate the importance of two satisfactions with 40 and 20 for example, I am merely saying that the first of the two satisfactions has twice the importance of the second to the economizing individual concerned.

here present. The importance a horse has to A is equal to 0, and the importance a second cow would have to him is equal to 40. On the other hand, a cow has a value of 0 to B, while a second horse would have a value of 40 (p. 131). Thus A and B could both provide considerably better for the satisfaction of their needs if A were to give B a horse and if B were to give A a cow in exchange. There is no doubt that they would actually undertake this exchange if they are economizing individuals.

The importance of the satisfactions that are provided for by the possessions of the two persons after this first exchange will be as follows:

A		B	
Horses	Cows	Horses	Cows
50	50	50	50
40	40	40	40
30			30
20			20
10			10

It is easily seen that each of the two traders obtained an economic gain from this first exchange equivalent to the gain that would accrue to him if his wealth had been increased by a good whose value to him is equal to 40.[4] But it is just as certain that the basis for economic exchange operations has by no means been exhausted by this first exchange. For a horse still has much less value to A than an additional cow would have (10 as compared with 30), whereas a cow has a value of only 10 to B while an additional horse would have a value of 30 (three times the value of a cow). It is therefore in the economic interest of both economizing individuals to undertake a second exchange operation.

The situation after the second exchange can be represented as follows:

4. These considerations completely disprove the contention of a number of economic writers (Lotz and Rau, for example, among the more recent German writers) who have denied the productivity of trade. The effect of an economic exchange of goods upon the economic position of each of the two traders is always the same as if a new object of wealth had entered his possession. Trade is therefore no less productive than industrial or agricultural activity.

A		B	
Horses	*Cows*	*Horses*	*Cows*
50	50	50	50
40	40	40	40
30	30	30	30
20			20

It can be seen that each of the two persons derived an economic gain that is no less than if their wealth had been increased by a good valued at 20.

Let us see whether there is a basis for further economic exchange operations even in this situation. A horse has an importance of 20 to A; an additional cow would also have an importance of 20 to him; and B is in a similar position. From what has been said, it is evident that an exchange of one of A's horses for one of B's cows under such conditions would not be worth while since there would be no economic gain at all.

But suppose that A and B should nevertheless enter into a third exchange. If performance of the exchange did not require any appreciable economic sacrifices (costs of transport, loss of time, etc.) it is evident that the economic positions of the two men would be neither injured nor improved.[5] After this third exchange their positions would be as follows:

A		B	
Horses	*Cows*	*Horses*	*Cows*
50	50	50	50
40	40	40	40
30	30	30	30
	20	20	

Let us now ask what would be the economic result of still further exchanges of one of A's horses for one of B's cows. The situation after a fourth exchange would be:

A		B	
Horses	*Cows*	*Horses*	*Cows*
50	50	50	50
40	40	40	40
	30	30	
	20	20	
	10	10	

5. I classify indifferent exchanges such as this as definitely non-economic since in them the provident activity of men is set in motion aimlessly quite apart from all the economic sacrifices they may entail.

As can be seen, the economic positions of A and B are both less favorable after the fourth exchange than they were before. By acquiring a fifth cow, A has indeed assured the satisfaction of a need that has an importance of 10 to him. But to obtain it he has given up a horse that had the importance to him of satisfactions that were assumed equal to 30. His economic position after this exchange is exactly the same as it would be if his wealth had been reduced without compensation by a good with a value equal to 20. The same result can be observed with B. The economic disadvantage of the fourth exchange operation is mutual. Instead of gaining from it, A and B would both suffer an economic loss.

If the two persons, A and B, should continue to exchange horses for cows, the situation after the fifth exchange would appear as follows:

A		B	
Horses	Cows	Horses	Cows
50	50	50	50
	40	40	
	30	30	
	20	20	
	10	10	
	0	0	

And after the sixth exchange it would be:

A		B	
Horses	Cows	Horses	Cows
	50	50	
	40	40	
	30	30	
	20	20	
	10	10	
	0	0	
	0	0	

It is easily seen that after the fifth exchange of one of A's horses for one of B's cows the two traders would have returned to the same situation, with respect to completeness of provision for the satisfaction of their needs, that they were in at the outset of exchange operations. After the sixth exchange they would have worsened their economic positions considerably more.

They could do nothing better than to revoke these uneconomic exchanges.

What has been shown here in a single instance can be observed wherever quantities of different goods are in the possession of different persons and a basis for economic exchange operations is present. If we were to select other examples, we would find differences in secondary circumstances but not in the nature of the relationship explained.

Above all we would find, in each instance and at any given point in time, a limit up to which two persons can exchange their goods to their mutual economic advantage. But we would find that they cannot overstep this limit without placing themselves in a less favorable economic position. In short, we would everywhere observe a limit at which the total economic gains to be derived from an exchange relationship are exhausted, and beyond which these gains would be diminished by further exchange operations, making the exchange of any further portions uneconomic. *This limit is reached when one of the two bargainers has no further quantity of goods which is of less value to him than a quantity of another good at the disposal of the second bargainer who, at the same time, evaluates the two quantities of goods inversely.*

Thus we see that in the reality of practical life men do not trade indefinitely and without limit. We see instead that particular persons, at any given time, with respect to any given kinds of goods, and in any given economic situation, reach a certain limit at which they cease to make further exchanges.[6]

A social economy is made up of individual economies, and what has been said above is therefore just as valid for the trade of entire peoples as it is for single economizing individuals. Two nations, one chiefly engaged in agriculture and the other primarily in industry, will be in a position to satisfy their needs much more completely if each exchanges a portion of its produce for the produce of the other (the first nation a portion of its agricultural produce and the second a portion of its manufactures). But they will not undertake the exchange indefinitely and without limit. At any given point in time they will reach a limit beyond which any further exchange of agricul-

6. The next paragraph appears here as a footnote in the original.—TR.

tural produce for manufactures will be uneconomic for both nations.

It is, of course, true that in the trade of individuals, and still more in the commerce between whole peoples, the values goods actually have for men can generally be observed to be subject to constant fluctuations. These fluctuations occur principally because new quantities of goods are continually coming into the hands of the various economizing individuals through the production process. As a result, the foundations for economic exchanges are constantly changing, and we therefore observe the phenomenon of a perpetual succession of exchange transactions. But even in this chain of transactions we can, by observing closely, find points of rest at particular times, for particular persons, and with particular kinds of goods. At these points of rest, no exchange of goods takes place because an economic limit to exchange has already been reached.

Another observation made earlier concerned the gradually diminishing economic gains obtained by given economizing individuals from the exploitation of a given opportunity for trade. The first trading contacts of economizing individuals are usually the most advantageous economically. It is usually only later that opportunities for trade that promise smaller economic gains are also exploited. This is true not only of trade between individuals but also of the commerce between whole nations. If two peoples whose ports or boundaries were always or for some time previous closed to mutual intercourse open them suddenly to trade, or even if only some previous impediments to trade are removed, a very lively trade in goods develops immediately. For the number of trading opportunities to be exploited and the economic gains to be made are at first very great. Later, trade moves in the channel of normally profitable business. But if the full gains from the new trade are sometimes not immediately forthcoming, the reason is that the other two prerequisites of economic exchange, knowledge of the trading opportunities and power to carry through exchange operations recognized to be economic, are ordinarily acquired by the participants only after a certain period of time. Some of the most strenuous efforts of trading nations are directed toward removing impediments to trade in both these categories (by careful study of the commercial situation, by the construction of good roads and other means of transport and communication, etc.).

Before I close this discussion of the foundations and limits of economic exchange, I wish to direct attention to an important factor that must be taken into consideration if the principles expounded in this chapter are to be correctly interpreted. I refer to the economic sacrifices that exchange operations demand.

If men and their possessions (the economies of individuals [7]) were not separated in space, and if the mutual transfer of command of goods between one economizing individual and another did not therefore generally require the shipping of goods and many other economic sacrifices, the full economic gains resulting from an exchange transaction would accrue to the two participants. But such cases are very rare. Cases are indeed conceivable in which the economic sacrifices of an exchange operation fall to a minimum neglected in practical life. But it is not easy to find an actual case in which an exchange operation can be performed without any economic sacrifices at all, even if they are confined only to the loss of time. Freight costs, loading charges, tolls, excise taxes, premiums for marine and other insurance, costs of correspondence, commissions and other sales costs, brokerage charges, weighages, packaging costs, storage charges, the entire cost of the commercial banking system, even the expenses of traders [8] and all their employees, etc., are nothing but the various economic sacrifices which are required for the conduct of exchange operations and which absorb a portion of the economic gains resulting from the exploitation of existing exchange opportunities. Indeed, these economic sacrifices often render exchange impossible when it would be possible if only these "expenses," in the general economic sense of the term, did not exist.

Economic development tends to reduce these economic sacrifices, with the result that even between the most distant lands

7. *"die menschlichen Wirthschaften"*—TR.
8. Carey's portrayal of merchants as economic parasites because they claim a portion of the gain arising from the exploitation of the available opportunities for economic exchange transactions (*op. cit.*, III, 23-25) is based on his erroneous ideas about the productivity of trade.

more and more economic exchanges become possible which previously could not have taken place.

Implicit in what has been said is an explanation of the source from which all the thousands of persons who are intermediaries in trade derive their incomes. Because they do not contribute directly to the physical augmentation of goods, their activity has often been considered *unproductive*. But an economic exchange contributes, as we have seen, to the better satisfaction of human needs and to the increase of the wealth of the participants just as effectively as a physical increase of economic goods. All persons who mediate exchange are therefore—provided always that the exchange operations are economic—just as productive as the farmer or manufacturer. For the end of economy is not the physical augmentation of goods but always the fullest possible satisfaction of human needs. Tradespeople contribute no less to the attainment of this end than persons who were, for a long time, and from a very one-sided point of view, exclusively called productive.

CHAPTER V | THE THEORY OF PRICE

HOWEVER much prices, or in other words, the quantities of goods actually exchanged, may impress themselves on our senses, and on this account form the usual object of scientific investigation, they are by no means the most fundamental feature of the economic phenomenon of exchange. This central feature lies rather in the better provision two persons can make for the satisfaction of their needs by means of trade. Economizing individuals strive to better their economic positions as much as possible. To this end they engage in economic activity in general. And to this end also, whenever it can be attained by means of trade, they exchange goods. Prices are only incidental manifestations of these activities, symptoms of an economic equilibrium between the economies of individuals.

If the locks between two still bodies of water at different levels are opened, the surface will become ruffled with waves that will gradually subside until the water is still once more. The waves are only symptoms of the operation of the forces we call gravity and friction. The prices of goods, which are symptoms of an economic equilibrium in the distribution of possessions between the economies of individuals, resemble these waves. The force that drives them to the surface is the ultimate and general cause of all economic activity, the endeavor of men to satisfy their needs as completely as possible, to better their economic positions. But since prices are the only phenomena of the process that are directly perceptible, since their magnitudes can be measured exactly, and since daily living brings them unceasingly before our eyes, it was easy to commit the error of regarding the magnitude of price as the essential feature of an exchange, and as a result of this mistake, to commit the further error of regarding the quantities of goods in an exchange as *equivalents*. The result was incalculable damage to our science since writers in the field of price theory lost themselves in attempts to solve the problem of discovering the causes of an alleged *equality* between two quantities of goods.[1] Some found the cause in equal quantities of labor expended on the goods. Others found it in equal costs of production. And a dispute even arose as to whether the goods are given for each other because they are equivalents, or whether they are equivalents because they are exchanged. But such an equality of the values of two quantities of goods (an equality in the objective sense) nowhere has any real existence.

The error on which these theories were based becomes immediately apparent as soon as we free ourselves from the one-sidedness that previously prevailed in the observation of price phenomena. The only quantities of goods that can be called equivalents (in the objective sense of the term) are quantities which, at a given point in time, can be exchanged at will—that is, in such a way that if one of two quantities of goods is offered, the other can be acquired for it, and *vice versa*. But equivalents of this sort are nowhere present in human economic

1. See Appendix F (p. 305) for the material originally appearing at this point as a footnote.—TR.

life. If goods were equivalents in this sense, there would be no reason, market conditions remaining unchanged, why every exchange should not be capable of reversal. Suppose A had exchanged his house for B's farm or for a sum of 20,000 Thalers. If these goods had become equivalents in the objective sense of the term as a result of the transaction, or if they had already been equivalents before it took place, there is no reason why the two participants should not be willing to reverse the trade immediately. But experience tells us that in a case of this kind neither of the two would give his consent to such an arrangement.

The same observation can also be made under the most highly developed conditions of trade, and even with respect to the most saleable commodities. Let anyone buy grain on a grain exchange or securities on a stock exchange and try to sell them again before a change in market conditions occurs, or let him try to sell and buy separate units of the same commodity at the same time, and he will easily be convinced that the difference between supply prices and demand prices is no mere accident but a general feature of social economy.

Thus commodities that can be exchanged against each other in certain definite quantities (a sum of money and a quantity of some other economic good, for instance), that can be exchanged for each other at will by a *sale* or a *purchase*, in short, commodities that are *equivalents in the objective sense of the term*, do not exist—even on given markets and at a given point in time. And what is more important, deeper understanding of the causes that lead to the exchange of goods and to human trade in general teaches us that equivalents of this sort are utterly impossible in the very nature of the case and cannot exist in reality at all.

A correct theory of prices cannot, therefore, have the task of explaining an alleged "equality of value" between two quantities of goods when such an equality does not, in truth, exist anywhere. In this setting, the subjective character of value and the nature of exchange would be completely misunderstood. A correct theory of price must instead be directed to showing how economizing men, in their endeavor to satisfy their needs as fully as possible, are led to give goods (that is, definite quan-

tities of goods) for other goods. In this investigation, I shall
proceed in accordance with the methods followed generally in
this work, beginning with the simplest phenomena and gradually passing on to the more complex phenomena of price formation.

1. PRICE FORMATION
IN AN ISOLATED EXCHANGE

In the previous chapter, we saw that the possibility of an
economic exchange of goods is dependent on an economizing
individual having command of goods that have a smaller value
to him than other goods at the command of another economizing individual who values the two goods in reverse fashion. The
mere statement of this condition, however, strongly implies the
existence of limits within which price formation must, in any
given instance, take place.

By way of illustration, we will suppose that 100 units of A's
grain have the same value to him as 40 units of wine. It is clear
from the beginning that A will, under no circumstances, be
prepared to give more than 100 units of grain for 40 units of
wine in an exchange, since if he were to do so, his needs would
be less well provided for after the exchange than before. He will
agree to an exchange only if it enables him to make better
provision for his needs than would be possible without the exchange. He will be willing to exchange his grain for wine only
if he has to give less than 100 units of grain for 40 units of
wine. Thus whatever the price of 40 units of wine may eventually be in an exchange of A's grain for the wine of some other
economizing individual, this much is certain, that it cannot,
owing to the economic position of A, reach 100 units of grain.

If A can find no other economizing individual to whom a
smaller quantity than 100 units of grain has a greater importance than 40 units of wine, he will never be in a position to exchange his grain for wine. In this event, the foundations for an
economic exchange of the two goods would not be present so
far as A is concerned. But if A does find a second economizing
individual, B, to whom only 80 units of grain, for example,
have a value equal to 40 units of wine, the prerequisites for an

economic exchange between A and B are certainly present (provided the two men recognize the situation and no barriers stand in the way of execution of the exchange), and at the same time a second limit is set to price formation. If it follows from the economic situation of A that the price of 40 units of wine must be below 100 units of grain (since he would otherwise derive no economic gain from the transaction), it follows from the economic situation of B that a greater quantity than 80 units of grain must be offered for his 40 units of wine. Hence, whatever the price that is finally established for 40 units of wine in an economic exchange between A and B, this much is certain, that it must be formed between the limits of 80 and 100 units of grain, above 80 and below 100 units.

It is easily seen that A could provide better for the satisfaction of his needs even if he should have to give 99 units of grain for the 40 units of wine, and that B would be acting economically on the other side if he were to accept as little as 81 units of grain in exchange for his 40 units of wine. But since there is an opportunity for both economizing individuals to exploit a much larger economic advantage, each of them will direct his efforts to turning as large a share as possible of the economic gain to himself. The result is the phenomenon which, in ordinary life, we call *bargaining*. Each of the two bargainers will attempt to acquire as large a portion as possible of the economic gain that can be derived from the exploitation of the exchange opportunity, and even if he were to try to obtain but a fair share of the gain, he will be inclined to demand higher prices the less he knows of the economic condition of the other bargainer and the less he knows the extreme limit to which the other is prepared to go.

What will be the numerical result of this price duel?

It is certain, as we saw, that the price of 40 units of wine will be higher than 80 units and lower than 100 units of grain. But it appears equally certain to me that the outcome of the exchange will prove sometimes more favorable to one and sometimes more favorable to the other of the two bargainers, depending upon their various individualities and upon their greater or smaller knowledge of business life and, in each case, of the situation of the other bargainer. In the formulation of general principles, however, there is no reason for assuming that one or the other of the two bargainers will have an overwhelming economic talent, or that other circumstances will operate more in the favor of one than the other. Under the assumption of economically equally capable individuals and equality of other circumstances, therefore, I venture to state, as a general rule, that the efforts of the two bargainers to obtain the maximum possible gain will be mutually paralyzing, and that the price will therefore be equally far from the two extremes between which it can be established.

In our case, the price for a quantity of wine of 40 units upon which the two bargainers will finally agree will lie within the limits of 80 and 100 units of grain, with the further restriction that it must be higher than 80 and lower than 100 units. As concerns its position between these limits, if the two bargainers are otherwise equally situated, it will be equal to 90 units of grain. But if this equality in their situations does not prevail, an exchange at another price between the two limits would not be economically impossible.

What has been said of price formation in this case holds in a similar fashion for every other. Wherever the foundations for an economic exchange of two goods between two economizing individuals exist, the nature of the relationship itself sets definite limits within which price formation must take place if the exchange is to have economic character at all. These limits are given by the different quantities of the goods that are equivalents for each bargainer (equivalents in a subjective sense). (In the example just considered, for instance, 100 units of grain are the equivalent of 40 units of wine for A, and 80 units of grain are the equivalent of the same quantity of wine for B.) Within these limits, the price tends to be determined at the average of the two equivalents (and hence, in our example, at 90 units of grain, the average of 80 and 100 units).

The quantities of goods that are given for each other in an economic exchange are therefore precisely determined by the economic situation obtaining in each case. It is true that human caprice has some degree of influence on the result since varying quantities of goods may be exchanged, within definite limits,

without a resultant loss of the economic character of the exchange operation. But it is equally certain that the opposing
efforts of the bargainers to derive the greatest possible gain from
the transaction will balance out in most cases, and that prices
will therefore have a tendency to settle at the average of the extreme possible limits. If other factors, founded on the personalities of the two economizing individuals or on other external
conditions affecting the transaction, enter the picture, prices
can deviate from this natural middle position between the
limits explained earlier without causing the exchange operations to lose economic character. But these deviations are not
economic in nature, being founded on personal characteristics
or on special external causes that are not of an economic character.

2. PRICE FORMATION UNDER MONOPOLY

In the previous section, I directed attention to the fact that
price formation and the distribution of goods conform to definite laws by first considering the simplest possible case in which
an exchange of goods takes place between two economizing individuals who are not influenced by the economic activity of
other persons. This case, which could be termed isolated exchange, is the most common form of human trade in the early
stages of the development of civilization. Its importance has
survived to later times in sparsely populated backward regions
and it is not completely absent even under advanced economic
conditions, since it can be observed in highly developed economies wherever an exchange of goods that have value only to
two economizing individuals takes place, or where other special
circumstances economically isolate two persons.

But with the progress of civilization, instances in which the
foundations for an economic exchange of goods are present
merely for two economizing individuals occur less frequently.
If, for example, A owns a horse that has a value to him equal
to the value of 10 bushels of grain if he were to acquire them,
he would be better able to provide for the satisfaction of his
needs even if he were to exchange the animal for but 11 bushels

of grain. To farmer B, on the other hand, who has a large stock of grain but lacks horses, a horse if acquired would be an equivalent for 20 bushels of his grain, and he would be better able to provide for the satisfaction of his needs even if he were to give 19 bushels of grain for A's horse. Farmer B_2 would be prepared to give 29 bushels of grain for the horse and farmer B_3 to give 39 bushels. In this case, according to what was said before, not only does a foundation exist for an exchange of the two goods between A and one other farmer, but A can, in an economic exchange, give his horse to any one of the grain farmers, and any one of the latter can economically acquire it in exchange.

What has just been said becomes still more evident if we consider the case in which foundations for economic exchange operations with the grain farmers exist not only for A, but also for several other owners of horses, A_2, A_3, etc. Suppose that only 8 bushels of grain for A_2, and but 6 for A_3, would, if acquired, have a value equal to one of their horses. There can be no doubt that, in this case, foundations for economic exchanges would exist between each of the animal breeders and each of the grain farmers.

In both these cases we have to deal with much more complicated relationships than the one presented in the first section of this chapter. In the first case, foundations for economic exchange operations exist between a monopolist (in the widest sense of the term) and each of several other economizing individuals who, in their efforts to exploit the exchange opportunities confronting them, are in competition with each other for the monopolized good. In the second case, the foundations for economic exchange operations are present simultaneously on the one side for each of several owners of one good, and on the other side for each of several owners of another good; on each side, therefore, these persons are in competition with one another.

I shall begin with the simpler of the two cases, in which there is competition between several economizing persons for a monopolized good, and later pass on to the more complicated case of price formation when there is competition on both sides.

A. *Price formation and the distribution of goods when there is competition between several persons for a single indivisible monopolized good.*

In the description of price formation in isolated exchange (p. 194), we saw that in each particular case there is a certain range of indeterminacy within which price formation can take place without the exchange losing its economic character, and that the extent of this range depends upon the nature of the particular exchange situation. We also saw that the price that tends to be formed is one that divides the economic gains that can be obtained from exploitation of the relationship confronting two bargainers between them equally, and that there is thus, in each given case, a certain average toward which the price tends to move. But in this connection, I pointed out that economic influences do not in any way, within this range of freedom, fix the point at which price formation must, of necessity, take place.

If, for example, an economizing individual, A, has a horse that has a value to him no higher than 10 bushels of grain if he were to acquire them, while to B, who has had a rich harvest of grain, 80 bushels have a value equal to a horse if he were to acquire one, it is clear that the foundations for an economic exchange of A's horse for B's grain are present, provided that A and B both recognize this relationship and have the power actually to perform the exchange of these goods. But it is equally certain that the price of the horse can be formed between the wide limits of 10 and 80 bushels of grain and can approach either of the two extremes without causing the economic character of the exchange to disappear. It is, of course, extremely improbable that the price of the horse will settle at 11 or 12 bushels or at 78 or 79 bushels of grain. But it is certain that no economic causes whatsoever are present that exclude completely the possibility of the formation of even these prices. At the same time, it is also clear that the transaction can take place naturally only between A and B only as long as B finds no competitor in his endeavor to acquire A's horse by trade.

But suppose that B_1 does have a competitor, B_2, who either

does not have as great an abundance of grain as B_1 or requires a
horse less urgently. Still, B_2 values a horse as highly as 30 bushels of grain, and could thus provide better for the satisfaction
of his needs if he were to give 29 bushels of grain for A's horse.
It is clear that the foundations for an economic exchange of a
horse for some quantity of grain exist between B_2 and A as well
as between B_1 and A. But since only one of the two competitors for A's horse can actually acquire it, two questions arise:
(a) With which of the two competitors will the monopolist A
conclude the exchange transaction? and (b) What will be the
limits within which price formation will take place?

The answer to the first question arises from the following
considerations. The value of A's horse to B_2 is equal to 30
bushels of his grain. He would thus provide better for the satisfaction of his needs if he were to give as much as 29 bushels of
his grain to A for his horse. This is not, by any means, to say
that B_2 will immediately offer A 29 bushels for the horse. But
it is certain that he will decide to make even this offer to meet
the competition of B_1 as far as possible, since he would be acting
very uneconomically if, as a last resort, he would not be satisfied with even as small a gain from trade as he could derive
from an exchange of 29 bushels of grain for A's horse. On the
other hand, B_1 would obviously be acting uneconomically if,
in the competition for A's horse, he were to permit B_2 to acquire it for the price of 29 bushels of grain, since the economic
gain of B_1 would still be considerable if he were to give 30
bushels of grain or more for the horse and thereby *economically
exclude* B_2 from the exchange transaction.[2]

Thus the fact that there is a price range within which an
exchange transaction would have become uneconomic for B_2
but still be economic for B_1 places B_1 in a position to obtain for

2. When I say that B_1 *economically excludes* B_2, I do not mean that B_2 is
excluded from the exchange by the use of physical force or because
of legal incapacity. The distinction is important, since B_2 could easily
own several hundred bushels of grain and thus have the power,
physically and legally, to acquire A's horse and still not choose to
acquire it. If he does not acquire it, his reason must be economic in
nature—that is, by giving up a larger quantity of grain than 29 bushels,
he would not provide better for the satisfaction of his needs than he
would without the exchange.

himself the gains resulting from the exchange by making the transaction economically impossible for his competitor.

Since A would certainly be acting uneconomically if he did not transfer his monopolized good to the competitor who is in a position to offer him the highest price for it, nothing is more certain than that the exchange transaction will, in this particular economic situation, take place between A and B_1.

As concerns the second question (the limits within which price formation will take place), it is certain that the price that B_1 will give A cannot reach 80 bushels of grain since at this price the transaction would lose its economic character for B_1. Nor can the price fall below 30 bushels of grain. For price formation would then fall within the limits where the exchange transaction would still be advantageous for B_2, who would therefore have an economic interest in competing until the price should again reach the limit of 30 bushels. In our case therefore, the price must, of necessity, be formed between the limits of 30 and 80 bushels of grain.[3]

Thus the effect of the competition of B_2 is that price formation, in the exchange of goods between A and B_1, will no longer take place between the wide limits of 10 and 80 bushels of grain, as would otherwise have been the case, but between the narrower limits of 30 and 80 bushels of grain. For only if the price is fixed between these limits does an economic gain from the transaction accrue to A and B_1 simultaneously with an economic exclusion of the competition of B_2. The simple relationship of the isolated exchange thus reappears, the only dif-

---

3. The opinion could arise that instead of the price in the case we have been discussing being formed between 30 and 80 bushels of grain it will be established at exactly 30 units. This conclusion would be correct if we were dealing with an auction sale in which no minimum price had been set in advance or if it had been set below 30 bushels of grain. In either case A would be compelled by the very nature of an auction to be satisfied with the price of 30 bushels, and the causes of the unusual price formation in auctions in general are to be sought in analogous relationships. But if economizing individual A does not bind himself from the beginning with an auction contract and can pursue his interest with complete freedom, there is no economic reason why the price of a horse should not reach 79 bushels of grain in an exchange between A and B, just as there is no reason why it should not be set at 30 bushels.

ference being that the limits between which price formation takes place have become narrower. Aside from this difference, the principles already explained for the case of isolated exchange become fully applicable here.

Suppose now that the two previous competitors for A's horse, B_1 and B_2, are joined by a third competitor, B_3. If the value of the horse to this third individual would be equal to 50 bushels of grain, it is clear from what has just been said that the transaction again will take place between A and B_1, but the price will be formed between the limits of 50 and 80 bushels. If a fourth competitor, B_4, appears, to whom A's horse would have a value equal to 70 bushels of grain, the transaction will still take place between A and B_1, but the price will be formed between the limits of 70 and 80 bushels.

Only when a competitor, for instance the economizing individual B_5, appears on the scene, to whom the monopolized good has a value of as much as 90 bushels of grain, will the transaction take place between A and this last competitor and the price of the horse be fixed between 80 and 90 bushels of grain. It is clear that the new competitor will exploit the exchange opportunity confronting him to his economic advantage, and that he will be in a position economically to exclude all other competitors (including B_1) from the exchange. Price formation will take place between 80 and 90 bushels of grain because, on the one hand, the competitor B_1 can only be economically excluded from the transaction by a price of at least 80 bushels of grain, which prevents the price from falling below this level, and because, on the other hand, the price cannot exceed or even reach 90 bushels of grain, since the transaction would then lose its economic character for B_5.

What has been said is valid for every other case in which the foundations for exchange operations exist between a monopolist exchanging an indivisible good for some other good offered by several other economizing individuals. Summarizing, we obtain the following principles: (1) When several economizing individuals, for each of whom the foundations for an economic exchange are present, compete for a single indivisible monopolized good, the competitor who will obtain the good will be the one for whom it is the equivalent of the largest quantity of the good offered for it in exchange. (2) Price formation takes place between limits that are set by the equivalents of the monopolized good in question for the two competitors who are most eager, or who are in the strongest competitive position, to perform the exchange. (3) Within these limits, the price is fixed according to the principles of price formation already demonstrated for isolated exchange.

B. *Price formation and the distribution of goods when there is competition for several units of a monopolized good.*

In the preceding section we selected as the subject of our investigation the simplest case of monopoly in which a monopolist brings a *single indivisible* good to market, and in which the process of price formation takes place under the influence of the competition of several economizing individuals for the good.

The more complex case that I wish to discuss now is one in which the foundations for economic exchange operations exist simultaneously between a monopolist who has command of a *quantity* of a monopolized good on the one hand and several economizing individuals on the other hand who have quantities of some other good at their disposal.

Suppose that a newly acquired horse would have a value to farmer B_1, who has a large quantity of grain but no horses, equal to 80 bushels of his grain. To farmer B_2 a newly acquired horse would have a value equal to 70 bushels of grain, to B_3 60, to B_4 50, to B_5 40, to B_6 30, to B_7 20, and to B_8 only 10 bushels of grain. A second horse would have a value, to each of these farmers of 10 bushels less than the value of the first, a third a value of 10 bushels less than the second, and so on, each additional horse having a value of 10 bushels less than the preceding one (provided in each case that an additional horse is needed at all). The essential features of this economic situation can be presented in a table (see next page).

If the monopolist A brings only *one* horse to market, it is certain, in accordance with the argument of the previous section, that B_1 will acquire it at a price somewhere between 70 and 80 bushels of grain.

NUMBER OF BUSHELS OF GRAIN THAT ARE EQUAL IN VALUE TO AN ADDITIONAL HORSE ACQUIRED BY TRADE

	1st horse	2nd horse	3rd horse	4th horse	5th horse	6th horse	7th horse	8th horse
To B_1	80	70	60	50	40	30	20	10
To B_2	70	60	50	40	30	20	10	
To B_3	60	50	40	30	20	10		
To B_4	50	40	30	20	10			
To B_5	40	30	20	10				
To B_6	30	20	10					
To B_7	20	10						
To B_8	10							

But suppose that the monopolist brings not merely one but three horses to market. Here we are concerned with the case that forms the subject of investigation in the present section, and the question is: which one (or which ones) of the eight farmers will acquire the horses brought to market by the monopolist and what price will be charged?

For the answer let us turn to our table. It appears that a first horse acquired by B_1 would have a value to him equal to 80 bushels, a second a value equal to 70 bushels, and a third a value equal to only 60 bushels of grain. In this situation, B_1 would be acting economically if he were to acquire *one* horse at a price between 70 and 80 bushels, thereby economically excluding all his competitors from the exchange. But he would act uneconomically with respect to the second horse if he were to offer 70 bushels or more for it, since by such an exchange the satisfaction of his needs would not be better provided for than before. With the third horse, at a price that would exclude B_2 from the transaction and which must therefore be at least equal to 70 bushels of grain, the economic disadvantage to B_1, and hence the non-economic character of such an exchange, would become still more obvious.

The economic situation in this case is therefore such that, on the one hand, B_1 can exclude all his competitors from acquiring any of the three horses only by conceding for each of them a price of 70 bushels of grain or more, while, on the other hand, he can purchase only *one* horse economically at this price and would worsen his economic position if he were also to buy the other two at the same price.

Since we are assuming that B_1 is an individual behaving economically, he will not exclude his competitors from the exchange purposelessly or to his own detriment. He will exclude them from acquiring quantities of the monopolized good only if, and to the extent to which, he can thereby obtain for himself an economic advantage he would have to forgo if he were to permit the other competitors to purchase quantities of the monopolized good. In our case, therefore, where an exclusion of all competitors for the monopolized good is rendered economically impossible for B_1 by the economic situation, he will find himself in the position of being obliged to let B_2 participate in the purchase of quantities of the monopolized good. He will even have a common interest with B_2 in establishing the price of a unit of the monopolized good, in this case the price of a horse, at as low a level as possible under the existing circumstances. Far from driving the price of a horse to 70 bushels of grain or more, B_1 as well as B_2 will therefore have an interest in seeing that the price is fixed as much below 70 bushels of grain as is possible in the given economic situation.

In these efforts, B_1 and B_2 will be limited by the competition of the other competitors, above all by that of B_3. They will have to agree to a price at which the other competitors for the monopolized good (including B_3) will be economically excluded from the transaction. Thus, in the case of three horses, the price will be formed between 60 and 70 bushels of grain. At a price fixed between these limits, B_1 could acquire two horses and B_2 could acquire one, in each case economically, while all other competitors would, at the same time, be excluded from acquiring quantities of the monopolized good.

Price formation between these limits is the only possible result. If the price were less than 60 bushels, B_3 would not be excluded from the transaction, and would therefore attempt to obtain for himself the gain that would result from the exploitation of the opportunity confronting him. But since B_1 and B_2 are economizing individuals, and since they are in a position to gain a considerable economic advantage at an even higher price, they will not allow this to happen. If the price were, on the other hand, to reach or to exceed the limit of 70 bushels of grain, B_1 would be able to purchase only *one* horse and B_2 none at all, and only one of the horses offered for sale would therefore actually be sold. In the case of three horses, therefore, price formation outside the limits of 60 and 70 bushels of grain is economically impossible.

If A were to bring 6 horses to market, we could show by similar reasoning that B_1 would acquire 3 horses, that B_2 would acquire 2 horses, that B_3 would acquire one horse, and that the price of a horse would be formed between 50 and 60 bushels of grain. If A were to bring 10 horses to market, B_1 would acquire 4 horses, B_2 3 horses, B_3 2 horses, B_4 one horse, and the price would be formed between 40 and 50 bushels of grain. If the monopolist A should offer still larger quantities of the monopolized good for sale, there is no doubt, on the one hand, that an ever smaller number of farmers would be economically excluded from purchasing quantities of the monopolized good, and on the other hand, that the price of a given quantity of the monopolized good would be pressed down to successively lower levels.

By imagining the symbols B_1, B_2, etc., to stand, not for single individuals, but for groups of the population of a country (using B_1 to designate the group of economizing individuals who are most eager and in the strongest competitive positions to exchange grain for the monopolized good, B_2 to designate the group of economizing individuals who are next in eagerness and in competitive strength, and so on) we obtain a model of monopoly trade as it actually appears under the conditions of everyday life.

We find classes of people of very different purchasing power competing for the quantities of monopolized goods reaching the market. As was demonstrated for single individuals, we find some of these classes economically excluding others from purchasing. We observe that the classes of people that must forgo the consumption of a monopolized good become more numerous the smaller the quantity of the good brought to market, and *vice versa* that a monopolized good penetrates to classes that are lower in purchasing power the larger the quantity marketed.

With these changes, the prices of monopolized goods are seen to rise and fall.

Summarizing what has been said, we obtain the following principles: (1) The quantity of a monopolized good offered for sale by a monopolist is acquired by those competitors for it to whom the largest quantities of the good offered in exchange for it are the equivalents of the units of the monopolized good. The monopolized good is distributed in such a way that the quantity of the good given in exchange that is the equivalent of one unit of the monopolized good is equal for each of the purchasers of portions of the monopolized good (50 bushels of grain equal to one horse, for example).

(2) Price formation takes place between limits that are set by the equivalent of one unit of the monopolized good to the individual least eager and least able to compete who still participates in the exchange and the equivalent of one unit of the monopolized good to the individual most eager and best able to compete of the competitors who are economically excluded from the exchange.

(3) The larger the quantity of the monopolized good offered for sale by the monopolist, the fewer will be the competitors for it who will be economically excluded from acquiring portions of it, and the more completely will those economizing individuals be provided with it who would have been in a position to acquire portions even if smaller quantities of it had been offered for sale.

(4) The larger the quantity of a monopolized good offered for sale by the monopolist, the lower in terms of purchasing power and eagerness to trade will he have to descend among the classes of competitors for the monopolized good in order to sell the whole quantity, and hence the lower also will be the price of one unit of the monopolized good.

C. *The influence of the price fixed by a monopolist on the quantity of a monopolized good that can be sold and on the distribution of the good among the competitors for it.*

As a rule, a monopolist does not bring given quantities of a monopolized good to market with the intention of selling the whole amount under all circumstances, and of awaiting the result of competition in the determination of the price, as at an auction. His usual procedure is rather to bring a quantity of his monopolized good to market or keep it ready for sale, and to ask a fixed per unit price for it. The reason for this is generally to be found in practical considerations, especially in the fact that the method of selling goods described in the preceding section requires both the simultaneous congregation of the largest possible number of the competitors for the monopolized good and the observance of numerous formalities if the price is to be determined by the joint influence of all the effective economic factors involved. These considerations appear to make employment of this method of marketing appropriate only in particular, and not too frequent, cases.

Whenever the monopolist can count on congregating all or at least a sufficient number of competitors, and when the necessary formalities can be observed without disproportionate economic sacrifices (as in the case of an auction of a monopolized article in a well-known auction hall, announced some time in advance), he will of course use the method described in the previous section as the one most certain to enable him to dispose of the entire amount of the monopolized good at his command in the most economic manner. He will also choose an auction when he must sell out a substantial stock of a monopolized good completely within a limited period of time. But the ordinary procedure adopted by a monopolist in marketing his commodities will, as has been said, be one in which he has the available quantities of the monopolized good ready for sale but offers only partial quantities to the competitors for it at a price set by him.

Where a monopolist sets the price of a unit of the monopolized good and lets the competing purchasers choose the quantities to meet their requirements for the good at the given price, and where the question of price formation is therefore excluded from the immediate problem from the first, the questions we must investigate are: (1) Which competitors will be economically excluded from acquiring quantities of the monopolized good at each given level of the price of a unit of it? (2) What will be the influence of the higher or lower level at which the price is set by the monopolist on the quantities of the monopolized good sold? and (3) In what manner will the quantity of the monopolized good actually sold be distributed among the various competitors for it?

To begin with, it is evident that if the monopolist were to fix the price of a unit of the monopolized good at so high a level that a unit of it would not have a value equal to the price demanded by the monopolist even for the competitor who is most eager and best able to make the exchange, all the competitors for the monopolized good would be excluded from acquiring any portions of it, and no sales could take place at all. This would be the case, in the situation described in the table of page 204, if the monopolist A were to fix the price of a horse at 100, or even at only slightly more than 80 bushels of grain, since it is clear that an economic exchange would be an impossibility at so high a price for any of the eight competitors for the monopolized good mentioned in our example.

But suppose that the monopolist fixes the price of a horse at a lower level than that which would economically exclude all the competitors for the monopolized good from acquiring quantities of it. In their endeavor to improve their economic positions, they will doubtless grasp the proffered opportunity and actually enter into exchange transactions with the monopolist within the limits explained in the previous section. But it is clear that the level of the price will be an essential determinant of the scope of these transactions. If, for example, A were to set the price of a horse at 75 bushels of grain, B_1 could economically purchase one horse. If the price were fixed at 62 bushels of grain, B_1 would purchase two horses and B_2 one horse. If the price were 54 bushels of grain, B_1 would purchase three, B_2 two, and B_3 one horse. At a price of 36 bushels of grain, B_1 would buy five, B_2 four, B_3 three, B_4 two, and B_5 one horse, and so on.

If our example is extended as before, and we imagine the symbols B_1, B_2, B_3, etc., to represent groups of competitors who differ in purchasing power and in their desire to trade, we see most distinctly the influence exercised on the economy by prices fixed by a monopolist at different levels. The higher the price, the more numerous will be the individuals, or classes of individuals, who are excluded completely from consuming the monopolized good, the scantier will be the provisioning of the other classes of the population who are not completely excluded, and the smaller will be the quantities of the monopolized good that the monopolist can sell. With reductions in price, on the other hand, progressively fewer economizing individuals, or classes of individuals, will be excluded completely from acquiring any quantities of the monopolized good, the provisioning of individuals who were already participating in the trade at higher prices will be more complete, and the sales of the monopolist will progressively increase.

What has just been said can be stated more precisely in terms of the following principles:

(1) When a monopolist sets the price of a unit of a monopolized good, the competitors for the monopolized good who are excluded from acquiring quantities of it are those for whom one unit of the monopolized good is the equivalent of a quantity of the good offered in exchange that is equal to or less than the price of the monopolized good.

(2) Competitors for quantities of a monopolized good for whom one unit of it is the equivalent of a quantity of the good offered in exchange that is larger than the price fixed by the monopolist will supply themselves with quantities of the monopolized good up to the limit at which one unit of it becomes for them the equivalent of an amount of the good offered in exchange that is equal to the monopoly price. The quantity of the monopolized good that will be acquired by each of these competitors at each price set by the monopolist is determined by the foundations for economic exchange operations existing for each individual at that price.

3) The higher a monopolist sets the price of a unit of a monopolized good, the larger will be the class of competitors for the monopolized good who are excluded from acquiring it, the less completely will the other classes of the population be provided with it, and the smaller will be the sales of the monopolist. Opposite relationships hold in the reverse case.

D. *The principles of monopoly trading (the policy of a monopolist).*

In the two previous sections, I have explained the influence of a larger or smaller quantity of a monopolized good offered for sale on the determination of its price, and the influence of a higher or lower price set by the monopolist on the quantity of a monopolized good that will be sold. In both cases I discussed the influence of the policy adopted on the distribution of the monopolized good among the various competitors for it.

Throughout the analysis, we have seen that the monopolist is not the only person determining, or decisive in, the course of economic events. Not only does the general principle of all economic exchanges of goods, according to which both parties must derive an economic advantage from an exchange, maintain its validity unimpaired in the case of monopoly, but within the trading range delimited by this factor, the monopolist is not completely unrestricted in influencing the course of economic events. As we have seen, if the monopolist wishes to sell a particular quantity of the monopolized good, he cannot fix the price at will. And if he fixes the price, he cannot, at the same time, determine the quantity that will be sold at the price he has set. He cannot, therefore, sell large quantities of the monopolized good and at the same time cause the price to settle at as high a level as it would have reached if he had marketed smaller quantities. Nor can he set the price at a certain level and at the same time sell as large a quantity as he could sell at lower prices. But what does give him an exceptional position in economic life is the fact that he has, in any given instance, a choice between determining the quantity of a monopolized good to be traded or its price. He makes this choice by himself and without regard to other economizing individuals, considering only his economic advantage. It is thus in his power to regulate price by offering smaller or larger quantities of the monopolized good for sale, or to regulate the quantity of the monopolized good traded by raising or lowering the price, always in accordance with his economic interest.

A monopolist will therefore raise his price, within the limits between which exchange operations have economic character, if he anticipates a greater economic gain from selling small quantities of the monopolized good for a high price. He will lower his price if he finds it more to his advantage to market larger quantities of the monopolized good at a lower price. In the beginning, he will set the price as high as possible and thus market only small quantities of the monopolized good, later lowering the price step by step to increase sales and thereby exploiting all classes of the population in succession—if he can obtain the greatest economic gain by following this procedure. But he will market large quantities of the monopolized good at lower prices from the start if his economic advantage so dictates. Under some circumstances, he may even have occasion to abandon part of the quantity of the monopolized good at his disposal to destruction instead of bringing it to market, or, with the same result, to leave unused or to destroy part of the corresponding means of production at his command instead of employing them for the production of the monopolized good. He would adopt this policy if marketing the whole quantity of the monopolized good directly or indirectly available to him would oblige him to offer it to classes of the population who have so little purchasing power or desire for the good that, in spite of the larger quantities marketed, the resultant price would be so low that he would have a smaller profit than could be obtained by destroying a portion of the quantity of the monopolized good at his command and selling only the remainder, at a higher price, to classes of the population having greater purchasing power.[4]

It would be entirely erroneous to assume that the price of a monopolized good always, or even usually, rises or falls in an *exactly* inverse proportion to the quantities marketed by the monopolist, or that a similar proportionality exists between the price set by the monopolist and the quantity of the monopolized good that can be sold. If, for example, the monopolist brings 2,000 instead of 1,000 units of the monopolized good to market, the price of one unit will not necessarily fall from 6 florins, for example, to 3 florins. On the contrary, depending upon the economic situation, it may in one case fall only to 5 florins, for ex-

4. The next paragraph appears here as a footnote in the original.—TR.

ample, but in another to as little as 2 florins. Under some circumstances, therefore, the total receipts that the monopolist
obtains from the sale of a larger quantity of the monopolized
good may be exactly the same as the total receipts yielded by
the sale of a smaller quantity. Under other circumstances, however, they may be greater or less. If the monopolist in our example were to sell 1,000 units of the monopolized good, his total
receipts would be 6,000 florins. For 2,000 units he would not,
however, necessarily receive 6,000 florins also, but perhaps as
much as 10,000 or as little as 4,000 florins, according to the circumstances of the case. The reason for this lies ultimately in
the fact that there are very great differences in the scales of
equivalents for the various individuals with respect to different
goods. Thus B, for example, may evaluate the first unit that he
acquires of a certain good as the equivalent of 10 units of the
good he gives in exchange, the second as the equivalent of 9
units, the third as the equivalent of 4 units, and the fourth as
the equivalent of but one unit of the good given in exchange.
With respect to another good, on the other hand, the above
scale might appear as 8, 7, 6, 5, ... Suppose that the first
good is grain and that the second is some article of luxury. It
is clear that an increase beyond a certain point in the quantity
marketed would cause a much more rapid fall (and that a decrease in the quantity marketed would cause a much more
rapid rise) in the price of grain than in the price of the article
of luxury.

If it is assumed that all monopolists are economizing individuals aware of their advantage, then their policy is directed
naturally neither to fixing the lowest possible price, nor to selling the largest possible quantity of a monopolized good. It is
directed neither to making the monopolized good available to
the largest possible number of economizing individuals, or
groups of individuals, nor to providing each individual with
the monopolized good to the fullest extent possible. The monopolist has no interest in all this. His economic policy is directed to making a maximum profit from the quantity of the
monopolized good available to him. He does not, therefore,
auction off the whole amount of the monopolized good at his
disposal, but markets instead only such an amount as promises,

at the expected price, to yield him the greatest profit. He does not fix the price at the precise level at which he can sell the whole quantity of the monopolized good at his command, but instead at the level most likely to yield the maximum profit. The correct economic policy from his point of view is obviously to offer only such quantities of the monopolized good for sale, or to set the price at such a level, as will yield the greatest profit in either case.

From a monopolistic point of view, his policy would be in-correct if, in spite of the fact that he could make a higher profit by marketing a smaller quantity of the monopolized good, he were nevertheless to sell a larger quantity. His policy would be still more uneconomic if, instead of confining himself to the production of the quantity of the monopolized good whose sale promises him the highest profit, he were to increase this quan-tity, with an expenditure of economic goods and other sacri-fices on his part, and nevertheless cause his eventual profit to be smaller. It would be incorrect if he were to set the price so low that, although he could sell larger quantities, he would obtain a smaller profit than if he had set the price higher. Above all, his policy would be incorrect if he were to set the price of the monopolized good so low that he could not fully supply all the purchasers competing for it to whom exchange would be eco-nomic at this price, and if some of them had to go without the good. A situation of this sort would be a distinct proof that he had set the price too low.

What has been said here is supported by experience and by history. The policies of all monopolists have, as their economic activities clearly demonstrate, been conducted in accordance with the above considerations. The Dutch East-India Company in the seventeenth century caused part of the spice plants in the Moluccas to be destroyed. Large stocks of spices have frequently been burned in the East Indies, and tobacco in North America. The guilds sought, by various means, to limit the number of artisans as much as possible (by long apprenticeship, by prohi-bition of more than a certain number of apprentices, etc.). All these measures were correct from a monopolistic standpoint, since the quantities of the several monopolized commodities reaching the market were regulated in a manner favorable to the monopolists, or to the corporations of monopolists. When freer trade, the emergence of factories, and other influences prevented the guilds from regulating independently the quantities of goods entering the market, the entire guild organization became ineffective so far as its monopolistic character was concerned. Monopolistic fines and similar measures directly influencing price formation at once gave way before the impact of the larger quantities of goods brought to market. Originally these fines were intended to subject single individuals (called price-cutters!) who failed to appreciate the interest of the whole guild or corporate body of monopolists to limitations profitable to the monopolistic group. When the power of the guilds to control the quantities of goods brought to market was wrested from them, their regulations could no longer be enforced. The most anxious concern of all members of a guild was always the regulation of the marketing of handicraft products so that only such quantities would be sold as corresponded to their interest. Those who interfered in this regulation were always regarded by the guilds as their most dangerous opponents, against whom they incessantly appealed to governments for protection. The breach in their regulatory activity that was made by the great quantities of manufactured products supplied by large-scale industry signified the fall of the guild system.

Summarizing what has been said in this section, we find that, for each quantity of a good that a monopolist decides to sell, the price is determined independently of his will; that, at each price that he decides to set for a unit of the monopolized good, the quantity is determined independently; that the distribution of goods is governed, in either case, in accordance with exact laws; and that the entire course of economic events is throughout not fortuitous but capable of being reduced to definite principles.

Even the fact that it is in the power of the monopolist to choose either his price or the quantity sold does not, as we have seen, imply any indeterminacy of the economic phenomena resulting from his decision. Although the monopolist has the power to set higher or lower prices, or to market larger or smaller quantities of the monopolized good, there is only *one particular* price and only *one particular* quantity of the monopolized good brought to market that corresponds most exactly to his economic interest. If the monopolist is an economizing individual, therefore, he will not proceed in an arbitrary fashion in determining his price or the quantity of the monopolized good he will sell, but in accordance with definite principles. Each given economic situation sets definite limits within which price formation and the distribution of goods must take place, and any price and distribution of goods that is outside these limits is economically impossible. The phenomena of monopoly trade present us therefore with a picture of strict conformity, in every respect, to definite laws. Here too, of course, error and imperfect knowledge may give rise to aberrations, but these are the pathological phenomena of social economy and prove as little against the laws of economics as do the symptoms of a sick body against the laws of physiology.

3. PRICE FORMATION AND THE DISTRIBUTION OF GOODS UNDER BILATERAL COMPETITION

A. *The origin of competition.*

We would interpret the concept of the monopolist too narrowly if we limited it to persons who are protected from the competition of other economizing individuals by the state or by some other organ of society. There are persons who, as a result of their property holdings, or due to special talents or circumstances, can market goods that it is physically or economically impossible for other economizing persons to supply competitively. And even where special circumstances of these types are not present, there is often no social barrier to the emergence of monopolists. Every artisan who establishes himself in a locality in which there is no other person of his particular occupation, and every merchant, physician, or attorney, who settles in a locality where no one previously exercised his trade or calling, is a monopolist in a certain sense, since the goods he offers to society in trade can, at least in numerous instances, be had only from him. The chronicles of many a flourishing town tell of the first weaver to settle there when the place was still small and poorly populated. Even today, a traveller can find this particular kind of monopolist everywhere in Eastern Europe, and in the smaller villages even of Austria. Monopoly, interpreted as an actual condition and not as a social restriction on free competition, is therefore, as a rule, the earlier and more primitive phenomenon, and competition the phenomenon coming later in time. Anyone wishing to expound the phenomena prevailing under competition will therefore find it to his advantage to begin with the phenomena of monopoly trade.

The manner in which competition develops from monopoly is closely connected with the economic progress of civilization. The increase of population, the increased needs of the various economizing individuals, and their growing wealth, drive the monopolist, in many instances even while increasing production, to exclude progressively larger classes of the population from consuming the monopolized good, and permit him at the same time to drive his prices higher and higher. Society thus becomes a progressively more favorable object for his monopolistic policy of exploitation. A first artisan of any particular kind, a first physician, or a first lawyer, is a welcome man in every locality. But if he encounters no competition and the locality flourishes, he will, almost without exception, after some time acquire the reputation of a hard and self-seeking man among the less wealthy classes of the population, and even among the wealthier inhabitants of the place he will be regarded as selfish. The monopolist *cannot* always comply with the growing requirements of society for his commodities (or labor services), and if he could comply, a corresponding increase of his sales is not always in his economic interest. In most cases, therefore, he will be driven to make a choice between his clients, and some of the competitors for his monopolized good will either get nothing or will be supplied with it only reluctantly and inadequately. Even his wealthier clients will often find cause to complain of negligence of all sorts and of the costliness of his services.

The economic situation just described is usually such that the need for competition itself calls forth competition, provided there are no social or other barriers in the way. Our next task, then, will be to investigate the effects of the appearance of competition upon the distribution, sales, and price of a commodity in comparison with the analogous phenomena observed under monopoly.

B. *The effect of the quantities of a commodity supplied by competitors on price formation; the effect of given prices set by them on sales; and in both cases the effect on the distribution of the commodity among the competing buyers.*[5]

To facilitate comprehension, I shall utilize the case with which I illustrated my explanation of the principles of monopoly trade as the basis of the present investigation. In the table on p. 204,[6] B_1, B_2, B_3, etc., represent individual farmers or groups of farmers. To each farmer a first newly acquired horse is the equivalent of the quantity of grain appearing in the first column, and each additional horse is the equivalent of a quantity of grain 10 bushels less. The question before us is: what will be the influence of larger or smaller quantities of a commodity offered for sale by several competing sellers on the price and on the distribution of the commodity among the competitors for it?

To begin with, assume that there are two competitors in supply, A_1 and A_2, and that together they have 3 horses for sale, A_1 having two horses and A_2 one. From what was said earlier, it is clear that in this case farmer B_1 will buy 2 horses and farmer B_2 one horse. The price will be between 60 and 70 bushels of grain, a higher price being impossible because of the economic interest of the two farmers B_1 and B_2, and a lower price because of the competition of B_3. If A_1 and A_2 have six horses for sale, it is no less certain that B_1 will purchase three of them, B_2 two, and B_3 one, and that the price will be between 50 and 60 bushels of grain, etc.[7]

5. See John Prince-Smith, "Der Markt, eine Skizze," *Vierteljahrschrift für Volkswirthschaft und Kulturgeschichte*, I, (1863), part IV, 148 ff.
6. In the original Menger repeats the table printed on p. 204. Since the two tables are identical it was considered permissible to omit it the second time.—TR.
7. From this it is at once evident that the great importance to human economy of markets, fairs, exchanges, and all points of concentration of trade in general, is due to the fact that as trading relationships become more complex the formation of economic prices becomes virtu-

If we compare the price and the distribution of goods resulting from the sale of a given quantity of a commodity by several competing sellers with the situation observed under monopoly, we find a complete analogy. *Whether a given quantity of a commodity is sold by a monopolist or by several competitors in supply, and independent of the way in which the commodity was originally distributed among the competing sellers, the effect on price formation and on the resultant distribution of the commodity among the competing buyers is exactly the same.*

Although the larger or smaller quantity of a good sold has a very decisive influence on its price and distribution under monopoly as well as competitive trade, the fact that a particular quantity of a commodity is supplied by a monopolist alone or by several competitors in supply has no influence on the phenomena of economic life just mentioned.

We can observe a similar result where commodities are offered for sale at given prices. The higher or lower level of the price has, as we saw, a very important influence on the total sales of a commodity as well as on the quantity that each competing buyer will actually acquire. But whether the goods (at the fixed price) are brought to market by only one or by several economizing individuals has no direct and necessary influence either on the total sales or on the quantities that will be acquired by the various economizing individuals.

The principles developed with respect to the influence of given quantities of a monopolized commodity offered for sale on its price (p. 203), with respect to the influence of given prices on the quantities sold (p. 207), and in both cases also with respect to its distribution among the various competitors attempting to buy it, are therefore fully applicable to all cases where a number of economizing individuals (competitors in demand) compete for

ally impossible without these institutions. The speculation that develops on these markets has the effect of impeding uneconomic price formation from whatever causes it may arise, or of mitigating at least its harmful effects on the economy of men. (Prince-Smith, *op. cit.*, pp. 143 ff; Otto Michaelis, "Die wirthschaftliche Rolle des Spekulationshandels," *Vierteljahrschrift für Volkswirthschaft und Kulturgeschichte*, II, (1864) part IV, 130 ff, III (1865) part II, 77 ff; Karl Scholz, "Der Wochenmarkt," *ibid.*, V (1867) part I, 25 ff; A. Emminghaus, "Märkte und Messen," *ibid.*, 61 ff.)

quantities of a commodity offered for sale by several other economizing individuals (competitors in supply).

C. *The effect of competition in the supply of a good on the
quantity sold and on the price at which it is offered (the
policies of competitors).*

I have just explained that, for each particular quantity of a
good offered for sale, a definite price is established, that at any
set price there is a definite amount of sales, that in both cases
there is also a definite distribution of the goods sold, and that it
is irrelevant in these respects whether the quantity involved is
marketed by a monopolist or by several competitors in supply.

Other things being equal, the price and distribution of a good
will be the same whether 1,000 units of it, for example, are offered for sale by a monopolist or by several competitors in supply. Whether a commodity is offered for sale by a monopolist
or by several competitors at a given price—at 3 units of some
other commodity for one unit of the commodity being offered
for sale, for example—the total sales and the distribution of the
quantity sold among the various competing buyers will be exactly the same.

If, therefore, competition in supply is to exercise any effect
at all on price formation, total sales, and the distribution of a
good among its competing purchasers, either *different quantities* of the good must be offered for sale or the competing sellers
must find themselves obliged to set *different prices* under the
regime of competition in supply than under monopoly.

The influence of competition in the supply of a commodity
on the quantities offered for sale, on its distribution, and on
the prices at which it is offered, is the topic with which we shall
be occupied in what follows. To set the economic phenomena
involved clearly before us, let us consider the simple case in
which the quantity of a monopolized good available to a monopolist suddenly comes into the hands of two competitors.

A monopolist has died, and has left his holdings of the monopolized good and means of production to two heirs in equal
shares. This is an instance of the simple case just posited. It is
not impossible that the two heirs of the monopolist will, instead

of competing with each other, operate as associates in a single firm and carry on the monopoly policy (described above) of their testator. Or they may enter into a mutual understanding to exploit the consumers, and together regulate the quantities of the good they offer for sale or the prices they set. It is even conceivable that they may, without an express understanding but "in their mutual well-understood interest," pursue this same monopoly policy toward their customers if they find it in their own economic interest. In each of these cases, which can be observed everywhere in the economic development of men,[8] we would undoubtedly encounter the same phenomena that we observed earlier with monopoly trade. For the two economizing individuals would then not be *competitors* in supply but monopolists, and so not within the present field of discussion. But if we suppose each of the two heirs to be determined to pursue the sale of the previously monopolized good independently, we have a case of real competition before us, and the questions to be considered are: what quantities of the previously monopolized good will now, in contrast to the previous situation, be offered for sale, and what supply prices will be set by the two competitors?

In the previous section, we saw that it is frequently in the economic interest of the monopolist to abstain from marketing portions of the whole quantity of the monopolized good available to him, and to destroy them or let them spoil, since he can often obtain a larger profit from a smaller quantity of his goods than he would if he were to sell the entire available quantity at lower prices. Assume that a monopolist has 1,000 pounds of

8. No phenomenon is more common than that of a monopolist defending his position against the entry of a competitor in the most belligerent manner. But it is just as common to find him coming to an understanding with a competitor once the competitor has established himself. The monopolist's first interest is to prevent a competitor from becoming established. But if a competitor has nevertheless succeeded in firmly entrenching himself, his economic interest consists in pursuing a modified monopoly policy in combination with this second firm whenever a monopoly policy proves to be possible even after the establishment of a competitor. Sharp competition is usually disadvantageous to both economizing individuals in cases of this kind. Hence two competitors, initially so hostile to each other, generally come to a quick understanding.

a monopolized commodity and that he can, in the given economic situation, either sell 800 pounds at 9 ounces of silver per pound or dispose of the whole available quantity at 6 ounces of silver per pound. It is thus in his power to take 6,000 ounces of silver for the entire quantity of the monopolized commodity at his command, or to take 7,200 ounces of silver for 800 pounds of it. If the monopolist is an economizing individual pursuing his self-interest, the choice he will make is not subject to doubt. He will destroy 200 pounds of his monopolized commodity, permit them to spoil, or otherwise withdraw them from trade, and will offer only the remaining 800 pounds for sale—or, which amounts to the same thing, he will set his price at such a level that the same result will obtain.

But if the 1,000 pounds of the previously monopolized commodity are divided between two competitors, this policy immediately becomes economically impossible for each of them. If one of the two were to destroy part of the quantity available to him, or if he were to withdraw it from trade in some other way, he would of course elicit a definite increase in the price of a unit of his commodity. But never, or only in very rare instances, would he able to obtain a greater profit by so doing. If A_1, for instance, the first of the two competitors, were to destroy 200 of the 500 pounds of the previously monopolized commodity at his command or otherwise withdraw them from trade, he would doubtless cause the price of the good to rise— from 6 to 9 ounces of silver per pound, for example. But he would not cause a greater total profit to accrue to himself. The consequence of his action would be that A_2 would obtain 4,500 instead of 3,000 ounces of silver, while he himself would obtain only 2,700 ounces of silver (instead of 3,000) in exchange for the other 300 units sold. The intended gain would accrue solely to his competitor, and he himself would suffer a substantial loss.

The first effect, therefore, of the appearance of competition in supply is that none of the competitors selling a commodity can derive an economic advantage from destroying or withdrawing from exchange a part of the available quantity of the commodity—or, which amounts to the same thing, from leaving the means of production available for its production unused.

A second phenomenon of economic life that is peculiar to

monopoly is also removed by competition. I refer to the successive exploitation of the various social classes that was mentioned in the previous section. We saw that it can often be to the advantage of a monopolist to market only small quantities of the monopolized good in the beginning at high prices and to sell to classes of people of successively lower purchasing power only by degrees, in order to exploit all classes of people in a stepwise fashion. This procedure is immediately rendered impossible by competition. If A_1 were to attempt a stepwise exploitation of the social classes of this sort in spite of the competition of A_2, and market only small initial quantities of the good, he would probably not be able to raise the price sufficiently to elicit a gain for himself, but would instead only permit his competitor to fill the gaps created by his action and to capture the intended economic gain.

Whatever else may be the effect of true competition on the distribution of goods and on price formation, therefore, it is certain at any rate that two of the socially most injurious outgrowths of monopoly described earlier are removed by competition. Neither the destruction of part of the available quantity of a commodity subject to competition in supply, nor the destruction of a part of the factors serving for its production, is in the interest of separate competitors, and the successive exploitation of the various social classes becomes impossible.

But competition has still another, much more important, consequence for the economic life of men. I refer to the increase of the quantities of a previously monopolized commodity that become available to economizing men. Monopoly usually causes only part of the quantity of the goods at the command of the monopolist to be offered for sale, or only a part of the available means of production to be put to use. True competition always puts this malpractice to an end immediately. But competition usually has the further effect of increasing the available quantity of a previously monopolized commodity. It is a very rare occurrence, at any rate, for the means of production collectively at the command of two or more competing sellers to be as narrowly limited as those at the command of a monopolist. In the great majority of cases, therefore, several competitors will market a greater quantity of a commodity than a monopolist. Thus the existence of true competition not only causes the entire quantity of a commodity actually available to be offered for sale, but also has the further and much more important result of increasing significantly the quantity that becomes available. When there is no natural limitation to the means of production, this means that more and more classes of society are able to consume the commodity at falling prices, and that the provisioning of society in general becomes ever more complete.[9]

In the preceding section, I gave the reasons why a monopolist generally does not bring certain fixed quantities of his commodity to market and await the determination of the price as at an auction, but instead sets a definite price for his commodity and awaits its effect on sales. A similar thing occurs when there are several competitors selling a commodity. In this case too, each of them offers his commodity at a set price, which he computes so as to yield him the largest possible proceeds. What distinguishes his behavior from that of a monopolist is that the latter will often, as we have seen, find it to his interest to fix his price so high that only a part of the quantity available to him reaches the consumers, while competition forces every competitor to fix his price with regard to the entire quantity in his own and in his competitors' hands. Barring error and ignorance on the part of the economizing individuals involved, prices are therefore formed under the impact of the entire quantity at the disposal of all the competing suppliers. To this must be added the fact that competition generally considerably increases the available quantity of commodities, as we have seen. These are the factors that are responsible for the reductions in prices that are a consequence of competition.

Even the direction of the economic activity of the economizing persons engaged in the production of a good is powerfully affected by the existence of competition. A monopolist naturally endeavors to place the monopolized good only within the reach of the higher social classes and to exclude all classes of society of lower purchasing power from consuming it. As a rule, it is much more advantageous for him, and always more convenient, to obtain large profits on small quantities than small profits on larger quantities. But competition, which concerns itself with

9. The next paragraph appears here as a footnote in the original.—TR.

the exploitation of even the smallest economic gain wherever possible, tends to descend with its goods to the lowest social classes that the economic situation at any time permits. The monopolist has the power to regulate, within certain limits, either the price or the quantity of a monopolized good coming upon the market. He readily renounces the small profit that can be made on goods destined to be consumed by the poorest social classes in order to be able to exploit the classes of greater purchasing power more effectively. But under competition, where no single competitor has the power to regulate by himself either the price or the quantity of a good traded, each individual competitor desires even the smallest profit, and the exploitation of existing possibilities of making such profits is no longer neglected. Competition leads therefore to large-scale production with its tendency to make many small profits and with its high degree of economy, since the smaller the profit on each unit the more dangerous becomes every uneconomic waste, and the brisker the competition the less possible becomes an unthinking continuation of business according to old-established methods.

A. THE NATURE OF USE
VALUE AND EXCHANGE VALUE

A

S LONG AS the development of a people is so re-
tarded economically that there is no significant amount of trade
and the requirements of the various families for goods must be
met *directly* from their own production, goods obviously have
value to economizing individuals only if the goods are themselves capable of satisfying the needs of the isolated economizing individuals or their families *directly*.[1] But when men become increasingly more aware of their economic interests, enter
into trading relationships with one another, and begin to exchange goods for goods, a situation finally develops in which

1. See Gustav Schmoller, "Die Lehre vom Einkommen in ihrem Zusammenhang mit den Grundprincipien der Steuerlehre," *Zeitschrift für die
   gesammte Staatswissenschaft*, XIX (1863), 53.

possession of economic goods gives the possessors the power to obtain goods of other kinds by means of exchange. When this occurs, it is no longer absolutely necessary, if economizing individuals are to be assured of the satisfaction of their needs, that they have command of the particular goods that are *directly* necessary for the satisfaction of their particular needs. In this more developed social situation, economizing individuals can of course ensure the satisfaction of their needs as before by obtaining possession of the particular goods that will, when employed directly, produce the result that we call satisfaction of their needs. But they can also, in the new situation, bring this result about indirectly by obtaining command of goods that can, according to the existing economic situation, be exchanged for such other goods as they require for the direct satisfaction of their needs. The special requirement for the value of goods obtaining under isolated household economy ceases, therefore, to apply.

Value, we saw, is the importance a good acquires for us when we are aware of being dependent on command of it for the satisfaction of one of our needs—that is, when we are conscious that a satisfaction would not take place if we did not have command of the good in question. Without the fulfillment of this condition, the existence of value is inconceivable. But value is not tied to the condition of a direct, to the exclusion of an indirect, assurance of our requirements. To have value, a good must assure the satisfaction of needs that would not be provided for if we did not have it at our command. But whether it does so in a direct or in an indirect manner is quite irrelevant when the existence of value in the general sense of the term is in question. The skin of a bear that he has killed has value to an isolated hunter only to the exent to which he would have to forgo the satisfaction of some need if he did not have the skin at his disposal. After he enters into trading relations, the skin has value to him for exactly the same reason. There is no difference between the two cases that in any way affects the essential nature of the phenomenon of value. For the only difference is that the hunter would be exposed to the injurious influences of the weather or would have to forgo the satisfaction of some other need for which the skin can be used in a *direct* fashion if

it were unavailable to him in the first case, while he would have
to forgo the satisfactions he could achieve by means of goods
that are at his disposal *indirectly* (by way of exchange) because
of his possession of the skin if it were unavailable to him in the
second case.

The value of the skin in the first case and its value in the second case are therefore only two different forms of the same
phenomenon of economic life. In both cases value is the importance that goods acquire for economizing individuals when
these individuals are aware of being dependent on command of
them for the satisfaction of their needs. What lends a special
character, in each of the two cases, to the phenomenon of value
is the fact that goods acquire the importance, to the economizing individuals commanding them, that we call value by being
employed *directly* in the first case and *indirectly* in the second.
This difference is nevertheless of sufficient importance both in
ordinary life and in our science in particular to require specific
terms for each of the two forms of the *one* general value phenomenon. Thus we call value in the first case *use value,* and in
the second case we call it *exchange value.*[2]

Use value, therefore, is the importance that goods acquire for
us because they *directly* assure us the satisfaction of needs that
would not be provided for if we did not have the goods at our
command. Exchange value is the importance that goods acquire
for us because their possession assures the same result *indirectly*.

B. THE RELATIONSHIP BETWEEN THE USE VALUE AND THE EXCHANGE VALUE OF GOODS

In an isolated household economy, economic goods either
have use value or they have no value at all to the economizing
individuals possessing them. But even in a society that has un-
dergone considerable cultural development and in which there
is an active commerce, economic goods can frequently be observed that have no exchange value to the economizing individ-

2. See Appendix G (p. 306) for the material originally appearing here as a
footnote.—TR.

uals possessing them, even though their use value to these same persons is beyond all doubt.

The crutches of a peculiarly deformed person, notes that can be used only by the writer who made them, family documents, and many similar goods, frequently have considerable use value to particular individuals. But these same individuals would, in most cases, attempt in vain to satisfy any of their needs with these goods in an indirect fashion—that is, through exchange. In a developed civilization, the opposite relationship occurs much more frequently. The spectacles and optical instruments kept in stock by an optical goods dealer usually have no use value to him, just as surgical instruments have none to the persons who produce and market them, and as books in foreign languages that can be understood only by a few scholars have none to booksellers. But all these goods, in view of the potential opportunities for exchange, ordinarily have a definite exchange value to these persons.

In these and in all other cases where economic goods have either use value or exchange value but not both to the persons possessing them, the question as to which of the two is determining in the economic activity of the individuals concerned cannot arise. But these cases are only exceptions in the economic life of men. When commerce has developed to any appreciable extent, economizing individuals ordinarily have a choice between employing the economic goods at their command directly or employing them indirectly for the satisfaction of their needs. Economic goods usually have use value, therefore, as well as exchange value to their possessors. Most of the clothes, the pieces of furniture, the jewelry, and the thousands of other goods in our possession undoubtedly have use value to us. But it is just as certain that we can also apply them indirectly for the satisfaction of our needs when commerce has developed, and that they therefore also simultaneously have exchange value to us.

It is true, as we have seen, that the importance of goods to us with respect to a direct employment and with respect to an indirect employment for the satisfaction of our needs are only different forms of a single general phenomenon of value. But their importance to us may simultaneously be very different in degree in the two forms. A gold cup will undoubtedly have a high exchange value to a poor man who has won it in a lottery. By means of the cup he will be in a position (in an indirect manner, through exchange) to satisfy many needs that would not otherwise be provided for. But the use value of the cup to him will scarcely be worth mentioning at all. A pair of glasses, on the other hand, adjusted exactly to the eyes of the owner, probably has a considerable use value to him, while its exchange value is usually very small.

It is' certain, then, that numerous cases can be observed in the economic life of men in which economic goods have use value and exchange value simultaneously to the economizing individuals possessing them, and that the two forms of value are often of different magnitudes. The question that arises is which of these two magnitudes is, in any given case, the one that determines the economic calculations and actions of men—or, in other words, which of the two forms of value is the *economic* form of value in the given instance.

The solution to this question arises from reflection upon the nature of human economy and upon the nature of value. The leading idea in all the economic activity of men is the fullest possible satisfaction of their needs. If more important satisfactions of an economizing individual are assured by the *direct* use of a good than by its indirect use, it follows that more important needs of the individual would remain unsatisfied if he were to employ the good in an indirect fashion for the satisfaction of his needs than if he were to employ it directly. There can be no doubt that in this case the use value of the good will be determining in the economic calculations and actions of the economizing individual concerned, and that in the reverse case it will be the exchange value. In the first case, it is the satisfactions that are assured by a direct employment of the good that the economizing individual would choose if he had command of it; in the second case, it is the satisfactions that are assured by an indirect employment of the good that he would choose if he had command of it; hence in each case it is the satisfactions that would otherwise have taken place that he would be compelled to forgo if he did not have command of the good in question. In all cases, therefore, in which a good has both use value and exchange value to its possessor, the economic value is the one that is the greater. But from what was said in Chapter IV, it is evident, in every instance in which the foundations for an economic exchange are present, that it is the exchange value of the good, and when this is not the case that it is the use value, that is the *economic* value.

C. CHANGES IN THE ECONOMIC CENTER OF GRAVITY OF THE VALUE OF GOODS [3]

One of the most important tasks of economizing men is that of recognizing the economic value of goods—that is, of being clear at all times whether their use value or their exchange value is the economic value. The determination of which goods or what portions of them are to be retained and which it is in one's best economic interest to offer for sale depends on this knowledge. But judging this relationship correctly is one of the most difficult tasks of practical economy, not only because a survey of all available use and exchange opportunities is required even in well developed markets, but also and above all because the factors on which a correct solution of this problem must be based are subject to a multitude of changes. It is clear that anything that diminishes the use value of a thing to us may, other things being equal, cause the exchange value of the good to become the economic form of value, and that anything that increases the use value of a good to us can have the effect of pushing the significance of its exchange value into the background. An increase or decrease in the exchange value of a good will, other things being equal, have the opposite effect.

The chief causes of changes in the economic form of value are as follows: (1) Changes in the importance of the particular satisfaction that a good renders to the economizing individual who has it at his command, if its use value to him is increased or decreased by the change. Thus if a person loses his taste for tobacco or wine, the stock of tobacco or wine in his possession

3. "Center of gravity" is the literal translation for *"Schwerpunkt."* Menger's title is *"Ueber den Wechsel im ökonomischen Schwerpunkte des Güterwerthes."* A less awkward translation is not possible without loss of the flavor of the original.—TR.

will take on a predominating exchange value for him. And men who have been hunting or sporting enthusiasts will sell their hunting utensils, hunting animals, etc., when their pastimes have lost their previous importance to them, the diminution in the use value of these goods having caused their exchange value to come to the fore in importance.

Transitions from one stage of life to another especially are characterized by changes of this kind. Satisfaction of the same want has a different meaning to an adolescent than it has to a mature man, and a different meaning again to a mature man than it has to an old man. Even if no other factors existed, therefore, the natural course of human development would alone cause the use value of goods to undergo significant changes. The simple toys of the child lose their use value to the adolescent; the study materials used by the adolescent lose their use value to the mature man; and the instruments by which the mature man earns a living lose their use value to the old man. In each instance, the exchange value of the goods mentioned becomes predominant. Nothing is more common, therefore, than for an adolescent to sell the goods that had a predominating use value to him as a child. We see people entering maturity generally selling not only many of the means of enjoyment appropriate to adolescence but the study materials of their youth as well. Old men can be observed permitting not only many of the means of enjoyment of their prime that require strength and courage to use, but also the instruments they employed in earning a living (factories, business firms, etc.), to pass into other hands. If the economic phenomena that would appear to be the natural consequence of these facts do not appear as distinctly on the surface as we might expect, the reason is to be found in the family life of men. For the passage of goods from the older members of a family into the possession of younger members takes place, not as a result of monetary compensation, but as a result of affection. The family, with its special economic relations, is thus an essential factor in the stability of human economic relations.

Increases in the use value of a good to its possessor naturally have the opposite effect. The owner of a forest, for example, to whom the yearly cut of timber has only exchange value, will probably immediately discontinue exchanging his timber for other goods if he constructs a blast furnace to melt iron and needs the full output of his timberland for its operation. An author who previously sold his work to publishers will not do so in the future if he founds his own magazine, and so on.

(2) Mere changes in the properties of a good can shift the center of gravity of its economic importance if its use value to the possessor is altered by the change while its exchange value either remains unchanged or does not rise or fall to the same extent as its use value.

Clothes, horses, dogs, coaches, and similar objects, usually lose their use value to wealthy people almost entirely if they have an externally visible defect. Their exchange value, although also decreased, comes to the fore in importance since the loss in their use value is usually greater to these persons than the loss in their exchange value.

On the other hand, goods become altered in many instances in such a way that their exchange value, which previously was the economic form of value to the economizing individuals possessing them, recedes as compared with their use value. Thus innkeepers and grocers usually employ foods having some external defect for their own consumption, since the defect in these goods causes them to lose their exchange value almost completely while their use value often remains the same, or is at any rate not diminished to the same extent as their exchange value. The same phenomenon can be observed in other trades. Shoemakers, especially in smaller villages, often wear badly fitting shoes, tailors often wear imperfectly cut clothes, and hatters often wear hats in whose production some slight accident has occurred.

(3) We come now to the third, and most important, cause of changes in the economic center of gravity of the value of goods. I refer to increases in the quantities of goods at the disposal of economizing individuals. An increase in the quantity of a good a person has almost always, other things remaining the same, causes the use value of each unit of the good to him to diminish and its exchange value to become the more important. After the harvest, the exchange value of grain is almost without exception the economic form of value to farmers, and it remains so

until, as a result of successive sales of portions of the grain, its use value again becomes the more important. The grain that farmers still possess in summer generally has a predominating use value to them. At another place in this work (Chapter IV, section 2) I have shown at what limit the importance of the exchange value of goods passes into the background as compared with their use value. To an heir, who is already equipped with sufficient furniture before his succession, and who finds still another large set of furniture in the legacy of his testator, many pieces of the furniture will have a very low use value (and some perhaps no use value at all) and will therefore acquire a predominating exchange value. The heir will continue to sell pieces of furniture until the pieces remaining in his possession again have a predominating use value.

A decrease in the quantity of a good available to an economizing individual will, on the other hand, generally cause its use value to him to increase, and thus cause the quantities of the good previously destined for exchange now to acquire a predominating use value.

Of special importance in this connection is the effect of changes in total wealth. When commercial relations are well developed, an increase or decrease in wealth is equivalent, to the economizing individual experiencing the change, to an increase or decrease of almost every particular kind of economic good. A man who becomes poor is forced to retrench in the satisfaction of almost all his needs. He will satisfy some needs less completely, quantitatively or qualitatively. Other needs he will perhaps not satisfy at all. If, after his impoverishment, there are any of the choicer consumption goods or articles of luxury in his possession, which previously contributed to the harmonic satisfaction of his needs, but which do not correspond to his changed circumstances, he will, if he is an economizing individual, sell them in order to use the proceeds to satisfy more important needs of himself and his family that would otherwise remain unsatisfied. People who have lost a large part of their wealth by unlucky speculations or as the result of other misfortunes actually sell their jewelry, works of art, and other objects of luxury, in order to provide themselves with the necessities of life. Increasing wealth has a similar but opposite effect, since many goods that previously had a predominating use value to their owners lose this use value, and the economic importance of their exchange value is pushed to the fore. Thus people who have suddenly become rich usually sell their simple furniture, their shabby trinkets, their inadequate houses, and many other goods that had previously had a predominating use value to them.

CHAPTER VII | THE THEORY OF THE COMMODITY

1. THE CONCEPT OF THE COMMODITY IN ITS POPULAR AND SCIENTIFIC MEANINGS

IN AN ISOLATED household economy the productive activity of each economizing unit is directed solely to the production of goods necessary for its own consumption. The very nature of such an economy precludes the production of goods for the purpose of exchange. But the various tasks that must be performed to meet the requirements of the household could be assigned by the head of the family to the various members of the family and to any servants he has, with due regard to their special faculties and skills. Hence the characteristic feature of the isolated household economy is not the absence of any division of labor but its self-sufficiency, production being concerned exclusively with goods destined for the consumption of the household itself, and not at all with goods destined to be exchanged for other goods.

It is, of course, quite evident that the division of labor remains very narrowly limited in the confines of an isolated household economy. The requirements of a family for any single good are usually much too small to permit an individual to occupy himself fully with its production, much less with a single manual operation. The available food supplies, moreover, are in most cases much too small to feed any considerable number of laborers. Societies in the lower stages of development, therefore, furnish us with examples of a complex division of labor only in the household economies of a few nobles, while the other economizing individuals continue to have little division of labor and narrowly limited wants.

A people can be considered to have taken its first step in economic development when persons who have acquired a certain skill offer their services to society and work up the raw materials of other persons for compensation. The Thetes of Ancient Greece appear to have been artisans of this kind, and even today, in many regions of eastern Europe, there are still no other artisans. Yarn spun in the home of the consumer is worked into cloth by the weaver; grain grown by the consumer is milled into flour by the miller; and even the carpenter and the smith are supplied with the raw materials for products ordered from them by their larger customers.

A further step in the path of economic development to higher levels of well-being can be regarded as having been taken when the artisans themselves begin to procure the raw materials for their products, even though they still produce these products for the consumers only *on order*. This state of affairs can still, with few exceptions, be observed in small towns, and to some extent even in larger places in some trades. The artisan does not yet manufacture products for later, and hence uncertain, sale. But he is already, to the extent of his labor power, in a position to meet the needs of his customers by making it unnecessary for them to expend efforts on purchasing or producing raw materials in a frequently highly uneconomic manner.[1]

1. Wilhelm Roscher, *Ansichten der Volkswirthschaft aus dem geschichtlichen Standpunkte*, Leipzig, 1861, p. 117; Bruno Hildebrand, "Naturalwirthschaft, Geldwirthschaft und Creditwirthschaft," *Jahrbücher für National-Oekonomie und Statistik*, II (1864), 17; H. v. Scheel,

This method of providing society with goods already signi-
fies a considerable forward step in economy and comfort for
consumers as well as producers. But for both groups it is a step
that involves several serious disadvantages. The consumer must
still wait some time for his product, and is never quite certain
of its properties in advance. The producer is sometimes wholly
unengaged and at other times overburdened with orders, with
the result that he is sometimes forced to be idle while at other
times he cannot meet the demand. These drawbacks have led
to the production of goods for uncertain future sale, the producer keeping them in stock in order to be able to meet requirements at once as they arise. It is this method of supplying
society that leads, with continuing economic development, to
factories (mass production) on the one side and to the purchase
of ready-made (standardized) commodities by consumers on the
other side. Hence it offers the highest degree of economy to
the producer because of the possibility of full exploitation of the
division of labor and the employment of machines, and the
highest degree of safety (inspection before purchase) and comfort to the consumer.

Products that the producers or middlemen hold in readiness
for sale are called *commodities*. In ordinary usage the term is
limited in its application to movable tangible goods (with the
exception of money).[2] Since the fact that a person keeps a portion of his wealth ready for exchange is not always obvious to
other persons, it is understandable that the commodity concept
was narrowed down still more in ordinary life. In popular language, the term "commodities" came quite generally to refer
only to goods that are so plainly destined for sale by their owner
that his intention is obvious even to other persons. An owner
can express his intention in very different ways. Most commonly he expresses it by displaying his commodities at places
where purchasers are accustomed to assemble—such as markets,

"Der Begriff des Geldes in seiner historisch-ökonomischen Entwickelung," *ibid.*, VI (1866), 15; Gustav Schmoller, *Zur Geschichte der
deutschen Kleingewerbe im 19. Jahrhundert*, Halle, 1870, pp. 165,
180, 511 ff.

2. The remainder of this paragraph and the next paragraph appear here
as a single footnote in the original.—TR.

fairs, organized exchanges, or other special places that either are well known as sites at which commodities are concentrated or give evidence of being points of concentration by their external appearance or by prominently visible characteristic markings (e.g. shops, stores, warehouses, etc.). In popular usage, therefore, the commodity concept is narrowed down to a designation for those economic goods that are in such external circumstances that the intention of their owner to sell them can be easily discerned by anyone.

The higher the level of civilization attained by a people and the more specialized the production of each economizing individual becomes, the wider become the foundations for economic exchanges and the larger become the absolute and relative amounts of those goods that at any time have commodity character, until finally the economic gains that can be derived from the exploitation of the above relationship become sufficiently large to call forth a special class of economizing individuals who take care of the intellectual and mechanical parts of exchange operations for society and who are reimbursed for this with a part of the gains from trade. When this has occurred, economic goods no longer, for the most part, pass directly from producers to consumers but often follow very complex paths through the hands of more or less numerous middlemen. By occupation these persons are accustomed to treat certain economic goods as commodities and to keep special places open to the public for the purpose of selling them. Popular usage has now limited the term "commodity" to goods that are in the hands of these traders and in the hands of producers who produce them with the obvious intention of selling them. This usage doubtless arose because the intention of the owners of selling these goods (merchandise, *marchandises, Kaufmannsgüter, mercanzie,* etc.) is especially easy for anyone to discern.

But in scientific discourse a need was felt for a term designating all economic goods held ready for sale without regard to their tangibility, mobility, or character as products of labor, and without regard to the persons offering them for sale. A large number of economists, especially German economists, therefore defined commodities as *(economic) goods of any kind that are intended for sale.*

The commodity concept in the popular sense is nevertheless of importance not only because law-givers[3] and a large number of economists employ the term in the popular sense, but also because some of those who are aware of the wider, scientific, sense of the term sometimes employ this or that element of the narrower, popular, meaning in their definitions.[4]

From the definition just given of a commodity in the scientific sense of the term, it appears that commodity-character is nothing inherent in a good, no property of it, but merely a specific relationship of a good to the person who has command of it. With the disappearance of this relationship the commodity-character of the good comes to an end. A good ceases to be a commodity, therefore, if the economizing individual possessing it gives up his intention of disposing of it, or if it comes into the hands of persons who do not intend to exchange it further but to consume it. The hat that a hatter, and the silk cloth that a silk merchant, exhibit for sale in their shops are examples of commodities, but they immediately cease to be commodities if the hatter decides to use the hat himself and the silk merchant decides to give the silk cloth as a present to his wife. Packages of sugar and oranges are commodities in the hands of a grocer, but they lose their commodity-character as soon as they have passed into the hands of consumers. Coined metal also immediately ceases to be a "commodity" if its possessor intends to use it, not for exchange, but for some consumption purpose—if he hands his Thalers to a silversmith for the purpose of making silver plate, for instance.

Commodity-character is therefore not only no property of goods but usually only a *transitory* relationship between goods and economizing individuals. Certain goods are intended by their owners to be exchanged for the goods of other economizing individuals. During their passage, sometimes through several hands, from the possession of the first into the possession of the last owner, we call them *"commodities,"* but as soon as they have reached their economic destination (that is, as soon as

3. See the first paragraph of Appendix H (p. 308) for the material originally appearing here as a footnote.—TR.
4. See the last seven paragraphs of Appendix H (p. 309) for the material originally appended here as a footnote.—TR.

they are in the hands of the ultimate consumer) they obviously cease to be commodities and become *"consumption goods"* in the narrow sense in which this term is opposed to the concept of *"commodity."* But where this does not happen, as is the case very frequently, for example, with gold, silver, etc., especially in the form of coins, they naturally continue to be "commodties" as long as they continue in the relationship responsible for their commodity-character.[5]

Two things are evident from this: (1) the frequently-stated proposition that money is a "commodity" contributes nothing at all toward explaining *the unique position of money among commodities;* (2) the view of those who deny the commodity character of money because "money as such, especially in the form of coin, does not serve any consumption purpose" is untenable simply because the same argument can be advanced against the commodity-character of all other goods—even if we were to ignore the fact that there is a misconception of the important function of money in the assumption that it is not consumed. For no "commodities" *as such* serve a consumption purpose, and least of all in the forms in which they are traded (i.e., in the form of ingots and bales, and in cases, packages, etc.). To be consumed a good must cease to be a "commodity" and relinquish the form in which it has been traded (i.e., it must be melted down, divided, unpacked, etc.). The coin and the ingot are the most common forms in which the precious metals are traded, and the fact that these forms must be abandoned before the precious metals can be brought into consumption is therefore nothing that justifies doubting their commodity-character.

2. THE MARKETABILITY[6] OF COMMODITIES

A. *The outer limits of the marketability of commodities*

The problem of explaining the causes of the different and changing proportions in which quantities of goods are exchanged for each other has always been given special attention

5. The next paragraph appears here as a footnote in the original.—TR.
6. *"Absatzfähigkeit"*—TR.

by scholars in the field of economics. There have been as many attempts to solve this problem as there have been independent economic treatises. In fact some writers have actually turned their treatises into theories of prices. But the fact that different goods cannot be exchanged for each other with equal facility was given only scant attention until now. Yet the obvious differences in the marketability of commodities is a phenomenon of such far-reaching practical importance, the success of the economic activity of producers and merchants depending to a very great extent on a correct understanding of the influences here operative, that science cannot, in the long run, avoid an exact investigation of its nature and causes. Indeed, it is also clear that a complete and satisfactory solution to the still controversial problem of the origin of money, the most liquid of all goods, can emerge only from an investigation of this topic.

As far as I have been able to observe, the marketability of commodities is limited in four directions:

(1) *Their marketability is limited with respect to the persons to whom they can be sold.* The owner of a commodity does not have the power to sell it to any person of his choice. On the contrary, there is always only a definite number [7] of economizing individuals to whom it can be sold. He has no chance of selling his commodity to persons (a) who have no requirements for it, (b) who are prevented, by legal or physical circumstances, from purchasing it,[8] or (c) who have no knowledge of the exchange opportunity offered them,[9] or finally (d) to anyone to whom a given quantity of the commodity in question is not the

7. "*Kreis*"—TR.
8. Here must be mentioned, above all, the rectrictions placed on the marketability of commodities by sumptuary laws and police regulations. In the middle ages, for example, the sale of velvet was limited to members of the nobility and the clergy, and still today the sale of arms is limited in many countries to persons who have obtained an official permit to bear them.
9. Commodities that are little known ("articles that have not yet been introduced") have very small clienteles simply because they are not known. Producers are therefore accustomed to make their commodities "known," often at great economic sacrifice, in order to increase the numbers of persons to whom they are saleable. This accounts for the economic importance of public announcements, advertisements, publicity, etc.

equivalent of a larger quantity of the good that is tendered in exchange for it than is the case with the initial owner of the commodity.[10]

If we observe the numbers of persons to whom the marketability of different commodities is restricted, we are confronted with a picture of vast differences. Compare only the number of persons to whom bread and meat can be sold with the number to whom astronomical instruments can be sold. Or compare the number of persons who purchase wine and tobacco with the number who purchase works in Sanskrit. Similar differences can be observed, in perhaps a still more striking manner, in the marketability of goods of different subcategories but of the same general type or kind. Dealers in optical goods have glasses for all degrees of long- and short-sightedness ready for sale. Hat and glove merchants, shoemakers, and furriers, have hats, gloves, shoes, and furs of different sizes and qualities. But how great is the difference between the number of persons to whom the marketability of the most powerful glasses is limited and the number to whom glasses of medium strength can be sold! How great is the difference between the number of persons to whom the marketability of gloves or hats of medium sizes extends and the number of persons purchasing gloves and hats of very large sizes!

(2) *The marketability of commodities is limited with respect to the area within which they can be sold.* For a commodity to be sold in any one place, it is necessary, in addition to the previous requirement that there must be a number of persons to whom it can be sold, that (a) there be no physical or legal barrier to its transportation to that place or to its being offered there for sale, and that (b) the costs and expenses of transportation shall not exhaust the gain that can be derived from the expected exchange opportunity (p. 189).

The differences between different commodities are not less

10. The marketability of commodities is generally considerably increased by the growing needs and increasing wealth of a people. The marketability of a few commodities, however, is diminished by these factors. There are a number of commodities that can easily be sold in a poor country, but become practically unsaleable as soon as the country attains economic maturity (see pp. 234-5).

great with respect to the geographical *extent of the areas* in which they can be sold than the differences we have just observed with respect to the numbers of persons to whom they can be sold. There are commodities which, as a result of spatially limited requirements for them, can be sold only in a single town or village, others that can be sold only in a few provinces, some only in a certain country, others in all civilized countries, and still others that can be sold in all the inhabited parts of the world. The peculiar hats worn by the rural population in some of the valleys of the Tyrol can be sold only in a particular valley; the hats of Swabian or Hungarian peasants cannot easily be sold elsewhere than in Swabia or Hungary; but the markets of the entire civilized world stand open to hats of the newest French fashion. For the same reason, the marketability of heavy furs is restricted to northern regions, and the marketability of heavy woollens to regions in the northern and temperate zones, while light cotton goods can be sold almost anywhere in the entire world.

A no less important difference in the size of the sales area is founded on the economic sacrifices involved in transporting commodities to distant markets. Where there are no railroads, the sales area of common building stone taken from a quarry not situated on a waterway, and the sales areas of ordinary sand, clay, and manure, do not often extend farther than two or three miles. Even where railroads do exist, it is only in the rarest instances that the sales areas of these commodities exceed 15 or 20 miles. The sales areas of coal, peat, and firewood are, under the same conditions, more extended but still narrowly restricted. The sales areas of pig iron and wheat are considerably wider; those of steel and wheat flour are still wider; and the sales area of precious metals, precious stones, and pearls, comprises practically all parts of the globe where requirements for these goods exist and where the means of payment for them are at hand.

The economic sacrifices involved in transportation must be recovered from the difference between the price at the point of origin and the price at the destination. For commodities of low value this difference can evidently never be significant. Firewood can be purchased at infinitesimally low prices in the virgin forests of Brazil and even in some regions of eastern Europe. In many cases it can be obtained entirely free of charge. But the price of a hundredweight of firewood is nowhere high enough that the difference between it and the price at the place of origin, even if the latter were equal to zero, would suffice to cover the costs of a long overland haul. In the case of commodities of high value (watches, for example), on the other hand, the difference between the price of a hundredweight of the commodity at the place of production and at the most distant markets (at Geneva, and at New York or Rio de Janeiro, for instance) may easily, in spite of the already considerable price in the market of origin, be sufficiently high to compensate for the expense of transporting the commodity to the distant regions of sale. Hence the more *valuable* a commodity the greater, other things being equal, is its sales area.

(3) *Commodities are limited quantitatively in their marketability.* The marketability of a commodity is restricted quantitatively to the requirements for it that have still to be met—even further, it is restricted to those quantities with respect to which the foundations for economic exchange operations are present. However large the requirements of a single individual for a commodity, purchases of quantities exceeding this amount cannot be expected during a given time period. Even within the limits of his requirements, an individual will be prepared to take in exchange only those quantities of the commodity with respect to which the foundations for economic exchange operations are present for him. The demand for a commodity in general is composed of the demands of the various economizing individuals desiring it. The total quantity of a commodity that can be sold to the members of a society is, therefore, in any given economic situation, strictly limited, and sales beyond this limit are inconceivable.

The quantitative limits of marketability are remarkably different for different goods. There are commodities that can never be sold, at given points in time, except in narrowly limited quantities because of narrowly limited requirements for them. There are others for which requirements are larger, and for which, in consequence, the quantitative limits of market-

ability extend considerably further. And there are still others
that can be sold in almost any practically conceivable amounts.

The publisher of a work on the language of the Tupi Indians
could count on a sale of perhaps 300 copies at a moderate price
for the work. But even at the lowest price, he could not count
on a sale of more than 600 copies. A scholarly work in which
only a narrow group of specialists is interested, and which is intended for the needs of several generations of scholars, often
attains its sales only with the increasing fame of its author, and
can be sold only over a long period of time. But a work about
a science that is attracting general interest may, in spite of its
scholarly character, attain sales of several thousand copies. Popular scientific publications may attain sales of 20,000 to 30,000
copies or more. Important works of fiction may, under favorable circumstances, sell in editions of several hundred thousand
copies. Consider the differences in the quantitative limits of the
marketability of a work on Peruvian archeology and the poems
of Friedrich Schiller, or of a work on Sanskrit and the plays
of Shakespeare! But the differences in the quantitative limits
of the marketability of commodities are still greater if we consider bread and meat on the one hand, and quinine or cas-
toreum on the other, or cotton and woollen goods on the one
hand, and astronomical instruments and anatomical specimens
on the other. Finally, compare the quantitative limits of the
marketability of hats and gloves of medium and of extra large
sizes.

(4) *Finally, commodities are also limited in their marketability with respect to the time periods in which they can be sold.*
There are goods for which requirements exist only in winter;
others for which they exist only in summer; and still others
for which a demand exists only during some other more or less
fleeting period. Programs for coming festivals or fine art exhibits, and even, in a certain sense, newspapers and articles of
fashion, are goods of this sort. In fact, all perishable goods are,
by their very nature, restricted in their marketability to a narrow time period.

To this must be added the fact that keeping commodities "in
stock" usually involves not inconsiderable economic sacrifices
on the part of the owner. The effect of storage fees, costs of safe-

keeping, and loss of interest, on the limits of the marketability
of commodities in time is similar to the effect of freight charges
and other transportation costs on the spatial limits of their marketability. A cattle trader in our civilization who has a herd of
cattle ready for slaughter and sale must necessarily exercise care
to sell them within certain time limits because they will otherwise not be in prime condition, because of loss of interest, and
in general because of the other economic sacrifices unavoidably
associated with the possession of these animals as "commodities." A wool merchant or an iron merchant also has commodities whose marketability is restricted to certain time periods
partly for physical and partly for economic reasons (storage costs,
loss of interest).

Very great differences can be observed in the time periods
during which different commodities must be sold. The time
limits within which, for example, oysters, fresh meat, many
prepared foods and beverages, cut flowers, programs for coming
festivals, political tracts, and so forth, must be sold are, on the
whole, restricted to a few days and often to but a few hours.
The period within which most fresh fruit, game, potted plants,
many articles of fashion, etc., must be sold is limited to a few
weeks, and a few months in the case of other similar commodities, while the period within which still other commodities
can be sold, provided they can be preserved long enough and
requirements for them continue, extends to years, decades, and
even centuries.

The economic sacrifices involved in the preservation and storage of commodities vary considerably. From this fact arises a
further, very important, factor responsible for differences in the
time limits of the marketability of commodities. A person with
building stones or firewood for sale has commodities that can
be stored in an open field. He will not ordinarily be forced to
make his sales as quickly, therefore, as a furniture dealer, and
the latter is again under less compulsion to sell quickly than a
horse trader. The owner of gold, silver, precious stones, or other
commodities that can be stored almost without cost (if we omit
consideration of the loss of interest), has goods whose marketability extends much further in time than that of all the above-
mentioned commodities.

B. *The different degrees of marketability of commodities.*

In the previous section, we saw that the marketability of commodities is restricted sometimes to greater and sometimes to
smaller numbers of persons, and within sometimes narrower
and sometimes wider spatial, temporal, and quantitative limits.
In all this, however, I have described only the outside limits
within which, in any given economic situation, commodities
can be sold. The causes determining the greater or less facility
with which commodities can be sold within these limits of marketability remain still to be examined.

It is necessary, for this purpose, to begin with a few words
about the nature of commodities and the intentions of their
possessors. A commodity is an economic good *intended* for sale.
But it is not intended for sale *unconditionally.* The owner of a
commodity intends to sell it, but by no means at any price. A
jeweller with a stock of watches could sell off his entire stock,
in almost any situation imaginable, if he were willing to sell
his watches at one Thaler each. A leather merchant could clear
out his stock too if he were prepared to sell his leather at similar ruinous prices. Both merchants may nevertheless be justified if they complain of sluggish sales, since although their commodities are intended for sale, as has been stated, they are intended for sale, not at any price, but at prices that correspond
to the *general* economic situation.

The prices that become effective are always the product of
existing competitive conditions (p. 218), and corre∶   ⌐nd more
closely to the *general* economic situation the more complete
the competition on both sides. If there are any circumstances
that restrain a number of those who have requirements for a
commodity from competing for it, its price will fall below the
level corresponding to the general economic situation. If there
are any restraints upon competition on the supply side, the
price of the commodity will rise above this level.

If the competition for one commodity is poorly organized
and there is danger therefore that the owners will be unable to
sell their holdings of the commodity at economic prices, at a
time when this danger does not exist at all, or not in the same

degree, for the owners of other commodities, it is clear that this circumstance will be responsible for a very important difference between the marketability of that commodity and all others. The other commodities can be brought to their final destinations easily and safely, but the commodity whose market is poorly organized can be brought to its final destination only with economic sacrifices, and in some cases not at all.

Market places, fairs, exchanges, public auctions that are held periodically (as is the case in large sea-ports, for example), and other public institutions of a similar nature, are for the purpose of bringing all persons interested in the pricing of a commodity together at a particular place either permanently or periodically to ensure the establishment of an economic price. Commodities for which an organized market exists can be sold without difficulty by their owners at prices corresponding to the general economic situation. But commodities for which there are poorly organized markets change hands at inconsistent prices, and sometimes cannot be disposed of at all. The institution of an organized market for an article makes it possible for the producers, or other economizing individuals trading in it, to sell their commodities at any time at economic prices. Thus the opening of a wool or grain market in a city increases considerably the marketability of wool or grain in neighboring regions where these articles are produced. Similarly, the admission of a security to trade on a stock exchange (so-called "listing") contributes to the establishment of economic prices in the selling of that security and also, in an outstanding fashion, to increasing its marketability since the listing of the security assures the owners of sales at economic prices.

If every consumer knows where to find the owners of a commodity, this fact alone increases to a high degree the probability that the commodity will, at any time, be sold at an economic price. This is best achieved in wholesale trade because of the practice, quite commonly observed, of the dealers in a commodity locating their warehouses as near to each other as possible in order to evoke, by their concentration, a similar concentration of customers. The absence of such concentration in retail trade constitutes the major cause of less economic prices being established in this branch of commerce, even though the deficiency arises naturally from the desire of consumers for convenience and economy of time in making their purchases.

But the selling of a commodity at economic prices is not the only result of the existence of points of concentration of trading and price formation. The prices established in these centers of trade are continuously made public, thus making it possible for interested persons whose establishments are outside the trading centers also to do business at any time at prices corresponding to the economic situation. Large sellers or buyers of a commodity will very seldom, of course, adopt this method of doing business since their transactions have a determining influence on price formation. But small businessmen whose scales of operation are too insignificant to have any appreciable effect on prices are placed by these public announcements in a position to execute their transactions in an economic fashion even outside the trade center, and thus to participate in the advantages of a market they do not even visit. In the countryside surrounding London it may happen that a tenant farmer will do business with a miller on the basis of a quotation in *The Times* for the price of grain on Mark Lane. In Vienna small sales of kerosene are often concluded on the basis of the price quotation in the *Neue Freie Presse* or some other reliable newspaper. Thus points of concentration of trade in a commodity have the quite general result of placing the owners in a position to sell their holdings at economic prices to any economizing individual wishing to obtain them.

The first cause of differences in the marketability of commodities we have thus seen to be the fact that the number of persons to whom they can be sold is sometimes larger and sometimes smaller, and that the points of concentration of the persons interested in their pricing are sometimes better and sometimes less well organized.

Secondly, there are commodities that can be sold almost anywhere within the spatial limits of their marketability. Domestic animals, grains, metals, and similar goods in common use, have markets almost everywhere that trade exists. Every small town and even the smallest village becomes a market for these goods at certain times. There are other commodities (furs, tea, indigo) for which only a few widely separated markets exist.

These markets are not independent of each other in the formation of prices. If a market is of decisive importance, reports of transactions made there are transmitted to all other major markets. A special class of economizing individuals, speculators, takes care that the differences in price between the various markets do not significantly exceed the costs of transportation.

The second cause of differences in the marketability of commodities is thus the fact that the geographical areas within which their sale is confined are sometimes wider and sometimes narrower, and that while there are many trading points within this area at which some commodities can be sold at economic prices, there are only a few such points in the case of other commodities. Owners of commodities of the first category can sell them at will in many places over a wide trading area at economic prices, while owners of commodities of the second category can sell them only in a few places over a narrow trading area.

Thirdly, there are commodities for which a lively and well organized speculation exists that absorbs every portion of the available quantity of the commodities coming to market at any time, even though in excess of current requirements. There are other commodity markets in which speculation is not carried on, or at least not to the same extent, and in which, if they become oversupplied with commodities, either prices fall rapidly, or the commodities brought to market must be taken away unsold. Goods of the first kind can generally be sold in any quantity actually available at a given time with little sacrifice in price, while the owner of a commodity for which no speculation exists can sell quantities exceeding current requirements only with very severe losses or not at all.

I gave an example of this last class of commodities earlier when I cited the marketability of books written for specific groups of scholars. More important in this regard are commodities that have no independent use and are wanted only as parts of other commodities. Whatever the price of watch springs or the price of pressure gauges for steam engines may be, requirements for them are determined almost exactly by the number of watches or steam engines to be produced, and a considerably larger quantity of the former goods could not be sold at any price. On the other hand, gold and silver, and several other commodities whose narrowly limited available quantities stand opposite almost unlimited requirements, can be sold in any quantity whatsoever. There is no doubt that a quantity of gold a thousand times as large as that presently available, and a quantity of silver a hundred times as large, would still find buyers if brought to market. Such increases in the available quantities of these metals would cause them to fall severely in price, and they would then doubtless be used by persons of little wealth for utensils and ordinary plate, and even by poorer people for adornment. But even if they were brought to market in such enormously increased quantities, it would not be in vain. They could still be sold. A similar increase, however, of the best scholarly work, of the most excellent optical instruments, or even of such important commodities as bread and meat, would make them literally unsaleable. From these considerations, it follows that a possessor of gold and silver can very readily sell any portion of the quantity of these goods available at any time, in the worst case with a small loss in price. But the sudden accumulation of most commodities usually leads to a much greater fall in price, and there is always the possibility that they cannot be sold at all under such conditions.

The third cause of differences in the marketability of commodities, then, is the fact that the quantitative limits of the amounts of them that can be sold are sometimes wider and sometimes narrower, and that within these limits the quantities of some commodities brought to market can easily be sold at economic prices, while this is not true of other commodities, or at least not in the same degree.

Finally, there are commodities for which almost continuous markets exist. Securities and a number of raw materials, in places where there are commodity exchanges, can be marketed every day. There are other commodities that are traded on two or three days of the week. There are usually weekly markets for grains and other legumes, quarterly fairs for the products of industry, and two or more so-called annual fairs a year for horses and other domestic animals, etc.

The fourth cause of differences in the marketability of commodities is thus the fact that the time limits within which commodities can be sold are sometimes wider and sometimes narrower, and that within these limits some commodities can be sold at economic prices at any time, while others can be sold only at more or less distant points in time.

If we now turn briefly to the actual phenomena of economic life and observe the extraordinary differences in the marketability of the various commodities, it will not be difficult for us to reduce these differences to one or more of the causes explained above.

A person who owns a quantity of grain has in his possession a commodity he can dispose of at almost any moment he desires wherever there are grain exchanges. Where there are only weekly markets he can still sell it every week at prices that are in accord with the economic situation. He thus has a commodity which, to use a very significant mercantile term, is almost "liquid cash." The causes of this lie in the large number of persons who have requirements for grain, in the wide spatial, temporal, and quantitative limits of its marketability, in the usually efficient organization of grain markets, and in the lively speculation in this commodity.

A person who has a stock of furs will find himself in many ways in a somewhat more unfavorable situation. The quantitative limits of the marketability of this article are much narrower and the markets less well organized than those for grain. In addition, fur markets are frequently very distant from each other in space and time, and speculation in this article is much less lively than in grain. A person with wheat will be able to unload his holdings under almost any circumstances if he is willing to sell at a fraction of a penny below the current market quotation. This will not always be true of furs, and it may happen much more easily that the owner can sell his holdings only at relatively large losses or perhaps sometimes not at all, and that he may therefore be compelled to wait a considerable time before selling. We would obtain even greater contrasts if we were to compare the marketability of grain with the marketability of such articles as telescopes, meerschaum ornaments, and potted plants in general—or with the less marketable varieties of these commodities!

C. *The facility with which commodities circulate.*

In the preceding sections, I have explained the general and specific causes of differences in the marketability of commodities. In other words, I have shown the causes of the greater or less facility with which an owner of commodities can expect to sell them at economic prices. At this point one might be inclined to consider the problem of the greater or less facility with which commodities can circulate through several hands as also solved, since the circulation of a commodity through several hands simply consists of a number of single transactions, and to think that a commodity that can be passed without difficulty from the hands of its owner to some other economizing individual should find its way just as easily from the hands of the second owner into those of a third, and so on. But experience shows that this is not true of all commodities. In what follows, it will be our task to investigate the special causes responsible for the fact that some commodities can be observed to circulate easily from hand to hand while others, even some that have a high degree of marketability, do not.

Some commodities have almost the same marketability in the hands of every economizing individual. Gold nuggets extracted from the sands of the Aranyos River by a dirty Transylvanian gypsy are just as saleable in his hands as in the hands of the owner of a gold mine, provided the gypsy knows where to find the right market for his commodity. Gold nuggets can pass through any number of hands without any decrease whatsoever in marketability. But articles of clothing, bedding, prepared foods, etc., would be suspect and almost unsaleable, or at any rate of greatly depreciated value, in the hands of the gypsy, even if they had not been used by him, and even if he had, from the beginning, acquired them only with the intention of passing them on in exchange. However saleable commodities of this kind may be in the hands of their producers or certain merchants, they lose their marketability altogether, or at any rate in part, if even a suspicion arises that they have already been used or only been in unclean hands. They are therefore not suited in economic exchange to circulation from hand to hand.

Other commodities require special knowledge, skills, permits, or governmental licenses, privileges, etc., for their sale, and are not at all, or only with difficulty, saleable in the hands of an individual who cannot acquire these requisites. In any case they lose value in his hands. Commodities destined for trade with India or South America, pharmaceutical preparations, patented articles, etc., may be extremely saleable in the hands of certain persons, but lose a large part of their marketability in the hands of other persons. Hence they are as little suited as the commodities of the previous paragraph to free circulation from hand to hand.

Moreover, commodities that must be specially fitted to the needs of the consumer to be useable at all are not saleable in an equal degree in the hands of every owner. Shoes, hats, and similar articles, of all sizes, are always fairly saleable in the hands of a shoe merchant or a hatter in whose shops or stores large numbers of customers assemble, especially since these businessmen generally have facilities for fitting the commodities to the special needs of their customers. In the hands of another person, these commodities can be sold only with difficulty and almost always only at a heavy loss. These commodities too are not suited to free circulation from hand to hand.

Commodities whose prices are not well known or subject to considerable fluctuations also do not pass easily from hand to hand. A purchaser of such commodities faces the danger of "overpaying" for them, or of suffering a loss before he has passed them on due to a fall in price. A "lot" of grain on a grain exchange, or a parcel of popular securities on a stock exchange, can easily change hands ten times in a few hours, but farms and factories, whose value can be determined only after a careful investigation of all the relevant circumstances, are entirely unsuited to rapid circulation. Even people who are not members of a stock exchange will readily accept securities whose prices are not subject to any considerable fluctuation in place of cash payment. But commodities that are subject to violent price fluctuations can circulate easily only "below the market," since all persons who are not willing to speculate will want to protect themselves against loss. Thus commodities whose prices are uncertain or fluctuate severely are also not well suited to free circulation from hand to hand.

Finally, it is clear that the several factors limiting the marketability of commodities will have a multiple weight wherever commodities are transferred from hand to hand, from place to place, and from one time period to another. Commodities whose marketability is restricted to a small number of persons, whose area of sale is limited, which can be preserved only for a short time, whose preservation involves considerable economic sacrifices, which can be brought to market only in strictly limited quantities at any one time, or whose prices are subject to fluctuations, etc., may all retain some degree of marketability within certain (even though very narrow) limits, but they are not capable of circulating freely.

Thus we find that for a commodity to be capable of circulating freely it must be saleable in the widest sense of the term to every economizing individual through whose hands it may pass, and to each of these persons it must be saleable, not in one respect alone, but in all four of the senses discussed above.

CHAPTER VIII | THE THEORY OF MONEY

1. THE NATURE AND ORIGIN OF MONEY [1]

I

N THE EARLY stages of trade, when economizing individuals are only slowly awakening to knowledge of the economic gains that can be derived from exploitation of existing exchange opportunities, their attention is, in keeping with the simplicity of all cultural beginnings, directed only to the most

1. Theodor Mommsen, *Geschichte des römischen Münzwesens*, Berlin, 1860, pp. v-xx, and 167 ff.; Carnap, "Zur Geschichte der Münzwissenschaft und der Werthzeichen," *Zeitschrift für die gesammte Staatswissenschaft*, XVI (1860), 348-396; Friedrich Kenner, "Die Anfänge des Geldes in Alterthume," *Sitzungsberichte der Kaiserlichen Akademie der Wissenschaften zu Wien: Philologisch-Historische Classe*, XLIII (1863), 382-490; Roscher, *op cit.*, pp. 36-40; Hildebrand, *op. cit.*, p. 5; Scheel, *op. cit.*, pp. 12-29; A. N. Bernardakis, "De l'origine des monnaies et de leurs noms," *Journal des Economistes*, (Third Series), XVIII (1870), 209-245.

obvious of these opportunities. In considering the goods he will acquire in trade, each man takes account only of their use value to himself. Hence the exchange transactions that are actually performed are restricted naturally to situations in which economizing individuals have goods in their possession that have a smaller *use value* to them than goods in the possession of other economizing individuals who value the same goods in reverse fashion. A has a sword that has a smaller use value to him than B's plough, while to B the same plough has a smaller use value than A's sword—at the beginning of human trade, all exchange transactions actually performed are restricted to cases of this sort.

It is not difficult to see that the number of exchanges actually performed must be very narrowly limited under these conditions. How rarely does it happen that a good in the possession of one person has a smaller use value to him than another good owned by another person who values these goods in precisely the opposite way at the same time! And even when this relationship is present, how much rarer still must situations be in which the two persons actually meet each other! A has a fishing net that he would like to exchange for a quantity of hemp. For him to be in a position actually to perform this exchange, it is not only necessary that there be another economizing individual, B, who is willing to give a quantity of hemp corresponding to the wishes of A for the fishing net, but also that the two economizing individuals, with these specific wishes, meet each other. Suppose that Farmer C has a horse that he would like to exchange for a number of agricultural implements and clothes. How unlikely it is that he will find another person who needs his horse and is, at the same time, both willing and in a position to give him all the implements and clothes he desires to have in exchange!

This difficulty would have been insurmountable, and would have seriously impeded progress in the division of labor, and above all in the production of goods for future sale, if there had not been, in the very nature of things, a way out. But there were elements in their situation that everywhere led men inevitably, without the need for a special agreement or even government compulsion, to a state of affairs in which this difficulty was completely overcome.

The direct provision of their requirements is the ultimate purpose of all the economic endeavors of men. The *final end* of their exchange operations is therefore to exchange their commodities for such goods as have use value to them. The endeavor to attain this final end has been equally characteristic of all stages of culture and is entirely correct economically. But economizing individuals would obviously be behaving uneconomically if, in all instances in which this final end cannot be reached *immediately and directly*, they were to forsake approaching it altogether.

Assume that a smith of the Homeric age has fashioned two suits of copper armor and wants to exchange them for copper, fuel, and food. He goes to market and offers his products for these goods. He would doubtless be very pleased if he were to encounter persons there who wish to purchase his armor and who, at the same time, have for sale all the raw materials and foods that he needs. But it must obviously be considered a particularly happy accident if, among the small number of persons who at any time wish to purchase a good so difficult to sell as his armor, he should find any who are offering precisely the goods that he needs. He would therefore make the marketing of his commodities either totally impossible, or possible only with the expenditure of a great deal of time, if he were to behave so uneconomically as to wish to take in exchange for his commodities only goods that have use value to himself and not also other goods which, although they would have commodity-character to him, nevertheless *have greater marketability than his own commodity.* Possession of these commodities would considerably facilitate his search for persons who have just the goods he needs. In the times of which I am speaking, cattle were, as we shall see below, the most salcable of all commodities. Even if the armorer is already sufficiently provided with cattle for his direct requirements, he would be acting very uneconomically if he did not give his armor for a number of additional cattle. By so doing, he is of course not exchanging his commodities for consumption goods (in the narrow sense in which this term is opposed to "commodities") but only for goods that also have commodity-character to him. But for his less saleable commodities he is obtaining others of greater marketability. Possession of these more saleable goods clearly multiplies his chances of finding persons on the market who will offer to sell him the goods that he needs. If our armorer correctly recognizes his individual interest, therefore, he will be led naturally, without compulsion or any special agreement, to give his armor for a corresponding number of cattle. With the more saleable commodities obtained in this way, he will go to persons at the market who are offering copper, fuel, and food for sale, in order to achieve his *ultimate objective,* the acquisition by trade of the consumption goods that he needs. But now he can proceed to this end much more quickly, more economically, and with a greatly enhanced probability of success.

As *each* economizing individual becomes increasingly more aware of his economic interest, he is led by this *interest, without any agreement, without legislative compulsion, and even without regard to the public interest,* to give his commodities in exchange for other, more saleable, commodities, even if he does not need them for any immediate consumption purpose. With economic progress, therefore, we can everywhere observe the phenomenon of a certain number of goods, especially those that are most easily saleable at a given time and place, becoming, under the powerful influence of *custom,* acceptable to everyone in trade, and thus capable of being given in exchange for any other commodity. These goods were called *"Geld"* [2] by our ancestors, a term derived from *"gelten"* which means to compensate or pay. Hence the term *"Geld"* in our language designates the means of payment as such.[3]

The great importance of *custom* [4] in the origin of money can be seen immediately by considering the process, described above, by which certain goods became money. The exchange of less easily saleable commodities for commodities of greater market-

2. For obvious reasons, the words *"Geld"* and *"gelten"* in this and the following sentence are left untranslated.—TR.

3. See the first two paragraphs of Appendix I (p. 312) for material originally appearing here as a footnote.—TR.

4. Custom as a factor in the origin of money is stressed by Condillac, *op. cit.,* pp. 286-290 and by G. F. Le Trosne, *De l'intérêt social,* Paris, 1777, pp. 43 f.

ability is in the economic interest of *every* economizing individual. But the actual performance of exchange operations of this kind presupposes a knowledge of their interest on the part of economizing individuals. For they must be willing to accept in exchange for their commodities, because of its greater marketability, a good that is perhaps itself quite useless to them. This knowledge will never be attained by all members of a people at the same time. On the contrary, only a small number of economizing individuals will at first recognize the advantage accruing to them from the acceptance of other, more saleable, commodities in exchange for their own whenever a direct exchange of their commodities for the goods they wish to consume is impossible or highly uncertain. This advantage is *independent of a general acknowledgement of any one commodity as money*. For an exchange of this sort will always, under any circumstances whatsoever, bring an economizing individual considerably nearer to his final end, the acquisition of the goods he wishes to consume. Since there is no better way in which men can become enlightened about their economic interests than by observation of the economic success of those who employ the correct means of achieving their ends, it is evident that nothing favored the rise of money so much as the long-practiced, and economically profitable, acceptance of eminently saleable commodities in exchange for all others by the most discerning and most capable economizing individuals. In this way, custom and practice contributed in no small degree to converting the commodities that were most saleable at a given time into commodities that came to be accepted, not merely by many, but by all economizing individuals in exchange for their own commodities.[5]

Within the boundaries of a state, the legal order usually has an influence on the money-character of commodities which, though small, cannot be denied. The origin of money (as distinct from coin, which is only one variety of money) is, as we have seen, entirely natural and thus displays legislative influence only in the rarest instances. Money is not an invention of the state. It is not the product of a legislative act. Even the sanc-

5. See Appendix J (p. 315) for material originally appended here as a footnote.—TR.

tion of political authority is not necessary for its existence. Certain commodities came to be money quite naturally, as the result of economic relationships that were independent of the power of the state.

But if, in response to the needs of trade, a good receives the sanction of the state as money, the result will be that not only every payment to the state itself but all other payments not explicitly contracted for in other goods can be required or offered, with legally binding effect, only in units of that good. There will be the further, and especially important, result that when payment has originally been contracted for in other goods but cannot, for some reason, be made, the payment substituted can similarly be required or offered, with legally binding effect, only in units of the one particular good. Thus the sanction of the state gives a particular good the attribute of being a universal substitute in exchange, and although the state is not responsible for the existence of the money-character of the good, it is responsible for a significant improvement of its money-character.[6]

2. THE KINDS OF MONEY APPROPRIATE TO PARTICULAR PEOPLES AND TO PARTICULAR HISTORICAL PERIODS

Money is not the product of an agreement on the part of economizing men nor the product of legislative acts. No one invented it. As economizing individuals in social situations became increasingly aware of their economic interest, they everywhere attained the simple knowledge that surrendering less saleable commodities for others of greater saleability brings them substantially closer to the attainment of their specific economic purposes. Thus, with the progressive development of social economy, money came to exist in numerous centers of civilization independently. But precisely because money is a natural product of human economy, the specific forms in which it has

6. See Stein, *op. cit.*, p. 55; especially also Karl Knies, "Ueber die Geldentwerthung und die mit ihr in Verbindung gebrachten Erscheinungen," *Zeitschrift für die gesammte Staatswissenschaft*, XIV (1858), 266; and Mommsen, *op. cit.*, pp. vii-viii.

appeared were everywhere and at all times the result of specific and changing economic situations. Among the same people at different times, and among different peoples at the same time, different goods have attained the special position in trade described above.

In the earliest periods of economic development, cattle seem to have been the most saleable commodity among most peoples of the ancient world. Domestic animals constituted the chief item of the wealth of every individual among nomads and peoples passing from a nomadic economy to agriculture. Their marketability extended literally to all economizing individuals, and the lack of artificial roads combined with the fact that cattle transported themselves (almost without cost in the primitive stages of civilization!) to make them saleable over a wider geographical area than most other commodities. A number of circumstances, moreover, favored broad quantitative and temporal limits to their marketability. A cow is a commodity of considerable durability. Its cost of maintenance is insignificant where pastures are available in abundance and where the animals are kept under the open sky. And in a culture in which everyone attempts to possess as large herds as possible, cattle are usually not brought to market in excessive quantities at any one time. In the period of which I am speaking, there was no similar juncture of circumstances establishing as broad a range of marketability for any other commodity. If we add to these circumstances the fact that trade in domestic animals was at least as well developed as trade in any other commodity, cattle appear to have been the most saleable of all available commodities and hence the natural money of the peoples of the ancient world.[7]

The trade and commerce of the most cultured people of the ancient world, the *Greeks*, whose stages of development history has revealed to us in fairly distinct outlines, showed no trace of coined money even as late as the time of Homer. Barter still prevailed, and wealth consisted of herds of cattle. Payments were made in cattle. Prices were reckoned in cattle. And cattle were used for the payment of fines. Even Draco imposed fines in cattle, and the practice was not abandoned until Solon con-

---

7. See the last two paragraphs of Appendix I (p. 313) for material appended here as a footnote in the original.—TR.

verted them, apparently because they had outlived their usefulness, into metallic money at the rate of one drachma for a sheep
and five drachmae for a cow. Even more distinctly than with
the Greeks, traces of cattle-money can be recognized in the case
of the cattle breeding ancestors of the peoples of the *Italian*
peninsula. Until very late, cattle and, next to them sheep,
formed the means of exchange among the Romans. Their earliest legal penalties were cattle fines (imposed in cattle and sheep)
which appear still in the lex Aternia Tarpeia of the year
454 B.C., and were only converted to coined money 24 years
later.[8]

Among our own ancestors, the old *Germanic* tribes, at a time
when, according to Tacitus, they held silver and earthen vessels
in equal esteem, a large herd of cattle was considered identical
with riches. Barter stood in the foreground, just as it did among
the Greeks of the Homeric age, and cattle again and, in this
case, horses (and weapons too!) already served as means of exchange. Cattle constituted their most highly esteemed property
and were preferred above all else. Legal fines were paid in cattle and weapons, and only later in metallic money.[9] Otto the
Great still imposed fines in terms of cattle.

Among the *Arabs*, the cattle standard existed as late as the
time of Mohammed.[10] Among the peoples of eastern Asia
Minor, where the writings of Zoroaster, the Zendavesta, were
held sacred, other forms of money replaced the cattle standard
only quite late, after the neighboring peoples had long gone
over to a metallic currency.[11] That cattle were used as currency

8. August Böckh, *Metrologische Untersuchungen über Gewichte, Münz-
   fusse und Masse des Alterthums,* Berlin, 1838, pp. 385 ff., 420 ff.;
   Mommsen, *op. cit.,* p. 169; Friedrich O. Hultsch, *Griechische und
   römische Metrologie,* Berlin, 1862, pp. 124 ff., 188 ff.

9. Wilh. Wackernagel, "Gewerbe, Handel und Schifffahrt der Ger-
   manen," *Zeitschrift für deutsches Alterthum,* IX (1853), 548 ff.; Jakob
   Grimm, *Deutsche Rechtsalterthümer,* 4th edition prepared by A.
   Heusler and R. Hübner, Leipzig, 1899, II, 123-124; Ad. Soetbeer,
   "Beiträge zur Geschichte des Geld- und Münzwesens in Deutschland,"
   Forschungen zur deutschen Geschichte, I (1862), 215.

10. Aloys Sprenger, *Das Leben und die Lehre des Mohammad,* Berlin,
    1861-65, III, 139.

11. Friedrich v. Spiegel, *Commentar über das Avesta,* Wien, 1864-68,
    I, 94 ff.

by the Hebrews,[12] by the peoples of Asia Minor, and by the inhabitants of Mesopotamia, in prehistoric times may be supposed although we cannot find evidence of it. These tribes all entered history at a level of civilization at which they had presumably already gone beyond the cattle standard—if one may be permitted to draw general conclusions, by analogy, from later developments, and from the fact that it appears to be unnatural in a primitive society to make large payments in metal or metallic implements.[13]

But rising civilization, and above all the division of labor and its natural consequence, the gradual formation of cities inhabited by a population devoted primarily to industry, must everywhere have had the result of simultaneously diminishing the marketability of cattle and increasing the marketability of many other commodities, especially the metals then in use. The artisan who began to trade with the farmer was seldom in a position to accept cattle as money; for a city dweller, the temporary possession of cattle necessarily involved, not only discomforts, but also considerable economic sacrifices; and the keeping and feeding of cattle imposed no significant economic sacrifice upon the farmer only as long as he had unlimited pasture and was accustomed to keep his cattle in an open field. With the progress of civilization, therefore, cattle lost to a great extent the broad range of marketability they had previously had with respect to the number of persons to whom, and with respect to the time period within which, they could be sold economically. At the same time, they receded more and more into the background relative to other goods with respect to the spatial and quantitative limits of their marketability. They ceased to be the most saleable of commodities, the *economic* form of money, and finally ceased to be money at all.

In all cultures in which cattle had previously had the character of money, cattle-money was abandoned with the passage from a nomadic existence and simple agriculture to a more complex system in which handicraft was practised, its place being taken by the metals then in use. Among the metals that were at first principally worked by men because of their ease of

12. Moritz A. Levy, *Geschichte der jüdischen Münzen*, Leipzig, 1862, p. 7.
13. Roscher, *op cit.*, note 5 on p. 309.

extraction and malleability were copper, silver, gold, and in some cases also iron. The transition took place quite smoothly when it became necessary, since metallic implements and the raw metal itself had doubtless already been in use everywhere as money in addition to cattle-currency, for the purpose of making small payments.

Copper was the earliest metal from which the farmer's plough, the warrior's weapons, and the artisan's tools were fashioned. Copper, gold, and silver were the earliest materials used for vessels and ornaments of all kinds. At the cultural stage at which peoples passed from cattle-money to an exclusively metallic currency, therefore, copper and perhaps some of its alloys were goods of very general use, and gold and silver, as the most important means of satisfying that most universal passion of primitive men, the desire to stand out in appearance before the other members of the tribe, had become goods of most general desire. As long as they had few uses, the three metals circulated almost exclusively in finished forms. Later, circulating as raw metal, they were less limited as to use and had greater divisibility. Their marketability was neither restricted to a small number of economizing persons nor, because of their great usefulness to all peoples and easy transportability at relatively slight economic sacrifices, confined within narrow spatial limits. Because of their durability they were not restricted in marketability to narrow limits in time. As a result of the general competition for them, they could be more easily marketed at economic prices than any other commodities in comparable quantities (p. 227). Thus we observe an economic situation in the historical period following nomadism and simple agriculture in which these three metals, being the most saleable goods, became the exclusive means of exchange.

This transition did not take place abruptly, nor did it take place in the same way among all peoples. The newer metallic standard may have been in use for a long time along with the older cattle-standard before it replaced the latter completely. The value of an animal, in metallic money, may have served as the basis for the currency unit even after metal had completely displaced cattle as currency in trade. The Dekaboion, Tesseraboion, and Hekatomboion of the Greeks, and the earliest metallic money of the Romans and Gauls were probably of this nature, and the animal picture appearing on the pieces of metal was probably a symbol of this value.[14]

It is, to say the least, uncertain whether copper or brass, as the most important of the metals in use, were the earliest means of exchange, and whether the precious metals acquired the function of money only later. In eastern Asia, in China, and perhaps also in India, the copper standard experienced its most complete development. In central Italy an exclusively copper standard also developed. In the ancient cultures on the Euphrates and Tigris, on the other hand, not even traces of the former existence of an exclusively copper standard are to be found, and in Asia Minor and Egypt, as well as in Greece, Sicily, and lower Italy, its independent development was arrested, wherever it had existed at all, by the vast development of Mediterranean commerce, which could not be carried on adequately with copper alone. But it is certain that all peoples who were led to adopt a copper standard as a result of the material circumstances under which their economy developed, passed on from the less precious metals to the more precious ones, from copper and iron to silver and gold, with the further development of civilization, and especially with the geographical extension of commerce. In all places, moreover, where a silver standard became established, there was a later transition to a gold standard, and if the transition was not always actually completed, the tendency existed nevertheless.

In the narrow commerce of an ancient Sabine city with the surrounding region, and in keeping with the early simplicity of Sabine customs, when the cattle-standard had outlived its usefulness, copper best served the practical purposes of the farmers and of the city dwellers as well. It was the most important metal in use, certainly the commodity whose marketability extended to the largest number of persons, and the quantitative limits of

14. Plutarch, *Lives*, with an English translation by Bernadotte Perrin, London: William Heinemann, 1914, I, 55; Pliny, *The Natural History*, translated by John Bostock and H. T. Riley, London: H. G. Bohn, 1856, IV, 5-6; Heinrich Schreiber, "Die Metallringe der Kelten als Schmuck und Geld," *Taschenbuch für Geschichte und Alterthum*, II, 67-152, 240-247, and III, 401-408.

its marketability were wider than those of any other commodity
—the most important requisites of money in the primitive stages
of civilization. It was, moreover, a good whose easy and in-
expensive preservation and storage in small amounts and whose
relatively moderate cost of transportation qualified it to a sufficient degree for monetary purposes within narrow geographical limits. But as soon as the area of trade widened, as the rate
of commodity turnover quickened, and as the precious metals
became more and more the most saleable commodities of a new
epoch, copper naturally lost its capacity to serve as money. With
the trade of this people extending over the whole world, with
the rapid turnover of their commodities, and with the increasing division of labor, each economizing individual felt more
and more the need of carrying money on his person. With the
progress of civilization, the precious metals became the most
saleable commodities and thus the natural money of peoples
highly developed economically.

The history of other peoples presents a picture of great differences in their economic development and hence also in their
monetary institutions. When Mexico was invaded for the first
time by Europeans, it appears already to have reached an unusual level of economic development, according to the reports
published by eye-witnesses about the condition of the country
at that time. The trade of the ancient Aztecs is of special interest to us for two reasons: (1) it proves to us that the economic
thinking that leads men to activity directed to the fullest possible satisfaction of their needs is everywhere responsible for
analogous economic phenomena, and (2) ancient Mexico presents us with the picture of a country in the state of transition
from a pure barter to a money economy. We thus have the record of a situation in which we can observe the characteristic
process by which a number of goods attain greater prominence
than the rest and become money.

The reports of the conquistadors and contemporary writers
depict Mexico as a country with numerous cities and a well organized and imposing trade in goods. There were daily markets
in the cities, and every five days major markets were held which
were distributed over the country in such a way that the major
market of any one city was not impaired by the competition of

that of a neighboring city. There was a special large square in each city for trade in commodities, and in it a particular place was assigned for each commodity, outside of which trade in that commodity was forbidden. The only exceptions to this rule were foodstuffs and objects difficult to transport (timber, tanning materials, stones, etc.). The number of people assembled at the market place of the capital, Mexico, was estimated to have been 20,000 to 25,000 for the daily markets, and between 40,000 and 50,000 on major market days. A great many varieties of commodities were traded.[15]

The interesting question that arises is whether, in the markets of ancient Mexico, which were similar in so many ways to those of Europe, there had also already appeared phenomena analogous in nature and origin to our money.

The actual report of the Spanish invaders is that the trade of Mexico, at the time they first entered the country, had long since ceased to move exclusively within the limits of simple barter, and that some commodities had instead already attained the special status in trade that I discussed more extensively earlier—that is, the status of money. Cocoa beans in small bags containing 8,000 to 24,000 beans, certain small cotton handkerchiefs, golds and in goose quills that were accepted according to size (balances and weighing instruments in general being unknown to the Mexicans), pieces of copper, and finally, thin pieces of tin, appear to have been the commodities that were readily accepted by everyone (as money), even if the persons receiving them did not need them immediately, whenever a direct exchange of immediately usable commodities could not be accomplished.

Eye-witnesses mention the following commodities as being traded on the Mexican markets: live and dead animals, cocoa, all other foods, precious stones, medicinal plants, herbs, gums, resins, earths, prepared medicines, commodities made of the fibers of the century plant, of palm leaves, and of animal hair, articles made of feathers, and of wood and stone, and finally gold, copper, tin, timber, stones, tanning materials, and hides. If we

15. Francesco Saverio Clavigero, *The History of Mexico*, Richmond, 1806, II, 188 ff.

consider not only this list of commodities but also (1) the fact
that Mexico, at the time of its discovery by Europeans, was already a developed country with some industry and populous cities, (2) that since the majority of our domestic animals were unknown to them, a cattle-standard was entirely out of the question, (3) that cocoa was the daily beverage, cotton the most
common clothing material, and gold, copper, and tin the most
widely used metals of the Aztec people, and (4) that the nature
of these commodities and the fact of their general use gave
them greater marketability than all other commodities, it is not
difficult to understand exactly why these goods became the
money of the Aztec people. They were the natural, even if little
developed, currency of ancient Mexico.

Analogous causes were responsible for the fact that animal
skins became money among hunting peoples engaged in external trade. Among hunting tribes there is naturally an over-
supply of furs, since providing a family with food by means of
hunting leads to so great an accumulation of skins that at most
only a competition for especially beautiful or rare kinds of skins
can arise among the members of the hunting tribe. But if the tribe
enters into trade with foreign peoples, and a market for skins
arises in which numerous consumable goods can, at the choice
of the hunters, be exchanged for furs, nothing is more natural
than that skins will become the most saleable good, and hence
that they will come to be preferred and accepted even in exchanges taking place between the hunters themselves. Of course
hunter A does not need the skins of hunter B that he accepts in
an exchange, but he is aware that he will be able to exchange
them easily on the markets for other goods that he does need.
He therefore prefers the skins, even though they also have only
the character of commodities to him, to other commodities in
his possession that are less easily saleable. We can actually observe this relationship among almost all hunting tribes who
carry on foreign trade with their skins.[16]

16. A beaver skin is still the unit of exchange value in several regions of
the Hudson's Bay Company. Three martens are equal to one beaver,
one white fox to two beavers, one black fox or one bear equal to four
beavers, and one rifle equal to 15 beavers ("Die Jäger im nördlichen

The fact that slaves and chunks of salt became money in the interior of Africa, and that cakes of wax on the upper Amazon, cod in Iceland and Newfoundland, tobacco in Maryland and Virginia, sugar in the British West Indies, and ivory in the vicinity of the Portuguese colonies, took on the functions of money is explained by the fact that these goods were, and in some cases still are, the chief articles exported from these places. Thus they acquire, just as did furs among hunting tribes, a pre-eminent marketability.

The local money-character of many other goods, on the other hand, can be traced back to their great and general use value locally and their resultant marketability. Examples are the money-character of dates in the oasis of Siwa, of tea-bricks in central Asia and Siberia, of glass beads in Nubia and Sennar, and of ghussub, a kind of millet, in the country of Ahir (Africa). An example in which both factors have been responsible for the money-character of a good is provided by cowrie-shells, which have, at the same time, been both a commonly desired ornament and an export commodity.[17]

Thus money presents itself to us, in its special locally and temporally different forms, not as the result of an agreement, legislative compulsion, or mere chance, but as the natural product of differences in the economic situation of different peoples at the same time, or of the same people in different periods of their history.

Amerika," *Das Ausland*, XIX, no. 21, [Jan. 21, 1846], 84). The Estonian word *"raha"* (money) has in the related language of the Laplanders the meaning of fur (Philipp Krug, *Zur Münzkunde Russlands*, St. Petersburg, 1805). On fur money in the Russian middle ages, see the report by Nestor (A. L. Schlözer, translator, *Nestor, Russische Annalen*, Goettingen, 1802-1809, III, 90). The old word, *"kung"* (money) really means marten. As late as 1610 a Russian war chest containing 5450 rubles in silver and 7000 rubles worth of fur was taken. (See Nikolai Karamzin, *Geschichte des russischen Reichs*, Riga, 1820-1833, XI, 183). See also Roscher, *op. cit.*, p. 309, and Heinrich Storch, *Handbuch der National-Wirthschaftlehre*, ed. by K. H. Rau, Hamburg, 1820, III, 25-26.

17. Roscher, *op. cit.*, note 13 on pp. 313-314.

3. MONEY AS A "MEASURE OF PRICE"
AND AS THE MOST ECONOMIC FORM
FOR STORING EXCHANGEABLE WEALTH

Since the progressive development of trade and the functioning of money give rise to an economic situation in which commodities of all kinds are exchanged for each other, and since the limits within which prices are formed become progressively narrower under the influence of lively competition (p. 201), it was easy for the idea to arise that all commodities will stand, at a given place and at a given time, in a certain price relationship to each other, on the basis of which they can be exchanged for each other at will.

Suppose that the prices of the commodities listed below (assuming them to be of given qualities), established in a particular market at a given time, are as follows:

	EFFECTIVE PRICES (per cwt.)	AVERAGE PRICE (per cwt.)
Sugar	24-26 Thalers	25 Thalers
Cotton	29-31 "	30 "
Wheat flour	5½-6½ "	6 "

Now if it is assumed that the average price of a commodity is one at which it can be both bought and sold, then 4 hundredweight of sugar appears, in the example, as the "equivalent" of $3\frac{1}{3}$ hundredweight of cotton, this as the "equivalent" of $16\frac{2}{3}$ hundredweight of wheat flour, and of 100 Thalers, and *vice versa*. We need only call the equivalent (in this sense) of a commodity (or one of its many equivalents) its "exchange value," and the sum of money for which it can be both bought and sold its "exchange value in the preferred sense of the term," to arrive at the concept of exchange value in general and of money as the "measure of exchange value" in particular, which dominate our science.

"In a country in which there is a lively commerce," writes Turgot, "every kind of good will have a current price in terms of every other good, which means that a definite quantity of one good will be equivalent to a definite quantity of every other kind of good. To express the exchange value of a particular good, it is evidently sufficient to state the quantity of another known commodity that is regarded as its equivalent. From this it can be seen that all kinds of goods that can be objects of trade are measured, so to speak, against one another, and that any one of them can serve as a yardstick for all the others." [18] Similar thoughts have been expressed by almost all other economists who come, like Turgot in the course of his famous essay on the origin and distribution of national wealth, to the conclusion that money, among all possible "measures of exchange value," is the most suitable and hence also the most common. The only defect of this measure is said to lie in the fact that the value of money is not fixed, but changeable,[19] and that money therefore provides a reliable measure of "exchange value" for any given moment but not for different points in time.

In my discussion of price theory, however, I have shown that equivalents of goods in the objective sense of the term cannot be observed anywhere in the economy of men (p. 193), and that the entire theory that presents money as the "measure of the exchange value" of goods disintegrates into nothingness, since the basis of the theory is a fiction, an error.

When a hundredweight of wool of given quality is sold in a particular transaction on a wool market for 103 florins, it is often found that transactions are taking place at higher and at lower prices on the same market and at the same time, at 104, 103½, and at 102 and 102½ florins, for example. Often too, while the buyers on the market declare themselves ready to "take" at 101 florins, the sellers simultaneously declare that they are willing to "offer" only at 105 florins. What, in such a case, is the "exchange value" of wool? Or, to state the same question in an inverse fashion, what quantity of wool is the "exchange value" of 100 florins, for example? Obviously all that can be said is that a hundredweight of wool can be bought or sold on

18. *Réflexions sur la formation et la distribution des richesses*, reprinted in *Oeuvres de Turgot*, ed. by G. Schelle, Paris, 1913-23, II, 554. See also Roscher, *op. cit.*, pp. 297-303, Knies, *op. cit.*, p. 262.

19. See on this especially J. A. R. v. Helferich, *Von den periodischen Schwankungen im Werth der edeln Metalle von der Entdeckung Amerikas bis zum Jahre 1830*, Nürnberg, 1843.

that market at that time between the limits of 101 and 105 florins.[20] But a *particular* quantity of wool and a *particular* quantity of money (or any other commodity) that can mutually be exchanged for each other—that are equivalents in the objective sense of the term—can nowhere be observed for they do not exist. There can thus be no question of a measure of these equivalents (a measure of "exchange value").

It is true that several economic objectives of practical life have given rise to a need for valuations of approximate exactness, especially valuations in terms of money. Where only an approximate correctness of the estimates is required, average prices can properly serve as the basis of valuation, since they are generally most suitable for this purpose. But it is clear that this method of valuing goods must prove itself completely insufficient and even erroneous, even for practical life, wherever a higher degree of precision becomes necessary. When an exact valuation of goods is necessary, three things must be distinguished according to the intention of the person making the estimate. He must direct his attention to estimating: (1) the price at which certain goods, if brought to market, can be *sold,* (2) the price at which goods of a certain kind and quality can be *bought* on the market, and (3) the quantity of commodities or the sum of money that is the equivalent, *to the particular individual himself,* of a good or of a quantity of goods.

The basis for making the first two estimates follows from what has been said. Price formation, we have seen, always takes place between two extremes, the lower of which may also be called the *demand price* (the price at which the commodity is asked for on the market) and the higher of which may also be called the *supply price* (the price at which the commodity is of-

20. It is perhaps equally obvious that these are not the limits described in Chapter V as those between which price formation must take place. Other interpretations may be possible, but it seems likely that the "limits" of this passage are simply the bids and offers chosen by two bargainers as arbitrary starting points in a haggling process, the seller intending to come down and the buyer to come up. In spite of Menger's apparent implication in the second paragraph following that "the demand price" and "the supply price" of that paragraph are the limits described in Chapter V, they are evidently of the same character as the wool market "limits" here.—TR.

fered for sale on the market).[21] The former will generally be the basis for making the first estimate and the latter the basis for making the second. The third estimate is more difficult since it involves the special position that the good or quantity of goods whose equivalent (in the subjective sense of the term) is under consideration occupies in the economy of the economizing individual. For when he estimates this equivalent, he is also considering whether the good has predominant use value or predominant exchange value to him; when quantities of a good are involved, he is considering what portion has predominant use value and what portion has predominant exchange value to him.

Suppose that A possesses goods a, b, and c, which have a predominant use value to him, and also goods d, e, and f, which have a predominant exchange value to him. The sum of money he expects he could *obtain* by selling the first group would not be an equivalent of these goods to him since their use value to him is the higher, economic, form. Instead, only a sum of money that would *purchase* identical goods or such goods as have the same use value to him will be an equivalent of these goods to him. Goods d, e, and f, however, are commodities and hence intended for sale. In the ordinary course of events, they will be exchanged for money. The price expected for them *by* economizing individual A is generally indeed the equivalent of these goods.[22] The equivalent of a good can be correctly estimated therefore only with respect to the possessor and the economic status of the good to him. The prerequisite that is necessary for the determination of the equivalent of a complex of goods (a person's property) is the separate estimation of the equivalent of each consumption good and each commodity in the complex.[23]

21. See note 20 above.—TR.
22. That is, the subjective equivalent of these goods *to A* is the price expected *by A*. The original German passage runs as follows: *"der voraussichtlich dafür zu erzielende Preis ist für das wirthschaftende Subject A allerdings der Regel nach das Aequivalent dieser Güter."* —TR.
23. Although this difference has not yet been sufficiently observed in our science, it has long been the object of detailed investigations on the part of students of the law. This question is of practical interest to them in cases in which there are claims for damages as well as in

Although the theory of "exchange value" in general, and as a necessary consequence, the theory of money as a "measure of exchange value" in particular, must be designated as untenable after what has been said, observation of the nature and function of money teaches us nevertheless that the various *estimates* just discussed (as distinguished from measurement of the "exchange value" of goods) are usually most suitably made in terms of money. The purpose of the first two valuations is the estimation of the quantities of goods for which a commodity may be bought or sold at a given time on a given market. These quantities of goods will ordinarily consist only of *money* if the prospective transactions are *actually* performed, and knowledge of the sums of *money* for which a commodity can be purchased or sold is naturally, therefore, the immediate objective of the economic task of valuation.

Under conditions of developed trade, the only commodity in which all others can be evaluated without roundabout procedures is money. Wherever barter in the narrow sense of the term disappears, and only sums of money (for the most part) actually appear as prices of the various commodities, a reliable basis for valuation in any but monetary terms is lacking. The valuation of grain or wool, for example, is relatively simple in terms of money. But the valuation of wool in terms of grain, or of grain in terms of wool, involves greater difficulties, if for no other reason than because a direct exchange of these two goods never takes place, or only in the rarest exceptional cases, with the result that the foundation for such a valuation, the respective effective prices, is wanting. A valuation of this kind is therefore usually only possible on the basis of a computation involving, as a prerequisite, the prior valuation of the two goods in terms of money. The valuation of a good in terms of money,

---

many other cases (whenever there is substitute fulfillment of a contract, for example). Consider, for instance, the case of someone unlawfully preventing a scientist from using his library. The "market price" of the books would be a very insufficient compensation to the scientist for his loss. But the market price would be the rightful equivalent of the library to the scientist's heir, to whom the library would have a predominating exchange value.

on the other hand, can be made directly on the basis of the existing effective prices.

The valuation of commodities in terms of money thus not only answers, as we saw before, the ordinary practical purposes of valuation most effectively, but is also the most convenient and the simplest in practical operation. Valuation in terms of other commodities is a more complicated procedure that presupposes prior valuations in terms of money.

The same may be said about the estimation of the equivalents of goods in the subjective sense of the term, since again the first two valuations constitute its prerequisites and foundation.

Thus it is clear why the only commodity in terms of which valuations are usually made is money. In this sense, as the commodity in terms of which valuations are as a rule and most suitably made under conditions of developed trade, money may, if one desires, be called a measure of prices.[24, 25]

I have explained above the reasons why estimates can generally be most effectively made in terms of a commodity that has already attained money character whenever such a commodity exists, and thus why estimates are actually made in these terms unless peculiarities of the commodity that has become money prevent it. But this outcome is not a *necessary* conse-

24. Aristotle already observed that money serves as a measure in the trade of men (*Ethica Nicomachea* v. 5. 1133^b, 16; and ix. 1. 1164^a, 1). Among the writers who trace back the origin of money exclusively or predominantly to the need of economizing men for a measure of "exchange value," or of prices, and who regard the money character of the precious metals as due to their special suitability for this purpose, I should like to mention here the following: Carlo Antonio Broggia, *Trattato delle monete*, (published 1743) in *Scrittori classici Italiani di economia politica*, Milano, 1803-05, IV, 304; Pompeo Neri, *Osservazioni sopra il prezzo legale delle monete*, (published 1751) in *ibid.*, VI, 134 ff.; Ferdinando Galiani, *Della moneta*, in *ibid.*, XII, 23 ff. and 120 ff.; Antonio Genovesi, *Lezioni di economia civile*, in *ibid.*, XV, 291-313 and 333-341; Francis Hutcheson, *A System of Moral Philosophy*, London, 1755, II, 55-58; David Ricardo, *op. cit.*, p. 40; Storch, op. cit., I, 45 ff.; Lorenz v. Stein, *System der Staatswissenschaft*, Stuttgart, 1852, I, 217 ff.; Albert E. F. Schäffle, *Das gesellschaftliche System der menschlichen Wirthschaft*, Tübingen, 1873, I, 221 f.

25. The next two paragraphs appear here as a footnote in the original.— TR.

quence of the money character of a commodity. One can very easily imagine cases in which a commodity that does not have money character neverthless serves as the "measure of price," or cases in which only one or another of several commodities that have attained money character serve in this additional capacity. The function of serving as a measure of price is therefore not necessarily an attribute of commodities that have attained money character. And if it is not a *necessary* consequence of the fact that a commodity has become money, it is still less a prerequisite or cause of a commodity becoming money.

Actually, of course, money is generally a very suitable measure of price. This is especially true of metallic money because of its high divisibility and because of the relatively greater stability of the factors determining its value. There are other commodities that have attained money character (weapons, plate, bronze rings, etc.) but which have never been used as measures of price. The function of serving as a measure of price is not, therefore, contained in the *concept* of money. Several economists have fused the concept of money and the concept of a "measure of value" together, and have involved themselves, as a result, in a misconception of the true nature of money.

The same factors that are responsible for the fact that money is the only commodity in terms of which valuations are usually made are responsible also for the fact that money is the most appropriate medium for accumulating that portion of a person's wealth by means of which he intends to acquire other goods (consumption goods or means of production). The portion of his wealth that an economizing individual intends to use for purchasing consumption goods attains that form in which he may, at any time, satisfy his needs in the most certain and most rapid manner if it is first exchanged for money. The portion of an economizing individual's capital that does not already consist of specialized factors of intended production is also, for the same reason, more suitably held in the form of money than in any other form, since any other commodity must first be exchanged for money in order to be further traded for the desired means of production. In fact, daily experience teaches us that economizing men endeavor to convert that part of their store of consumption goods into money which consists

of goods that they no longer intend to use for the direct satisfaction of their needs but instead regard as commodities. Similarly, that part of their capital which does not consist of factors
of intended production they turn first into money and thereby
take a not inconsiderable step in furthering their economic
purposes.

But the notion that attributes to *money* as such the function
of also transferring "values" from the present into the future
must be designated as erroneous. Although metallic money, because of its durability and low cost of preservation, is doubtless
suitable for this purpose also, it is nevertheless clear that other
commodities are still better suited for it. Indeed, experience
teaches that wherever less easily preserved goods rather than
the precious metals have attained money-character, they ordinarily serve for purposes of circulation, but not for the preservation of "values." [26]

26. The chief representatives of this theory are the great English philosophers of the seventeenth century. Hobbes starts with the need of men
for conserving perishable wealth that they do not intend to use for
immediate consumption, and he shows how this end can be achieved
by transformation (*"concoctio"*) of the perishable wealth into metallic
money. He also shows how wealth can thereby be carried about more
easily (*Leviathan*, ed. by A. D. Lindsay, "Everyman's Library," London, 1914, p. 133). Locke makes the same point (*Two Treatises of
Government*, and *Further Considerations concerning Raising the
Value of Money*, in *The Works of John Locke*, 12th edition, London,
1824, IV, 364-365 and 139 ff.).

Sallustio Antonio Bandini develops a view that has its roots in the
work of Aristotle. He begins his exposition by showing the difficulties
to which pure barter leads, arguing that a person whose goods are
wanted by others was not always in a situation in which he could
make use of their goods, hence that a pawn (*"un mallevadore"*) became necessary whose transfer was to assure future compensation, and
that the precious metals were chosen for this function. (*Discorso
economico* in *Scrittori classici Italiani di economia politica*, Milano,
1803-05, VIII, 142 ff.) This theory was further developed in Italy by
Giammaria Ortes (*Della economia nazionale*, in *ibid.*, XXIX, 271-276,
and *Lettere* in *ibid.*, XXX, 258 ff.); by Gian-Rinaldo Carli (*Dell'
origine e del commercio della moneta*, in *ibid.*, XX, 15-26); and by
Giambattista Coriani (*Riflessioni sulle monete*, and *Lettera ad un
legislatore della Republica Cisalpina*, in *ibid.*, XLVI, 87-102 and
153 ff.). In France the theory was developed by Dutot, (*Réflexions politiques sur les finances et le commerce*, in E. Daire, ed., *Economistes*

If we summarize what has been said, we come to the conclusion that the commodity that has become money is also the commodity in which valuations answering the practical purposes of economizing men and in which accumulations of funds for exchange purposes can most appropriately be made provided that no impediments founded upon its properties stand in the way. *Metallic* money (which writers in our science always have primarily in mind when they speak of money in general) actually answers these purposes to a high degree. But it appears to me to be just as certain that the functions of being a "measure of value" and a "store of value" must not be attributed *to money as such,* since these functions are of a merely accidental nature and are not an essential part of the concept of money.

4. COINAGE

From the preceding exposition of the nature and origin of money, it appears that the precious metals naturally became the *economic* form of money in the ordinary trading relations of civilized peoples. But the use of the precious metals for monetary purposes is accompanied by some defects whose removal had to be attempted by economizing men. The chief defects involved in the use of the precious metals for monetary purposes are: (1) the difficulty of determining their genuineness and degree of fineness, and (2) the necessity of dividing the hard material into pieces appropriate to each particular transaction. These difficulties cannot be removed easily without loss of time and other economic sacrifices.

The testing of the genuineness of precious metals and their degree of fineness requires the use of chemicals and specific labor services, since it can be undertaken only by experts. The division of the hard metals into pieces of the weights needed for particular transactions is an operation which, because of the exactness necessary, not only requires labor, loss of time, and pre-

---

financiers du XVIIIe Siècle, Paris, 1843, p. 895). In Germany it was revised by T. A. H. Schmalz, (*Staatswirthschaftslehre in Briefen,* Berlin, 1818, I, 48 ff.), and in England recently by Henry Dunning Macleod, (*The Elements of Economics,* New York, 1881, I, 171 ff.).

cision instruments, but is also accompanied by a not inconsiderable loss of the precious metal itself (because of the loss of chips and as the result of repeated smelting).

A very penetrating description of the difficulties that arise from the use of the precious metals for monetary purposes has been given us by the well-known traveler [27] in southeastern Asia, Bastian, in his work on Burma, a country where silver still circulates in an uncoined state.

"When a person goes to market in Burma," Bastian relates, "he must take along a piece of silver, a hammer, a chisel, a balance, and the necessary weights. 'How much are these pots?' 'Show me your money,' answers the merchant, and after inspecting it determines a price at this or that weight. The buyer then asks the merchant for a small anvil and belabors his piece of silver with his hammer until he thinks he has found the correct weight. He thereupon weighs it on his own balance, since that of the merchant is not to be trusted, and adds to or takes away from the silver on the scales until the weight is right. Of course a good deal of the silver is lost as chips drop to the floor, and the buyer therefore usually prefers not to buy the exact quantity he desires but one equivalent to the piece of silver he has just broken off. In larger purchases, which are made only with silver of the highest degree of fineness, the process is still more complicated, since first an assayer must be called who determines the exact degree of fineness, and who must be paid for this task."

This description furnishes us a clear picture of the difficulties involved in the trade of all peoples before they learned to coin metals. Frequently repeated experiences with these difficulties must have made their removal seem most desirable to every economizing individual.

The first of the two difficulties, the determination of the degree of fineness of the metal, seems to have been the one whose removal appeared to be first in importance to economizing

27. Menger does not give references to the passages he quotes from Bastian and we were unable to find them in the published works of Adolph Bastian that were accessible to us. It is possible that Menger's information was based on an unpublished lecture or on a personal communication from Bastian.—TR.

men. A stamp impressed by a public official or some reliable person on a metal bar guaranteed, not its weight, but its degree of fineness, and exempted the possessor, when he passed the metal on to other persons who appreciated the reliability of the stamp, from the burdensome and expensive assay test. Metal so stamped still had to be weighed, as before, but its fineness required no further examination.

In some cases at the same time, and in other cases possibly somewhat later, economizing men appear to have hit upon the idea of also designating the *weight* of the pieces of metal in similar fashion, and of dividing the metals from the beginning into pieces that were reliably marked with their weight as well as their fineness. This was naturally best accomplished by dividing the precious metal into small pieces corresponding to the needs of trade, and by marking the metal in such a way that no significant part could be removed from the pieces without the removal becoming immediately apparent. This aim was achieved by coining the metal, and it was in this way that our coins came into being. Coins are thus, in their very nature, nothing but pieces of metal whose fineness and weight have been determined in a reliable manner and with an exactness sufficient for the practical purposes of economic life, and which are protected against fraud in as efficient a manner as possible. The fact of coinage makes it possible for us, in all transactions, simply to count out the necessary weights of the precious metals in a reliable manner without irksome assay tests, division, and weighing. The economic importance of the coin, therefore, consists in the fact that (apart from saving us from the mechanical operation of dividing the precious metal into the required quantities) its acceptance saves us the *examination* of its genuineness, fineness, and weight. When we pass it on, it saves us from giving *proof* of these facts. Thus it frees us from many irksome, wearisome, procedures involving economic sacrifices, and as a consequence of this fact, the naturally high marketability of the precious metals is considerably increased.

The best guarantee of the full weight and assured fineness of coins can, in the nature of the case, be given by the government itself, since it is known to and recognized by everyone and has the power to prevent and punish crimes against the coinage.

Governments have therefore usually accepted the obligation of stamping the coins necessary for trade. But they have so often and so greatly misused their power that economizing individuals eventually almost forgot the fact that a coin is nothing but a piece of precious metal of fixed fineness and weight, for which fineness and full weight the honesty and rectitude of the mint constitute a guarantee. Doubts even arose as to whether money is a commodity at all. Indeed, it was finally declared to be something entirely imaginary resting solely on human convenience. The fact that governments treated money as if it actually had been merely the product of the convenience of men in general and of their legislative whims in particular contributed therefore in no small degree to furthering errors about the nature of money.[28]

Originally the money metals were undoubtedly divided into pieces that corresponded to the weights already in general use in commerce. The Roman as was originally a pound of copper. In the time of Edward I, the English pound sterling contained a pound, Tower weight, of silver, of a certain fineness. Similarly, the French livre in the time of Charlemagne contained a pound of silver according to Troyes weight. The English shilling and penny were also weights customarily used in commerce. "When wheat is at twelve shillings the quarter," says an ancient statute of Henry III, "then wastel bread of a farthing shall weigh eleven shillings and four pence." [29] It is also known that the German mark, schilling, pfennig, etc., were originally commercial weights. But the repeated debasements of the currency that were brought about by the masters of the mints soon caused the ordinary weights of bullion and the weights according to which the precious metals were used in trade (counted out as coins) to become very different in most countries. This difference in turn contributed not a little toward causing money to be regarded as a special "measure of exchange value," even though the standard coin in every natural economy is nothing but a unit of weight defined by the weight according to which the precious metals are traded. Frequent attempts have been

28. The next paragraph appears in the original as a footnote appended at the end of the previous paragraph.—TR.

29. See Adam Smith, *op. cit.*, p. 26.

made in recent times to bring the unit of weight of bullion again into accord with the coinage unit, as in Germany and Austria where the *Zollverein* pound was chosen as the foundation of the coinage system.

The principal imperfections of our coins are that they cannot be made in perfectly exact weights, and that even the exactness that could be achieved is not attempted, for practical reasons (because of cost), in the customary manufacturing processes employed in the mints. The imperfections with which the coins originally leave the mint are augmented during their circulation by use, with the result that a perceptible inequality easily arises in the weights of coins of the same denomination.

Obviously these defects are more pronounced the smaller the quantities into which the precious metals are divided. The coining of the precious metals into pieces as small as retail trade requires would lead to the greatest technical difficulties, and even if it were done with moderate care, it would require economic sacrifices that would be out of all proportion to the face value of the coins. On the other hand, everyone familiar with trade can easily understand the difficulties to which a lack of coins of small denominations would lead.

"A smaller coin than 2 Annas," Bastian reports, "did not exist in Siam. Anyone wishing to buy anything below that price had to wait until the addition of a new want justified the expenditure of such a sum or join with other would-be buyers and split the purchase with them. Sometimes small cups of rice served as money substitutes, and it is said that in Sokotra small pieces of ghi, or butter, served as small change." In Mexican cities Bastian was given pieces of soap, and eggs in the country, as small change. In the highlands of Peru it is the custom of the natives to have a basket ready which they have divided into compartments. In one compartment there are sewing needles, in another spools of thread, and in others candles and other objects of daily use. They offer a selection of these things equal to the amount of small change needed. In upper Burma, lumps of lead are used for the smallest purchases, such as fruit, cigars, etc., and every merchant has a large case full of these lumps in his shop. They are weighed on a larger balance than that used for silver. In villages where one does not expect to get change for silver, a servant must follow with a heavy sack of lead for small purchases.

In most civilized countries, the technical and economic difficulties of coining the precious metals into very small pieces are evaded by coining pieces of some ordinary metal, usually copper or brass.

Since, as a matter of convenience if for no other reason, no-one will needlessly keep any sizeable part of his wealth in these coins, they have merely a subsidiary position in trade, and can be coined harmlessly at half weight, or even less, for the greater *convenience* of the public, provided only that they can, at any time, be exchanged at the mint for coins made of precious metals, or that only such small quantities of subsidiary coin are issued that they remain in circulation. The first is, in any case, the more correct method and at the same time a more certain protection against government abuses arising from the profit accruing to government from the issuance of these coins. Such pieces of money are called subsidiary coin. Their value is greater than the materials from which they are made, the additional value being attributable to the fact that a certain number of the subsidiary coins can be exchanged at the mint for a coin of larger denomination, and to the fact that anybody can use them to discharge his obligations to the issuing government and to any other person up to the amount of the smallest full-weight coin. Because of the greater convenience of subsidiary brass or copper coins, the public in this case readily tolerates the small economic anomaly, since the advantages of easier transportability and convenience are more important than fullness of weight in the case of coins that are never the center of important economic interests. In a similar manner, even light-weight silver coins are minted in many countries. This is not harmful as long as they are limited to denominations for which, for technical or economic reasons, no suitable full-weight coins can be made.

APPENDICES

ARISTOTLE (*Politics* i. 4. 1253^b, 23-25) calls the means of life and well-being of men "goods." The predominantly ethical standpoint from which the peoples of antiquity regarded human relationships is reflected in the views of ancient writers on the nature of utility and the nature of goods, just as the religious standpoint predominates in medieval writings. Ambrosius says "nihil utile, nisi quod ad vitae illius eternae prosit gratiam," [2] and even Louis Thomassin, whose economic views belong to the middle ages, writes in his *Traité du négoce et de l'usure* (Paris, 1697, p. 22), that "l'utilité même se mesure par les considérations de la vie éter-

1. To Chapter I. See notes 2 and 8 of Chapter I.—TR.
2. "nothing is useful but what serves to the salvation of one's eternal life."

286

nelle." [3] Among more recent writers, François V. de Forbonnais defines goods (biens) as "les propriétés qui ne rendent pas une production annuelle, telles que les meubles précieux, les fruits destinés à la consommation." [4] (*Principes économiques* in E. Daire [ed.], *Mélanges d'économie politique*, Paris, 1847, I, 174-175), and contrasts them with "richesses" (goods that yield a revenue). A similar distinction, in a different sense, is also made by Du Pont (*Physiocratie*, Leyden, 1768, p. cxviii).

The word "good," in the special meaning of present day science, was already used by Guillaume F. Le Trosne (*De l'intérêt social*, Paris, 1777, pp. 5-6) who contrasts needs with the means for their satisfaction and calls the latter goods (biens). See also Jacques Necker, *Sur la législation et le commerce des grains*, Paris, 1775, pp. 17-24. Jean Baptiste Say (*Cours complet d'économie politique pratique*, Paris, 1840, I, 65) defines goods (biens) as "les moyens que nous avons de satisfaire [nos besoins]."

The development of the theory of the good in Germany can be seen from what follows: Julius v. Soden (*Die National-Oekonomie*, Leipzig, 1805, I, 39-40) defined a good as an article of consumption; L. H. v. Jakob (*Grundsätze der National-Oekonomie*, Halle, 1825, p. 30) defined a good as "was zur Befriedigung menschlicher Bedürfnisse geschickt ist"; [5] Gottlieb Hufeland (*Neue Grundlegung der Staatswirthschaftskunst*, Wien, 1815, I, 15) defined it as "jedes Mittel zu einem Zwecke eines Menschen"; [6] Henri Storch (*Cours d'économie politique*, St. Petersbourg, 1815, I, 56-57) said: "L'arrêt que notre jugement porte sur l'utilité des choses . . . en fait des *biens*." [7] From these beginnings, Friedrich Carl Fulda (*Grundsätze der ökonomisch-politischen oder Kameralwissenschaften*, Tübingen, 1816, p. 2) defines goods as "diejenige [Sachen], welche der Mensch zu diesem Zweck [Befriedigung geistiger und physicher Bedürfnisse] als Mittel anerkennt" [8] (cf., however, Hufeland, *op. cit.*, I, 22 ff.). Wilhelm Roscher (*Grundlagen der Nationalökonomie*, Twentieth edition, Stuttgart, 1892, p. 2) defines them as "alles das-

3. "utility itself is measured by considerations of eternal life."
4. "possessions that do not yield an annual product, such as precious objects, products destined for consumption."
5. "what is suited to the satisfaction of human needs."
6. "every means to a purpose of a man."
7. "the judgment we pass upon the utility of things . . . makes *goods* of them."
8. "those [things] which man recognizes as means to this end [satisfaction of psychological and physical needs]."

jenige was zur . . . Befriedigung eines *wahren* menschlichen Bedürfnisses anerkannt brauchbar ist." [9]

Sir James Steuart, in *An Inquiry into the Principles of Political
Oeconomy* (London, 1767, I, 360 ff.), had already divided goods into
things, personal services, and rights. In the category of rights he
even included marketable privileges or immunities (p. 370). Say
(*op. cit.*, pp. 530-531) counted a law practice, the goodwill enjoyed
by a merchant, newspaper enterprises, and even the reputation of a
military leader as goods (biens). Friedrich v. Hermann (*Staatswirthschaftliche Untersuchungen*, München, 1874, pp. 103 ff.) includes a
large number of relationships under the concept of external goods
(relationships of hospitality, love, family, gainful employment, etc.)
and distinguishes them from material goods and personal services as
a special category of goods. Roscher (*op. cit.*, p. 8) counts the state
among "relationships," whereas Albert E. F. Schäffle (*Die nationalökonomische Theorie der ausschliessenden Absazverhältnisse*, Tübingen, 1867, p. 12) confines the concept "relationships" to "über-
tragbare, durch private Beherrschung des Absatzes und durch Ver-
drängung der Concurrenz ausschliessend gemachte Renten." [10] In
this passage Schäffle uses the term "rent" in a sense peculiar to
himself. (See Schäffle, *Das gesellschaftliche System der menschlichen
Wirtschaft*, Tübingen, 1873, I, 208 ff.; also Soden, *op. cit.*, I, 25 ff.;
and Hufeland, *op. cit.*, I, 30.)

APPENDIX B [1]

WEALTH

INVESTIGATIONS of the nature of economic goods began with attempts to define the *concept wealth* in the economy of an individual. Adam Smith barely touched upon the question, but the suggestions he made have had the most far-reaching effects on theories
of wealth. "After the division of labour has once thoroughly taken
place," he says, ". . . a man . . . must be rich or poor according to
the quantity of that labour which he can command or which he can
afford to purchase." (*Wealth of Nations*, Modern Library Edition,
New York, 1937, p. 30.) From this it may be concluded as a consist-

9. "all that is recognized as being applicable to the satisfaction of a *true*
   human need" (Menger's italics).
10. "transferable rents made exclusive by private control of supply and
    elimination of competition."
1. To Chapter II. See notes 9 and 14 of Chapter II.—TR.

ent extension of the Smithian theory that whether or not a good provides us with command of labor (or, which is the same thing as far as Smith is concerned, whether or not it has exchange value) is the criterion by which its character as an object of wealth (in the economy of an individual) is to be judged. Say also follows this line of reasoning. In his *Traité d'économie politique* (Paris, 1803, p. 2), he separates goods that have exchange value from goods that do not, and excludes the latter from wealth. ("Ce qui n'a point de valeur, ne saurait être une richesse. Ces choses ne sont pas du domaine d'économie politique." [2]) In his *Principles of Political Economy and Taxation* (ed. by E. C. K. Gonner, London, 1891, p. 258), Ricardo also distinguishes between value and goods ("riches"), and differs from his predecessors only in that he employs the word "riches" in a markedly different sense than that in which Say uses the word "richesse." Following Adam Smith (*op. cit.*, pp. 314 ff.), Malthus sought the criterion of the wealth-character of goods in whether or not they are tangible objects (*Principles of Political Economy*, London, 1820, p. 28), and in his later writings as well, he confines the concept wealth to material goods. Among German writers, this same opinion is held by H. Storch (*Cours d'économie politique*, St. Petersbourg, 1815, I, 108 ff.); F. C. Fulda (*Grundsätze der ökonomisch-politischen oder Kameralwissenschaften*, Tübingen, 1816, p. 2); J. A. Oberndorfer (*System der Nationalökonomie*, Landshut, 1822, pp. 64-65), K. H. Rau (*Grundsätze der Volkswirthschaftslehre*, Heidelberg, 1847, p. 1); J. F. E. Lotz (*Handbuch der Staatswirthschaftslehre*, Erlangen, 1837, I, 19); and Theodor Bernhardi (*Versuch einer Kritik der Gründe die für grosses und kleines Grundeigenthum angeführt werden*, St. Petersburg, 1849, pp. 134 ff., and especially pp. 143 ff.).

Writers who have argued against the exclusion of immaterial goods are: J. B. Say (*Cours complet d'économie politique pratique*, Paris, 1840, I, 89), J. R. McCulloch (*Principles of Political Economy*, London, 1830, pp. 6 ff.), F. v. Hermann (*Staatswirthschaftliche Untersuchungen*, München, 1874, pp. 21 ff.), and Wilhelm Roscher (*Grundlagen der Nationalökonomie*, Twentieth edition, Stuttgart, 1892, p. 16). Malthus had already recognized that the concept of wealth cannot be correctly defined by limiting it to material goods (*Principles of Political Economy*, Second Edition, London, 1836, p. 34), but I shall have occasion at a later point to discuss his shifting attempts to provide a definition of wealth.

2. "That which has no value cannot be wealth. These things are not within the domain of political economy."

The most recent representatives of political economy in England
tie the concept of wealth almost exclusively to objects having exchange value. See, for example, McCulloch (*op. cit.*, p. 6); J. S. Mill
(*Principles of Political Economy*, ed. by Sir W. J. Ashley, London,
1909, p. 9); and N. W. Senior (*An Outline of the Science of Political Economy*, London, 1836, p. 6). Among the recent French writers, Ambroise Clément and Auguste Walras (*De la nature de la richesse et de l'origine de la valeur*, ed. by Gaëtan Pirou, Paris, 1938,
pp. 146 ff.) in particular hold this view.

Whereas the English and French economists merely distinguish
between goods that are wealth and goods that are not, Hermann
(*op. cit.*, p. 12) goes much deeper, since he contrasts economic goods
(objects of economizing) with free goods. This distinction has since
been maintained in German economics with few exceptions. But
Hermann defines the concept economic goods too narrowly. For he
says that an economic good is "was nur gegen bestimmte Aufopfe-
rung, durch Arbeit oder Vergeltung hergestellt werden kann." [3] He
thus makes the economic character of goods depend on labor or on
trade between men (*ibid.*, p. 18). But are not the fruits that an isolated individual can gather without labor from trees economic
goods for him if they are available to him in smaller quantities
than his requirements for them? And is not spring water that is also
available to him without labor and in quantities exceeding his requirements a non-economic good?

Roscher who had defined economic goods in his *Grundriss zu
Vorlesungen über die Staatswirthschaft* (Göttingen, 1843, p. 3) as
goods "die in den Verkehr kommen," and who defined them in the
earlier editions of his *System der Volkswirthschaft* (Edition of 1857,
p. 3) as "Güter, welche des Verkehrs fähig sind, oder wenigstens den-
selben fördern können," [4] defines them in the more recent editions
of his major work (*Grundlagen der Nationalökonomie*, Twentieth
edition, Stuttgart, 1892, p. 4) as "Zwecke und Mittel der Wirthschaft." [5] This definition is merely a paraphrase of the concept to be
defined, and shows that the eminent scholar considers the question
of the criteria for distinguishing between economic and non-economic goods as still open. See also Schäffle's *Das gesellschaftliche
System der menschlichen Wirthschaft* (Tübingen, 1873, I, 66 ff.), and
his "Die ethische Seite der nationalökonomischen Lehre vom

3. "what can be obtained only for a definite sacrifice in the form of labor
   or monetary consideration."
4. "that are capable of being traded, or that, at least, facilitate trade."
5. "ends and means of economizing."

Werthe" (originally published in *Tübinger Universitätsschriften,* 1862, and reprinted in A. E. F. Schäffle, *Gesammelte Aufsätze* Tübingen, 1885, I, 184-195).

That the difficulties non-German economists have had in attempting to define the concept "wealth" stem from the fact that they do not know the concept "economic good" is most clearly illustrated by the writings of Malthus. In the first edition of his *Principles of Political Economy,* which was published in 1820, he defines wealth as "those *material* objects which are necessary, useful, or agreeable to mankind" (p. 28). Since this definition includes all (material) goods in the concept "wealth," it includes even non-economic goods, and is entirely too broad for this reason. In his *Definitions in Political Economy,* which appeared seven years later, he defines wealth as "the material objects necessary, useful or agreeable to man, which have required some portion of human exertion to appropriate or produce." (p. 234.) In the second edition of his *Principles* (London, 1836, pp. 33-34, note) he explains that "the latter part was added, in order to exclude air, light, rain, etc." But he recognizes that even this definition is untenable and says (*ibid.*) that "there is some objection to the introduction of the term industry or labour into the definition, because an object might be considered as wealth which has had no labour employed upon it." Finally, in the text of the second (1836) edition of the *Principles* (p. 33) he comes to the following definition of the concept: "I should define wealth to be the material objects, necessary, useful, or agreeable to man, which are voluntarily appropriated by individuals or nations." Thus he falls into a new error by making the fact that a good is the property of an economizing individual the source of its wealth-character (i.e. of its economic character).

We find similar shifting attempts to arrive at a definition of wealth in the writings of J. B. Say. In his *Traité d'économie politique* (Paris, 1803, p. 2), he makes value (exchange value) the source of the wealth-character of goods. He says that "ce qui n'a point de valeur, ne saurait être une richesse." This view was attacked by R. Torrens (*An Essay on the Production of Wealth,* London, 1821, p. 7), and Say then shifted in his *Cours complet d'économie politique pratique* (Paris, 1840, I, 66), to the following description of goods that constitute wealth: "Nous sommes forcés d'acheter, pour ainsi dire, ces . . . biens par des travaux, des économies, des privations; en un mot, par de véritables sacrifices." [6] In this passage, Say

6. "We are forced, so to speak, to buy these . . . goods by labor, economy, abstinence,—in a word by real sacrifices."

takes essentially the same position as that expressed by Malthus in his *Definitions in Political Economy*. But a little further on (*Cours complet*, p. 66) he says, "On ne peut pas séparer de ces biens l'idée de la propriété. Ils n'existeraient pas si la possession exclusive n'en était assurée à celui qui les a acquis. . . . D'un autre côté, la propriété suppose une société quelconque, des conventions, des lois. On peut en conséquence nommer les richesses ainsi acquises, des *richesses sociales*." [7]

APPENDIX C [1]

THE NATURE OF VALUE

ATTEMPTS to determine the factors common to all forms of the value of goods, and thus to formulate the general concept of "value," can be found in the works of all recent German authors who have independently treated the theory of value. Moreover, they have all tried to distinguish the use value of goods from mere utility.

Friedländer ("Theorie des Werthes," *Dorpater Universitäts Program*, 1852, p. 48) [2] defines value as "das im menschlichen Urtheil erkannte Verhältniss, wornach ein Ding Mittel für die Erfüllung eines erstrebenswerthen Zweckes sein kann." [3] (See also H. Storch, *Cours d'économie politique*, St. Petersbourg, 1815, I, 36.) Since the relationship described by Friedländer (provided that the end desired is the satisfaction of a human need or an end that is causally connected with the satisfaction of a human need) is what is responsible for the utility of a thing, his definition is identical with one in which the value of a good is conceived to consist in its *recognized*

7. "One cannot separate the idea of property from these goods. They would not exist if exclusive possession of them were not assured to the person who has acquired them. . . . On the other hand, property presupposes some form of society, contracts, and laws. Hence wealth so acquired may be called *social wealth*."

1. To Chapter III, Section 1. See note 1 of Chapter III.—TR.

2. We were unable to locate this item. We suspect, however, that Menger's reference is to the following work: Dorpat, Kaiserliche Universität, *Facultätsschriften der Kaiserlichen Universität Dorpat, dargebracht zur Feier ihres funfzigjährigen Bestehens*, etc. Dorpat, 1852, (see *Catalogue of the Printed Books in the Library of the British Museum*, London, 1881-1900, I, 202).—TR.

3. "the relationship recognized by human judgment that a thing can be a means to the fulfilment of some desired end."

fitness for attaining an end, or as the recognized utility of a thing. But utility is a general prerequisite of goods character and Friedländer's definition is therefore too broad, quite apart from the fact that it does not touch upon the nature of value. Indeed, Friedländer comes to the conclusion (*op. cit.*, p. 50) that non-economic goods are just as much objects of human valuation as economic goods.

Like many of his predecessors, Karl Knies ("Die nationalökonomische Lehre vom Werth," *Zeitschrift für die gesammte Stattswissenschaft*, XI [1855],423) sees in value the *degree* of suitability of a good for serving human ends. (See also the earlier editions of Wilhelm Roscher's *Die Grundlagen der Nationalökonomie*, e.g. the Fourth Edition, Stuttgart, 1861, p. 5.) I cannot concur in this view, because although value is a magnitude that can be measured, the measure of value belongs as little to the nature of value as the measure of space or time to the nature of space or time. In fact, Knies himself senses the difficulties to which his conception of value ultimately leads, since he also acknowledges usefulness, utility, and even goods-character as definitions of value and remarks that "die Werttheorie . . . [ist] . . . an einzelnen Stellen thatsächlich im Ganzen auf die Combination beider Bedeutungen des Wortes Werth aufgebaut" [4] (*ibid.*, pp. 423-424). He does not, therefore, reach any uniform principle of value.

A. E. F. Schäffle ("Die ethische Seite der nationalökonomischen Lehre vom Werthe" originally published in *Akademisches Programm zur Feier des Geburtsfestes Sr. Majestät des Königs Wilhelm*, Tübingen, 1862, and reprinted in A. E. F. Schäffle *Gesammelte Aufsätze* Tübingen, 1885, I, 184-195) proceeds from the view that "eine potentielle oder actuelle vom Menschen mit bewusstem Willen gestaltete Beziehung zwischen Person und unpersönlichen Aussendingen ist also stets erforderlich, wenn vom Wirthschaften und von wirthschaftlichen Gütern soll die Rede sein können. *Diese Beziehung lässt sich nun sowohl von Seite des wirthschaftlichen Objectes als von Seite des wirthschaftlichen Subjectes auffassen. Objectiv ist sie die Brauchbarkeit, subjectiv der Werth des Gutes.* Brauchbarkeit (Dienlichkeit, Nützlichkeit) ist die Tauglichkeit der Sache, einem menschlichen Zwecke . . . zu dienen. Werth aber ist die *Bedeutung*, welche das Gut vermöge seiner Brauchbarkeit für das ökonomische Zweckbewusstsein der wirthschaftlichen Persön-

---

4. "in a number of instances, the theory of value . . . [is] . . . actually erected entirely on a combination of the two meanings of the word value."

lichkeit hat." [5] (*Ibid.*, p. 186). But Schäffle himself shows that this definition of value is certainly too broad when, in his later writings (e.g. *Das gesellschaftliche System der menschlichen Wirthschaft,* Tübingen, 1873, I, 162) he defines value as "die Bedeutung eines Gutes, um der dafür zu bringenden Opfer." [6] His earlier definition is too broad because non-economic goods also have utility and may be consciously applied to the purposes of men even though they have no value. It does not, therefore, confine value to economic goods, although Schäffle, a penetrating scholar, is fully aware of the fact that value is never attributed to non-economic goods (*Gesammelte Aufsätze,* p. 187). His more recent definition, on the other hand, is clearly too narrow, for nothing is more certain than that there are numerous economic goods that come into the command of men without the least sacrifice (alluvial land, for instance), and still other economic goods that cannot be attained by any economic sacrifice at all (inborn talents, for example). But Schäffle nevertheless placed an important factor for the deeper understanding of the nature of value in the clearest possible light. For according to him it is not the objective suitability of a good in itself (*ibid.*, p. 186), nor the degree of its utility (*ibid.*, pp. 191-192), but the *importance* of a good to an economizing individual that constitutes the essence of its value.

An interesting contribution to the correct conception of value has been made by H. Roesler ("Zur Theorie des Werthes," *Jahrbücher für Nationalökonomie und Statistik,* XI [1868], 279-313 and 406-419). Roesler comes to the conclusion that "die herkömmliche Unterscheidung zwischen Gebrauchs- und Tauschwert unrichtig sei und mit dem Moment des nützlichen Gebrauchs der Dinge der Begriff des Werthes absolut nicht verbunden werden könne; dass vielmehr der Begriff des Werthes nur ein *einheitlicher* sei, die *Vermögensqualität* der Dinge bezeichne und durch Realisirung der Ver-

5. "in order to be able to speak of economizing or of economic goods, a potential or actual relationship between persons and impersonal external objects consciously established by men must always exist. *This relationship can be considered with reference to the economic object or from the standpoint of the economizing individual. Looked at objectively it is the utility of the good. Looked at subjectively it is the value of the good.* Utility (serviceability, usefulness) is the suitability of a thing to serve a human purpose. . . . But value is the *importance* the good has, because of its utility, for the conscious economic purposes of the economizing individual."

6. "the importance of a good because of the sacrifices made in obtaining it."

mögensrechtsordnung zur concreten Erscheinung komme." (*Ibid.*, p. 406.) [7] Roesler's peculiar point of view is evident in this passage, but so also is the fact that his conception is a forward step. For he correctly delimits the sphere of objects that constitute wealth and strictly separates the utility of goods from their value. But I cannot agree with Roesler if he makes the wealth-character of a good the determining principle of its value, since both a good's wealth-character and its value are consequences of the same quantitative relationship (the relationship described in the text above). Moreover, Roesler's conception of wealth character seems questionable to me because it was borrowed from jurisprudence (see *ibid.*, pp. 295 and 302 ff., and also Christian von Schlözer, *Anfangsgründe der Staatswirthschaft*, Riga, 1805, p. 14). Like their economic character the value of goods is independent of social economy, of the legal order and even of the existence of human society itself. For value can be observed in an isolated economy, and cannot therefore be founded upon the legal order.

Among earlier attempts to define the general concept of value I wish also to mention those of : Geminiano Montanari (*Della moneta*, in *Scrittori classici Italiani di economia politica*, Milano, 1803-5, II, 43); A. R. J. Turgot ("Valeurs et Monnaies" in *Oeuvres de Turgot*, ed. by G. Schelle, Paris, 1913–23, III, 79ff.); E. B. de Condillac (*Le commerce et le gouvernement*, reprinted in E. Daire, [ed.] *Mélanges d'économie politique*, Paris, 1847, I, 251ff.); G. Garnier (in the Preface to his French translation of A. Smith's *Wealth of Nations* under the title *La Richesse des Nations,* Paris, 1843, I, xlvi ff.); and H. Storch (*op. cit.*, I, 56ff.) Among these, it is Condillac's definition of value in particular that bears no small resemblance to the recent developments of the theory of value in Germany.

APPENDIX D [1]

THE MEASURE OF VALUE

As EARLY AS Aristotle we find an attempt to discover a measure of the use value of goods and to represent use value as the foundation

7. "the traditional distinction between use value and exchange value is incorrect, and the concept of value cannot by any means be tied to the factor of things having useful employments. On the contrary, the concept of value is *uniform*, designating the *wealth-character* of things, and becoming a concrete phenomenon as a result of the institution of laws with respect to property." (The italics in the quotation were added by Menger).—TR.

1. To Chapter III, Section 2. See note 11 of Chapter III.—TR.

of exchange value. In the *Ethica Nicomachea* (v. 5. 1133ᵃ, 26-1133ᵇ, 10) he says that "there must be something that can be the measure of all goods. . . . This measure is, in reality, nothing other than need, which compares all goods. For if men desire nothing or if they desire all goods in the same way, there would be no trade in goods." [2] In the same spirit Ferdinando Galiani (*Della moneta* in *Scrittori classici Italiani di economia politica*, Milano, 1803-5, X, 58) writes "ch'essendo varie le disposizioni degli animi umani e varj i bisogni, vario è il valor delle cose." [3]

A. R. J. Turgot deals with this problem in an essay of which only a fragment survives ("Valeurs et Monnaies" in *Oeuvres de Turgot*, ed. by G. Schelle, Paris, 1913-23, III, 79-98). He explains (pp. 85ff.) that when human civilization has reached a certain stage man begins to compare his needs one with another, in order to adjust his efforts in procuring different goods to the degree of necessity and utility of these goods (*besoins,* a word used frequently in this sense by the Physiocrats). In evaluating goods man also takes into account the greater or less difficulty of procuring them, and Turgot thus comes to the conclusion that "la *valeur estimative* d'un objet, pour l'homme isolé, est précisément la portion du total de ses facultés qui répond au désir qu'il a de cet objet, ou celle qu'il veut employer à satisfaire ce désir." [4] (*Ibid.,* p. 88.)

E. B. de Condillac comes to another result. In his *Le commerce et le gouvernement* (published originally in 1777 and reprinted in E. Daire [ed.], *Mélanges d'économie politique*, Paris, 1843, I, 247-445) he says: "On dit qu'une chose est utile, lorsqu'elle sert à quelques-uns de nos besoins; . . . D'après cette utilité, nous l'estimons plus ou moins; . . . Or cette estime est ce que nous appellons

2. The passage from Aristotle given here is a literal English translation of the German translation offered by Menger. In the standard English translation by W. D. Ross (*The Works of Aristotle*, London, Oxford University Press, 1925, Vol. IX), the passage runs as follows: "all goods must therefore be measured by some one thing. . . . That demand holds things together as a single unit is shown by the fact that when men do not need one another . . . they do not exchange, as we do when someone wants what one has oneself."—TR.

3. "since the dispositions of human minds vary, the value of things varies."

4. "the *esteem value* of an object, for an isolated individual, is precisely equal to the portion of his total faculties [labor] that answers his desire for the object or that he wishes to employ for its satisfaction."

valeur." [5] (*Ibid.,* pp. 250-251.) Whereas Turgot makes the effort a person employs in procuring a good the measure of its use value, Condillac contends that its utility is the measure of its use value. These two fundamental views have frequently reappeared since that time in the writings of English and French economists.

A deeper treatment of the problem of the measure of use value is to be found only among the German writers. In an often quoted passage, refuting Proudhon's arguments against the prevailing theory of value, Bruno Hildebrand (*Die Nationalökonomie der Gegenwart und Zukunft,* Frankfurt, 1848, pp. 318ff.) says: "Da der Nutzwerth immer eine Relation der Sache zum Menschen ist, so hat jede Gütergattung das Mass ihres Nutzwerthes an der Summe und Rangordnung der menschlichen Bedürfnisse, welche sie befriedigt, und wo keine Menschen und keine Bedürfnisse existiren, dort giebt es auch keinen Nutzwerth. Die Summe des Nutzwerthes, welche jede Gütergattung besitzt, bleibt daher, sobald sich nicht die Bedürfnisse der menschlichen Gesellschaft ändern, unveränderlich, *und vertheilt sich auf die einzelnen Stücke der Gattung, je nach der Quantität derselben.* Je mehr die Summe der Stücke vergrössert, desto geringer wird der Antheil, welcher jedem Stücke vom Nutzwerthe der Gattung zufällt und umgekehrt." [6] Hildebrand's treatment gave an incomparable impetus to investigation, but it suffered from two shortcomings, which were felt (as we shall see) by later students of the theory who endeavored to eliminate them. In the passage quoted, the only thing that the value of a given "species of goods" can possibly mean is the value to human society of the total available quantity of all goods of that one kind. This value, however, has no *real* existence. It cannot anywhere be observed in the real world. For value arises only for an individual and for him only with respect to concrete quantities of a good (see p. 116 of the text). And even if we were to overlook

5. "A thing is said to be useful when it serves for one of our needs; . . . according to this utility we esteem it more or less. . . . Now, this esteem is what we call *value.*"

6. "Since use value is always a relation of a thing to man, the use value of every species of goods is determined by the magnitude and rank of the human needs the species of goods satisfies. Where there are no men and no needs, no use value exists. The total use value of any species of goods remains unchanged, therefore, as long as the needs of human society remain unchanged, *and the use value of a single unit of the species is equal to this total use value divided by the number of units.* Hence the larger the total number of units, the smaller becomes the portion of use value attributed to each unit from the total use value of the species and *vice versa.*"

this inaccuracy and conceive of Hildebrand's "value of the species" as the sum of value of all concrete goods of a given kind for the different members of society possessing them, his statement would still be unacceptable, since it is clear that a different distribution of these goods, and even more a change in the quantity of them available, would change the "value of the species" in this sense, and in certain circumstances, reduce it completely to zero. If the term is taken literally, therefore, the "value of a species of goods" has no real nature and does not exist, unless "utility," "recognized utility," or the "degree of utility" is confounded with "value." On the other hand, the value of a species of goods, in the sense of the sum of the value to the various members of society of all concrete goods of a given kind, is not an unchanging magnitude, even if the needs of the various members of society remain unchanged. The foundation upon which Hildebrand builds his calculus is therefore contestable. To this must be added the fact that Hildebrand does not consider differences in the degree of importance of satisfaction of the various *concrete* needs of men, if he attributes the "value of a species" to the various units of the species *according to quantity*. (See already the essay by Karl Knies, "Die nationalökonomische Lehre vom Werth," *Zeitschrift für die gesammte Staatswissenschaft,* XI [1855], 463ff.) The correct element in Hildebrand's theory lies in the acute and universally valid observation that the use value of goods increases when their available quantity is diminished, and *vice versa*. But he definitely goes too far in assuming that there is always a strict proportionality between the two.

Friedländer ("Die Theorie des Werthes," *Dorpater Universitäts Schrift*, 1852, pp. 6off.) [7] adopts a different approach in his attempt to solve the problem, and comes to the conclusion that "die durchschnittliche concrete Bedürfnisseinheit (das Mittel der innerhalb der verschiedenen Classen der Gesellschaft gefundenen besonderen Bedürfnisseinheiten) der allgemeine Ausdruck für den objectiven volkswirthschaftlichen Gebrauchswerth sei, und der Bruch, welcher die Quoten ausdrückt, welche die einzelnen Brauchlichkeiten zur Bedürfnisseinheit beitragen und das Werthverhältniss derselben zur mittleren concreten Bedürfnisseinheit anzeigt, das Mass für den objectiven Werth der einzelnen Brauchlichkeiten abgebe." [8] I believe

7. See note 2 of Appendix C concerning this work.—TR.
8. The average concrete need-unit (the average of all the separate need-units found among the various classes of society) is the general expression for objective economic use value. The fraction that expresses the shares that the various useful things contribute toward [satisfac-

that this solution of the problem is vulnerable, above all, in that it involves a complete misunderstanding of the subjective character of value if an "average man" with "average needs" is posited. For the use value of one and the same good is usually very different for two different individuals, since it depends upon the requirements of and quantities available to each of them. The "determination of the use value to the average man" does not, therefore, really solve the problem, since we are interested in a measure of the use value of goods that can be observed in real cases and with respect to specific persons. Friedländer therefore arrives merely at the definition of a measure of the *"objective value"* of different goods (*ibid.*, p. 68), although a measure of this sort does not, in reality, exist.

Karl Knies too has made a penetrating attempt to solve the problem in the essay to which I have already referred. He says quite correctly on p. 429 that "die Bedingungen für die Abschätzung des Gebrauchswerthes der Güter können in nichts Anderem als in den wesentlichen Elementen für den Begriff des Gebrauchswerthes gefunden werden." [9] But the fact that Knies does not circumscribe the concept of use value narrowly enough (as we have seen earlier in Appendix C, p. 293) leads him to several doubtful conclusions about the determination of the measure of value. Knies continues: "Sonach hängt die Grösse des Gebrauchswerthes der Güter ab (a) von der Intensivität des menschlichen Bedürfnisses, welches sie befriedigen, (b) von der Intensivität, in welcher sie ein menschliches Bedürfniss befriedigen. . . . Hiernach stellt sich eine Classification und Stufenleiter der menschlichen Bedürfnisse ein, mit welcher eine Classification und Stufenleiter der Gütergattungen correspondirt." [10] But the need for water is one of the most intense of human needs, since our lives depend on its satisfaction, and no one will deny that fresh spring water satisfies this need most adequately. Hence, if Knies' principle of the measure of value were correct, fresh spring water would occupy one of the highest points on the

tion of] the need-unit, and that indicates their value relationship to the average concrete need-unit, furnishes the measure for the objective value of the various useful things.

9. "the requisites for the estimation of the use value of goods cannot be found anywhere but in the fundamental elements of the concept of use value itself."

10. "Thus the magnitudes of the use value of goods depend (a) on the intensity of the human needs they satisfy, and (b) on the intensity with which they satisfy these human needs. . . . Hence we find a classification and scale of human needs to which corresponds a classification and scale of species of goods."

scale of species of goods. But *concrete quantities* of this good normally have no value, and *species of goods* cannot have value at all, as I already have shown. Although, in the course of his article, after an extensive examination of the measure of the "abstract value of goods," Knies also touches upon the use value of concrete goods in the economy of a single individual (*ibid.*, p. 461) he does so only in order to elucidate the difference between the "value of a species of goods" (really "utility") and the value of concrete goods, thus very correctly formulating the proposition that the measure of the utility of a thing is something fundamentally different from the measure of its value. But Knies does not succeed in formulating a principle for determining the magnitude of use value in its *concrete* form, although he comes very close to it at one point (*ibid.*, p. 441) in his richly suggestive essay.

A. E. F. Schäffle has approached the solution of the problem from another standpoint ("Die ethische Seite der nationalökonomischen Lehre vom Werthe," in *Gesammelte Aufsätze,* Tübingen, 1885, I, 184-195). This penetrating scholar writes: "Die Thätigkeit des Wirthschaftens wird um so energischer in Anregung kommen, je dringender das persönliche Bedürfniss für ein Gut, und je schwieriger das diesem Bedürfniss entsprechende Gut zu beschaffen ist. Je mehr diese beiden Factoren: Intensivität des Begehrens und Intensivität der Schwierigkeit des Erlangens, auf einander wirken, desto stärker tritt die Bedeutung des Gutes in das die wirthschaftliche Thätigkeit leitende Bewusstsein. Auf dieses Grundverhältniss führen alle Sätze über Mass und Bewegung des Werthes zurück." [11] I fully agree with Schäffle when he says that the more pressing one's need for a good the more energetic will be one's economizing ac-

11. "Economic activity will be engaged in more energetically the more urgent a person's need for a good and the more difficult it is to procure the good corresponding to that need. The more these two factors (intensity of desire and degree of difficulty of procurement) *operate upon one another,* the more strongly does the importance of the good enter into the consciousness that guides economic activity. All propositions about the magnitude of value and its changes are reducible to this fundamental relationship." This passage could not be located in the reprinted edition of Schäffle's essay, which alone was available to us. It is likely that the reprint constitutes only an incomplete version of Schäffle's original article. But whether or not this is the case, it is quite clear from Schäffle's other writings, for example, *Das gesellschaftliche System der menschlichen Wirthschaft* (Tübingen, 1873, I, 172), that Menger's quotation accurately represents Schäffle's thought.—TR.

tivity whenever it is necessary to procure the good in question. But it is just as certain that many goods for which we experience the most urgent needs (water, for instance) ordinarily have no value, while other goods that are only suitable for the satisfaction of needs of much less importance (hunting lodges, artificial duck ponds, etc.) have a considerable value to us. The urgency of the needs a good can satisfy cannot therefore by itself be the *determining* factor of the value of that good, even if we were to overlook the fact that most goods are suited to the satisfaction of several different needs that differ in intensity. Hence in this proposition, since the determining magnitude is not established with certainty, the very thing that was in question remains in doubt. But it is equally certain that the degree of difficulty of procuring a good is not, by itself, a measure of its value. Goods of very little value can often be procured only with the greatest difficulty, and it is not true that the economizing activity of men becomes more energetic the greater the difficulty. On the contrary, men always direct their economizing activity toward the procurement of those goods which, given equal urgency of the needs for them, can be acquired with the least difficulty. Neither the one nor the other part of Schäffle's two-horned principle provides, by itself, the determining principle for the measure of value. Although he says that the more these two factors (intensity of desire and difficulty of procurement) *operate upon one another,* the more strongly does the importance of the good enter into the consciousness that guides the economic activity, and even if we assume, as Schäffle explicitly does, that economizing activity is "mit Bewusstsein gerichtet auf die allseitige Erfüllung der sittlich vernünftigen Lebenszwecke," [12] (*ibid.,* p. 185) (that is, in other words, even if we assume goods to be in the hands of rational economizing individuals, a fact that constitutes, as Schäffle quite correctly sees, an essential factor for the resolution of his dilemma) the question how these two factors influence each other, and *how* in consequence of this mutual influence each good attains a *definite* magnitude of importance for economizing men, still remains unsolved.

Among the most recent economists who have treated the theory of the measure of value as parts of their systems, L. v. Stein must be mentioned in particular because of his original treatment of the subject. Stein defines value as "das Verhältniss des Masses eines be-

12. "consciously directed to the all-around fulfilment of ethically rational purposes of life."

stimmten Gutes zum Leben der Güter überhaupt." [18] (*System der Staatswissenschaft*, Stuttgart, 1852, I, 169-170.) On page 171 he arrives at the following formula for the determination of the measure of value: "Das wirkliche Wertmass eines Gutes wird daher gefunden, indem die Masse *der übrigen Güter mit der Masse des fraglichen Gutes dividirt wird.* Um dieses aber zu können, muss zuerst für die gesammte Gütermasse ein *gleichnamiger Nenner* gefunden werden. Dieser gleichartige Nennner oder die Gleichartigkeit der Güter ist für sie aber nur gegeben in ihrem gleichartigen *Wesen;* darin dass alles wirkliche Gut wieder aus den sechs Elementen des Stoffes, der Arbeit, des Erzeugnisses, des Bedürfnisses, der Verwendung und der wirklichen Consumtion besteht, indem, wo eins dieser Elemente wegfällt, das Objekt ein Gut zu sein aufhört. Diese Elemente eines jeden wirklichen Gutes sind nun in diesem Gute wieder in bestimmtem Masse enthalten, und das Mass dieser Elemente bestimmt das Mass *des einzelnen,* wirklichen Gutes *für sich.* Daraus folgt, dass das Massenverhältniss aller einzelnen Güter untereinander, oder ihr *allgemeines Wertmass* gegeben ist in *dem Verhältniss der Güterelemente und ihrer Masse innerhalb des einen Gutes zu demjenigen innerhalb des andern.* Und die Bestimmung und Berechnung dieses Verhältnisses ist mithin die Bestimmung des wirklichen Wertmasses." [14] (See also *ibid.,* pp. 181 ff. for a formula of the value equation.)

13. "The relationship of the measure of a given good to the run of goods in general."
14. "The true measure of the value of a good is found *by dividing the magnitude of the good in question into the magnitudes of other goods.* In order to be able to do this a *common denominator* for the magnitudes of all goods must be found. But this common denominator, or homogeneous element in goods can be found only in their homogeneous *nature*—that is, in the fact that all true goods originate from the six elements, matter, labor, production, need, usefulness, and true consumability, since if one of these elements disappears, an object ceases to be a good. These elements are contained in a given good only to a particular degree, and their magnitude determines the measure of each true good *taken separately.* From this it follows that the quantitative relationship of all the separate goods to one another, or the *general measure of their value,* is given by the ratio between these component elements of goods and their magnitude in one good relative to another. To determine and calculate this relationship is therefore to determine the true measure of value."

APPENDIX E [1]

THE CONCEPT OF CAPITAL

THE MOST frequent mistake that is made not only in the classification but also in the definition of capital, consists in the stress laid on the *technical* instead of the *economic* standpoint. (Against this practice see also J. F. E. Lotz, *Handbuch der Staatswirthschaftslehre* Erlangen, 1837, I, 60 ff., and F. B. W. v. Hermann, *Staatswirthschaftliche Untersuchungen* München, 1874, pp. 221 ff.) The classification of goods into means of production and consumption goods (goods of higher order and goods of first order) is scientifically justified, but does not coincide with a classification of *wealth* into capital and non-capital. The opinion of those who use the term "capital" to refer to all items of wealth that yield a permanent *income* seems to me to be equally untenable. For if the concept of wealth is stretched to include *labor power,* and if the concept of *income* is extended to include the services of consumption goods to their owners (see Hermann, *op. cit.,* pp. 582 ff. and G. v. Schmoller, "Die Lehre vom Einkommen in ihrem Zusammenhang mit den Grundprincipien der Steuerlehre," *Zeitschrift für die gesammte Staatswissenschaft,* XIX (1863), 53 ff. and 76 ff.), a consistent extension of this doctrine leads one to the proposition that *labor power* (see already N. F. Canard, *Principes d'économie politique* Paris, 1801, p. 9, and J. B. Say, *Cours complet d'économie politique pratique* Paris, 1840, p. 144), *land* (see Ehrenberg, *Die Staatswirthschaft nach Naturgesetzen,* Leipzig 1819, p. 13; J. A. Oberndorfer, *System der Nationalökonomie* Landshut, 1822, p. 207; "Lord Lauderdale on Public Wealth," *The Edinburgh Review,* IV, no. 8, [July, 1804], 364; Hermann, *op. cit.,* pp. 221 ff.; and L. v. Hasner, *System der politischen Oekonomie* Prague, 1860, p. 294), and finally also all consumption goods of any durability (Hermann, *op. cit.,* pp. 225-226) must all be called capital.

Correctly understood, however, capital consists only of those quantities of economic goods that are available to us in the present for future periods of time and are capable of being applied to uses whose nature and economic character I have discussed at length in the text of the present work (p. 152). This means that the following conditions must be met simultaneously: (1) the time period during which an economizing individual has command of the necessary

1. To Chapter III, Section 3. See note 15 of Chapter III.—TR.

quantities of economic goods must be long enough to permit a
production process (in the economic sense of the term, p. 157) to
take place; and (2) the amounts and kinds of the available quantities of goods must be such that through them, the economizing individual has either direct or indirect command of the complementary goods of higher order that are necessary for the production
of goods of lower order. Hence quantities of economic goods that
are at the command of economizing individuals for such short time
periods or in such amounts, kinds, or forms that their productivity
is lost are not capital.

The most important difference between capital on the one hand
and items of wealth that yield an income (land, buildings, etc.) on
the other is that the later are *concrete* durable goods whose services
themselves have both goods character and economic character,
whereas capital represents, directly or indirectly, a *combination* of
economic goods of higher order (i.e. complementary quantities of
these goods) whose services also have economic character and therefore yield income, but whose productivity is of an essentially different nature than that of durable wealth that is not capital. Almost
all the theoretical difficulties that have arisen in the theory of capital can be traced to the linguistic confusion involved in including
both of the above sources of income in the concept capital.

The fact that under developed trading conditions capital is usually reckoned in terms of money and also most frequently offered
in the convenient form of money to persons requiring it, has re-
sulted in capital generally being interpreted in ordinary life as a
sum of money. It is plain that this concept of capital is much too
narrow, and that a particular form of capital has been elevated to
the status of the genus itself. On the other hand, the opposite error
has been made by those who do not regard money capital as true
capital at all, but only as representing it. The first of the two views
is analogous to that of the mercantilists who regarded only money
as "wealth," while the latter view is that of a number of opponents
of mercantilism who have gone too far in their opposition and do
not even accord sums of money the status of true wealth. (Among
more recent writers, see, above all, Michel Chevalier, *Cours d'économie politique* Paris, 1866, III, 584 ff., and H. C. Carey, *Principles
of Social Science* Philadelphia, 1858, II, 337.) In reality, money capital is only one convenient form of capital that is especially suitable
for use under advanced trading conditions. (See H. Brocher, "Zwei
Worte über Kapital und Geld," *Jahrbücher für Nationalökonomie
und Statistik*, VII (1866), 33-37.) Karl Knies emphasizes this fact

most effectively in his *Die politische Oekonomie vom Standpunkte der geschichtlichen Methode* (Braunschweig, 1853, p. 87): "Wir finden bei allen einzelnen Nationen in sofern eine Analogie der Entwicklung, als überall das Capital seine wirthschaftliche Kraft erst nach der Einführung und der verbreiteteren Anwendung des Metallgeldes stärker entwickeln, seine ausgedehntere Macht erst auf den höheren Culturstufen entfalten kann." [2] Money does, of course, facilitate the transfer of capital from one hand to another, and especially also the transfer of capital goods and the transformation of capital into any desired form (its application to any desired use), but the concept of money is entirely foreign to the concept of capital. (See E. Dühring, "Kritik des Kapitalbegriffs und seiner Rolle in der Volkswirthschaftslehre," *Jahrbücher für Nationalökonomie und Statistik*, V [1865], 318-343, and F. Kleinwächter, "Beitrag zur Lehre vom Kapitale," *ibid.*, IX [1867], 369-421).

APPENDIX F [1]

EQUIVALENCE IN EXCHANGE

THE ERROR of regarding the quantities of goods in an exchange as equivalents was made as early as Aristotle, who says: "To have more than one's own is called gaining and to have less than one's original share is called losing, e.g. in buying and selling . . . but when they get neither more nor less but just what belongs to themselves, they say that they have their own and that they neither lose nor gain." (*Ethica Nicomachea*, v.5. 1132^b, 13-18.) Continuing, he says: "If, then, first there is proportionate equality of goods, and then reciprocal action takes place, the result we mention will be effected. . . . And this proportion will not be effected unless the goods are somehow equal." (*Ibid.*, 1133^a, 10-26.) A similar view is expressed by Geminiano Montanari (*Della moneta*, in *Scittori classici Italiani di economia politica*, Milano, 1803-5, III, 119f.). François Quesnay (*Dialogue sur les travaux des artisans*, reprinted in E. Daire (ed.), *Physiocrates*, Paris, 1846, p. 196) says that "le commerce n'est qu'un échange de valeur pour valeur égale." See also A. R. J. Turgot,

2. "We find that the development of all nations was analogous to this extent, that capital was everywhere able to develop its economic power strongly only after the introduction and widespread use of metallic money and to reveal its more extensive power only at higher levels of civilization."

1. To Chapter V. See note 1 of Chapter V.—TR.

Réflexions sur la formation et la distribution des richesses, reprinted in *Oeuvres de Turgot,* ed. by G. Schelle, Paris, 1913-23, II, 555; G. F. Le Trosne, *De l'intérêt social,* Paris, 1777, p. 33; Adam Smith, *An Inquiry into the Nature and Causes of the Wealth of Nations,* Modern Library Edition, New York, 1937, p. 33; David Ricardo, *Principles of Political Economy and Taxation,* ed. by E. C. K. Gonner, London, 1891, p. 11; and J. B. Say, *Cours complet d'économie politique pratique,* Paris, 1840, I, 303ff.

As early as 1776, we find E. B. de Condillac opposing this view, although his reasons were one-sided (*Le commerce et le gouvernement,* reprinted in E. Daire (ed.), *Mélanges d'économie politique,* Paris, 1847, I, 267). The objections that Say advances against Condillac (Say, *op. cit.,* pp. 305-306) rest on a confusion between use value, which Condillac has in mind (Condillac, *op. cit.,* p. 250), and exchange value in the sense of an equivalence between goods, which Say has in mind. The confusion seems to be due, however, to an improper use of the word *"valeur"* on the part of Condillac. Theodor Bernhardi has presented a penetrating criticism of English price theories (*Versuch einer Kritik der Gründe die für grosses und kleines Grundeigenthum angeführt werden,* St. Petersburg, 1849, pp. 67-236). Recently, the earlier price theories have been criticized exhaustively by H. Roesler ("Zur Theorie des Preises," *Jahrbücher für Nationalökonomie und Statistik,* XII [1869], 81-138) and Johann Komorzynski ("Ist auf Grundlage der bisherigen wissenschaftlichen Forschung die Bestimmung der natürlichen Höhe der Güterpreise möglich?," *Zeitschrift für die gesammte Staatswissenschaft,* XXV [1869], 189-238). (See also Karl Knies, "Die nationalökonomische Lehre vom Werth," *Zeitschrift für die gesammte Staatswissenschaft,* XI [1855], 467.)

APPENDIX G [1]

USE VALUE AND EXCHANGE VALUE

THEODOR BERNHARDI (*Versuch einer Kritik der Gründe die für grosses und kleines Grundeigenthum angeführt werden,* St. Petersburg, 1849, p. 79) says that it has frequently been noted in recent times that Aristotle had already mentioned the difference between use value and exchange value in his *Politics* (i.6.), and that Adam Smith distinguished between the two concepts independently of the Greek philosopher. Against this, it must be said that the greater part of Adam Smith's famous passage (*An Inquiry into the Nature*

1. To Chapter VI. See note 2 of Chapter VI.—TR.

and Causes of the Wealth of Nations, Modern Library Edition, New York, 1937, p. 28) coincides almost word for word with a passage in John Law's *Money and Trade Considered,* London, 1720, p. 4. Moreover, A. R. J. Turgot ("Valeurs et Monnaies" in *Oeuvres de Turgot,* ed. by G. Schelle, Paris, 1913-23, III, 86-93) not only makes a sharp distinction between use value and exchange value (*valeur estimative* and *valeur échangeable*) but goes into the matter in considerable detail. Also of interest for the history of doctrine is a passage in the work of the Scottish moral philosopher Francis Hutcheson, the famous teacher of Adam Smith, in which a differentiation between use value and exchange value can be found, although not in the terminology employed by Smith (F. Hutcheson, *A System of Moral Philosophy,* London, 1755, II, 53 ff; see also John Locke, "Some Considerations of the Consequences of lowering the Interest and raising the Value of Money," in *The Works of John Locke,* London, 1823, V, 34 ff; and G. F. Le Trosne, *De l'intérêt social,* Paris, 1777, pp. 7-8).

More recently, several writers mentioned in Appendix D (pp. 298)—Friedländer, Knies, Schäffle, Roesler—who have made the theory of value their special subject, have dealt at length with the difference between use value and exchange value. Others that should be mentioned are Otto Michaelis, "Das Kapitel vom Werthe," *Vierteljahrschrift für Volkswirthschaft und Culturgeschichte,* I (1863), 1-28; A. Lindwurm, "Die Theorie des Werthes," *Jahrbücher für Nationalökonomie und Statistik,* IV (1865), 165-218; Julius v. Soden, *Die Nazional-Oekonomie,* Leipzig, 1805-10, I, 38ff. and IV, 23ff; Gottlieb Hufeland, *Neue Grundlegung der Staatswirthschaftskunst,* Wien, 1815, I, 95ff; Henri Storch, *Cours d'économie politique,* St. Petersbourg, 1815, I, 57ff; J. F. E. Lotz, *Handbuch der Staatswirthschaftslehre,* Erlangen, 1837, I, 21ff; Karl Rau, *Grundsätze der Volkswirthschaftslehre,* Heidelberg, 1847, pp. 73ff; Theodor Bernhardi, *op. cit.,* pp. 67ff; Wilhelm Roscher, *Grundlagen der Nationalökonomie,* Twentieth Edition, Stuttgart, 1892, pp. 9-16; Karl Thomas, *Theorie des Verkehrs,* Berlin, 1841, p. 11; and L. Stein, *System der Staatswissenschaft,* Stuttgart, 1852, I, 168ff.

Perhaps nothing reveals the German tendency toward philosophical penetration of economics and the practical sense of the English better than a comparison of the treatments given the theory of value by German and English writers. Like Adam Smith, David Ricardo (*Principles of Political Economy and Taxation,* ed. by E. C. K. Gonner, London, 1891, pp. 361-369), Thomas Robert Malthus (*Principles of Political Economy,* London, 1820, p. 51, and

Definitions in Political Economy, London, 1827, p. 234), and John
Stuart Mill (*Principles of Political Economy*, ed. by W. J. Ashley,
London, 1909, pp. 436-437) employ "value in use" as synonymous
with "utility." Indeed, Robert Torrens (*An Essay on the Production
of Wealth*, London, 1821, p. 8) and J. R. McCulloch (*The Principles of Political Economy*, London, 1830, p. 4) even employ the term
"utility" instead of "value in use." Among recent French writers,
the same thing is done by Frédéric Bastiat (*Harmonies économiques*,
in *Oeuvres complètes de Frédéric Bastiat*, Paris, 1893, VI, 141). Lord
Lauderdale (*An Inquiry into the Nature and Origin of Public
Wealth*, Edinburgh, 1804, p. 12) and N. W. Senior (*An Outline of
the Science of Political Economy*, London, 1836, pp. 6ff.) recognize
utility as a prerequisite of exchange value, but not as use value,
which is a concept they repudiate altogether. What is understood
in England by the concept exchange value is best illustrated by the
following passage from John Stuart Mill (*op. cit.*, p. 437): "The
words Value and Price were used as synonymous by the early political economists, and are not always discriminated even by Ricardo. But the most accurate modern writers, to avoid the wasteful
expenditure of two good scientific terms on a single idea, have employed Price to express the value of a thing in relation to money;
the quantity of money for which it will exchange . . . by the value
or exchange value of a thing, [we shall, therefore, understand] its
general power of purchasing; the command which its possession
gives over purchaseable commodities in general."

APPENDIX H [1]

THE COMMODITY CONCEPT

EVEN in the German commercial code the term "commodity" is
employed in the popular and not in the technical sense. Thus one
sometimes finds "good" (Articles 365, 366, and 367), "object" (Articles 349 and 359), or "movable thing" (Articles 272, 301, and 342)
used in place of the word "commodity." Article 271 refers to "Commodities, or other movable things, or securities destined for
trade. . . ." *Real estate* and *labor services* are never considered to
be commodities in the German commercial code. Firms are not included either. According to Article 23, firms, just like all other
"res extra commercium," cannot be commodities at all in a legal
sense apart from the business bearing the firm name. In German

1. To Chapter VII. See notes 3 and 4 of Chapter VII.—TR.

commercial law, *ships* are not considered to be commodities (Article 67), but in several other codes they are looked upon as "movable things" and able to attain commodity character (see L. Goldschmidt, *Handbuch des Handelsrechts*, Erlangen, 1868, I, 527). Goldschmidt discusses the legal literature on the commodity concept (*ibid.*, p. 525), but his own definition of the term is too narrow from the legal standpoint since he excludes goods kept ready for sale by producers (*ibid.*, I, 298). In Roman legal sources, "merx," "res promercalis," "mercatura," etc., are used sometimes in the narrower sense of objects of trade and sometimes in the wider sense of things that are offered for sale (L. 73, §4, Dig. de legat. 32,3; L. 32, §4, Dig. de aur. arg. 34,2; L.1, pr. §1, Dig. de cont. emt. 18,1; L. 42, Dig. de fidejus. 46,1). The Austrian Civil Code distinguishes commodities from claims of debt (Article 991).

With few exceptions, the theory of the commodity has not been independently treated by English, French, and Italian writers. The words "goods," *"marchandises," "merci,"* etc., are almost always used, not in the technical sense, but in the popular meanings of "articles of trade," "purchasable goods," etc., and in an extremely heterodox manner. *Commodities* have often been opposed to *labor services* and *money* (Jacques Necker, *Sur la législation et le commerce des grains*, Paris, 1775, pp. 52-53; Antonio Genovesi, *Lezioni di economia civile*, in *Scrittori classici Italiani di economia politica*, Milano, 1803-5, XV, 294). They have regularly been contrasted with immovable goods (Horace Say, "Marchandises," in Ch. Coquelin and Guillaumin, eds., *Dictionnaire de l'économie politique*, Paris, 1873, II, 131), and have sometimes been pictured as products of industry in opposition to raw materials (François Quesnay, *Maximes générales du gouvernement économique d'un royaume agricole*, reprinted in E. Daire, ed., *Physiocrates*, Paris, 1846, p. 98) or to consumption goods (*denrées*), (Dutot, *Réflexions politiques sur les finances et le commerce*, ed. by Paul Harsin, Paris 1935, I, 72). On the other hand, Montesquieu uses the term *"marchandises"* in the sense of *"denrées"* (*De l'esprit des lois*, in *Oeuvres complètes de Montesquieu*, ed. by E. Laboulaye, Paris, 1877, V, 12.) Lewes Roberts, a contemporary of Thomas Mun, defines "the things wherewith the merchants negotiate and traffick" as "merchandises," and divides "merchandises" into "wares" and "money" (*The Merchants Map of Commerce*, Third ed., London, 1677, pp. 6-7). The Dictionary of the French Academy (Institut de France, *Dictionnaire de l'Académie Française*, Sixth ed., Paris, 1835, II, 165) defines "commodities" as "ce qui se vend, se débite, soit en gros, soit en détail, dans les boutiques, magasins, foires, marchés, etc." [2]

On such occasions as a need for designating commodities in the wider scientific sense of the term has arisen, circumlocutions like the following are used: "Quantité à vendre" (Necker), "superflu autant qu'il peut être échangé" (Forbonnais), "things which have not reached the hands of those who are finally to use them" (Adam Smith), and "cio que soprabonda in alcuni per sussistere essi stessi, e ch'essi passano ad altri" [3] (Ortes). Yet as early as 1776, E. B. de Condillac (*Le commerce et le gouvernement,* reprinted in E. Daire, ed., *Mélanges d'économie politique,* Paris, 1847, I, 261) defined "marchandises" as "ces choses qu'on offre d'échanger," thereby becoming a precursor of Henri Storch who (writing in French) gives the following definition: "Les choses destinées à l'échange se nomment *marchandises.*" (*Cours d'économie politique,* St. Petersbourg, 1815, I, 82.)

Among the German writers, Justi, Büsch, Sonnenfels, and Jakob still employ the word "commodity," in its popular meaning. Julius v. Soden defines "commodities" as "all production materials" (*Die Nazional-Oekonomie,* Leipzig, 1810, IV, 96), and understands all raw materials and manufactured products to be included under "production materials" (*ibid.,* p. 17). Gottlieb Hufeland's definition is also too broad: "Waare [ist] alles . . . was . . . weggegeben, besonders für etwas anderes weggegeben, werden kann." [4] (*Neue Grundlegung der Staatswirthschaftskunst,* Wien, 1815, II, 15). Karl H. Rau adopts the definition given by Storch when he defines commodities as "Vorräthe von Gütern, welche zum Tausche bereit liegen" [5] (*Grundsätze der Volkswirthschaftslehre,* Heidelberg, 1847, p. 164). He adds that land can be a commodity, and that although money is not a commodity as such, the materials of which it is made are commodities (*ibid.,* p. 336 and p. 537). From Rau's general view of the concept "good," it is clear that he regards only material goods as commodities. Almost parallel with the views of Rau are those of Karl Murhard (*Theorie des Handels,* Göttingen, 1831, p. 22). Karl S. Zachariä (*Vierzig Bücher vom Staate,* Heidelberg, 1832, V, part I, 2) also extends the concept of commodity to include land, whereas Eduard

2. "what is sold or supplied, wholesale or retail, in shops, stores, at fairs, markets, etc."

3. "what is superfluous to a person for his support and which he passes on to others."

4. "A commodity is anything . . . that . . . can be given to someone else, especially in exchange for something else."

5. "stocks of goods that are kept ready for exchange."

Baumstark (*Kameralistische Encyclopädie*, Heidelberg, 1835, p. 450) confines the concept again to movable goods and furthermore demands that a good have a certain degree of marketability to be classed as a commodity. Thus he approaches the popular concept of a commodity which again becomes dominant in the works of Fulda, Lotz, Schön, and Hermann.

A. F. Riedel and Wilhelm Roscher reestablish the scientific concept of commodity. Riedel defines a commodity as "die zum Tausch oder Verkauf bereit liegenden Güter" [6] (*Nationalöconomie*, Berlin, 1838, p. 336). Roscher says that a commodity is "jedes zum Vertauschen bestimmte Gut," [7] but means "economic good" (*Grundlagen der Nationalökonomie*, Stuttgart, 1892, p. 227 and p. 4). The lead of these two authors is followed by H. v. Mangoldt (*Grundriss der Volkswirthschaftslehre*, Stuttgart, n.d., p. 45); by Karl Knies ("Ueber die Geldentwerthung und die mit ihr in Verbindung gebrachten Erscheinungen," *Zeitschrift für die gesammte Staatswissenschaft*, XIV, 1858, 266) who defines commodities as "für den Verkehr überschüssige Gütern"; [8] by H. Rentzsch (Article "Waare" in *Handwörterbuch der Volkswirthschaftslehre*, Leipzig, 1870, p. 1042) who defines them as "Tauschwerthe und zum Tausch bestimmte Güter"; [9] and in the main also by Leopold v. Hasner who elaborates the concept of "abstract trading stocks" which he divides into two chief subgroups, "commodity stocks" and "cash funds" (*System der politischen Oekonomie*, Prag, 1860, pp. 288 and 302 ff.).

Among recent writers who adhere to the idea that commodities are products must be mentioned: J. C. Glaser, who defines a commodity as "jedes Product welches in den Handel kommt" (*Die allgemeine Wirthschaftslehre*, Berlin, 1858, p. 115); Hermann Roesler who defines commodities as "die für den Umlauf bestimmten oder im Umlauf befindlichen Producte" [10] (*Grundsätze der Volkswirthschaftslehre*, Rostock, 1864, p. 217); and H. v. Scheel, who applies the term commodities to "die einzelnen zum Tausch bestimmten Produkte" [11] ("Der Begriff des Geldes in seiner historisch-ökonomischen Entwickelung," *Jahrbücher für Nationalökonomie und Statistik*, VI [1866], 15).

L. v. Stein also uses the term commodity to mean "das *einzelne*

6. "goods kept ready for exchange or sale."
7. "every good intended for sale."
8. "surplus goods intended for trade."
9. "valuables and goods destined for sale."
10. "products that circulate or are destined for circulation."
11. "the various products intended for trade."

Product der Unternehmung, als selbstständiges Gut dargestellt" [12]
(*Lehrbuch der Volkswirthschaft*, Wien, 1858, p. 152). Currently, a
considerable number of very respected scholars have returned to the
use of the *word* commodity in its popular meaning. Among others
are Bruno Hildebrand and A. E. F. Schäffle who contrast commodities with services (Bruno Hildebrand, "Naturalwirthschaft, Geldwirthschaft, und Creditwirthschaft," *Jahrbücher für Nationalökonomie und Statistik*, II [1864], 14, and A. E. F. Schäffle, *Das gesellschaftliche System der menschlichen Wirthschaft*, Tübingen,
1873, II, 124-126). But the scientific *concept* of the commodity has
not been lost. Schäffle sharply distinguishes between commodities in
the popular sense and commodities in the scientific sense, and calls
the latter "exchangeable material goods" (*ibid.*, II, 142 and passim).

Like many of his other theories, T. A. H. Schmalz's doctrine of
commodities is also very peculiar. Because of an erroneous conception of the relationship between money and commodities, he con-
fuses commodities with consumption goods in the narrow sense of
the term, and therefore arrives (*Staatswirthschaftslehre in Briefen*,
Berlin, 1818, I, 63 f.) at precisely the opposite of the scientific definition of commodity given in the present work.

APPENDIX I [1]

DESIGNATIONS FOR MONEY

In Old High German, the term *"scaz"* generally takes the place of
our word money. In Gothic the word *"skatts"* is employed, although
Ulpilas translates the word ἀργύριον (which appears in Mark,
14, 11, where it refers to money in general) by *"faihu"* (cattle,
money). The Old High German word *"gelt"* can be found in a
tenth century glossary to the Bible with the meaning of "payment,"
"ransom," or "fine," as a translation of the Latin word *"aes."* In Old
Norse, on the other hand, the word *"giald"* was already commonly
used in the sense of our present-day term money. In Middle High
German the term *"gelt"* was customarily used to designate "payment" (kind and object of payment), "wealth," or "income," but was
also frequently used with the present-day meaning of "money"—by
Hugo von Langenstein, for example, in *Martina* (ed. by Adelbert

12. *"each* product of an enterprise appearing as an independent good."
1. To Chapter VIII, Sections 1 and 2. See notes 3 and 7 of Chapter VIII.
   —TR.

von Keller, *Bibliothek des Litterarischen Vereins in Stuttgart,* Stuttgart, 1856, XXXVIII, 543) where he employs the form *"ze gelte keren"* (to measure in money); and by Peter Suchenwirt, *Werke* (ed. by Alois Primisser, Wien, 1827, pp. 29, 115 and passim, esp. p. 329). (See E. G. Graff, *Althochdeutscher Sprachschatz,* Berlin, 1838, IV, 191; G. F. Benecke and Wilhelm Müller, *Mittelhochdeutsches Wörterbuch,* Leipzig, 1854, I, 522 ff.; Lorenz Diefenbach, *Vergleichendes Wörterbuch der gothischen Sprache,* Frankfurt am Main, 1851, II, 403.)

It is interesting to consider how other peoples designate money. The Greeks, the Hebrews, and in one manner of speech the Romans as well, used the word silver (ἀργύριον, *keseph, argentum*) for money. The French do so today (*argent*). The English, Spaniards and Portuguese, and in another manner of speech, the Hebrews, Greeks and French also, employ words meaning coin to designate money (money, *moneda, moeda, maoth,* νόμισμα, *monnaie*). The Italians and Russians speak of pieces of monetary metal (denars) if they wish to designate money in general (*danaro, dengi*) and the same is true of the Spanish and Portuguese in an alternative manner of speech. The Poles, Czechs, and Slovenes designate money by pennies, i.e. pieces of monetary metal (*pienadze, penize, penize*), and the Croatians, Bosnians, and Dalmatians do the same. The Danes, Swedes, and Magyars also speak of pieces of monetary metal, i.e. pennies, when they wish to designate money (*penge, penningar, penz*). The Arabs do the same, since their word for money, *"fulus,"* really means "coins." In the language of the Bari, who live on the upper Nile, the word *"naglia"* means glass beads as well as money (Friedrich Müller, "Die Sprache der Bari," *Sitzungsberichte der Kaiserlichen Akademie der Wissenschaften zu Wien, Philosophisch-Historische Classe,* XLV [1864], 117). Among the Nubians, metallic money is called *"shongir"* which means lettered shell (i.e. a cowrie shell with letters imprinted on it—coinage!).

There is a connection between the designations for money and cattle, the earliest medium of exchange, in most languages. In Old Norse the word *"naut"* means both cow and money, and in Old Frisian the word *"sket"* means both cattle and money. The Gothic *"faihu,"* the Anglo-Saxon *"feoh,"* the Northumbrian *"feh"* and corresponding expressions in all the other Germanic dialects were used interchangeably to designate cattle, wealth, money, etc. (See Wilh. Wackernagel, "Gewerbe, Handel und Schifffahrt der Germanen," *Zeitschrift für deutsches Alterthum,* IX 1853, 549, note 101; Diefenbach, *op. cit.,* I, 350 ff. and II, 758; and the interesting note in Richard C. Trench, *A Select Glossary of English Words Used formerly in Senses Different from their Present*, London, 1873, p. 30.) In the Lex Frisionum, Additio Sapientium, Tit. X, (in *Monumenta Germaniae Historica*, Hannover, 1863, XV, 695) we read "equum . . . vel quamlibet aliam pecuniam"; [2] and in the *Glossa Cassellanae* we read *"pecunia fihu"* (in Johann Georg Eckhart, *Commentarii de Rebus Franciae Orientalis et Episcopatus Wirceburgensis*, Frankfurt, 1729, I, 853-855). The Old Slavic word *"skotum,"* meaning "cattle" is used in its Lithuanian diminutive form, *"skatikas"* or *"skatiks,"* in the meaning of groat (see Georg H. F. Nesselmann, *Wörterbuch der littauischen Sprache*, Königsberg, 1850). The derivation of the Latin words *pecunia, peculium*, etc., from the word *pecus* (cattle) has frequently been pointed out. Similarly, a legend mentioned by Julius Pollux has often been cited, since according to it the earliest money of the Athenians was called βοῦς, a designation which is said to have been preserved in the proverb βοῦς ἐπὶ γλώττης. The terms dekaboion, tesseraboion and hekatomboion are also known to have served as designations for amounts of money. The view that these terms came, not from cattle money which was once in existence, but from the earliest metallic money that bore an animal sign, can be found already in the writings of Pollux and Plutarch, and has been revived more recently by Beulé and others. But I am inclined to consider as more correct the alternative view that with the gradual transition from a customary cattle standard to a metallic standard, the value of an animal in terms of metal originally constituted the principal denomination of the new currency, and hence that term that designated quantities of animals was transferred to metallic coins and to amounts of such coins.

The concepts cattle and money are also related in Arabic. There is evidence of this in the fact that the word *"mâl"* means property, or cattle in the singular, and wealth or money (*amwâl*) in the plural. (See Georg W. Freytag, *Lexicon Arabico-Latinum*, Halle, 1837, IV, 221; and Maninski, p. 4225.[3])

2. "a horse . . . or some other monetary payment."
3. We were unable to verify this reference.—TR.

APPENDIX J [1]

HISTORY OF THEORIES OF THE ORIGIN OF MONEY

THE great thinkers of antiquity, and following them a long series of the most eminent scholars of later times up to the present day, have been more concerned than with any other problem of our science with the explanation of the strange fact that a number of goods (gold and silver in the form of coin, as civilization develops) are readily accepted by everyone in exchange for all other commodities, even by persons who have no direct requirements for them or whose requirements have already been fully met. A person of the most ordinary intelligence realizes that the owner of a good will give it in exchange for one that is more useful to him. But that every economizing individual of an entire society should be eager to exchange his commodities for small discs of metal, which ordinarily only a few men can use directly, is something that is so contradictory to the ordinary course of events that we cannot be surprised that it appears "mysterious" to even so brilliant a thinker as F. K. v. Savigny (*Das Obligationenrecht als Theil des heutigen römischen Rechts*, Berlin, 1851–53, II, 406). The problem that science must solve is thus the explanation of human behavior that is *general* and whose motives do not lie clearly upon the surface. Considering these two features of the problem it is easy to understand why the idea arose of attributing the behavior in question to an agreement between men or to the expression of their collective will (the law), especially with respect to money in its minted form. Plato and Aristotle take this position. Plato calls money a "token for purposes of exchange" (*Republic*, II. 371; see B. Jowett, trans. & ed., *The Dialogues of Plato*, London, Oxford University Press, 1892, III, 52), and Aristotle, in a much quoted passage, says that money originated by convention, not by nature but by law (*Ethica Nicomachea*, v. 5, 1133^a, 29-32). He expresses this view even more distinctly in his *Politics*, where he says that "men agreed to employ in their dealings with each other something . . . for example iron, silver, and the like," and offers this as his explanation of the origin of money (i.9. 1257^a, 36-40).

The Roman jurist Paulus, whose views on the origin of money have been preserved in Justinian's code (L.1. Dig. de contr. emt. 18, 1), solves the problem in a way similar to that of the Greek philos-

1. To Chapter VIII, Section 1. See note 5 of Chapter VIII.—TR.

ophers. He points to the difficulties involved in pure barter and gives
it as his opinion that these difficulties were removed by a public institution (money). Paulus writes that "A substance was selected
whose *public* evaluation exempted it from the fluctuations of the
other commodities, thus giving it an always stable external (nominal) value. A mark (of its external value) was stamped upon this
substance by society. Hence its exchange value is based, not upon
the substance itself, but upon its nominal value." Thus Paulus also
attributes the origin of money to public authority.

Alongside the views just described, we can also discern attempts
of the writers of antiquity to trace the special position occupied by
the precious metals as compared with the rest of commodities back
to special qualities of the former. Aristotle points to the ease with
which they can be handled and transported (*Politics*, i. 9. 1257^a, 39-
41) and in another place to their relative stability of price (*Ethica
Nicomachea*, v. 5. 1133^b, 13-15). Xenophon even observes the wide
quantitative limits within which the precious metals, chiefly silver,
can be marketed. He argues that if the products of smiths or copper-
smiths, or even wine or grain were to arrive on a market in unusually large quantities, they would severely fall in price, whereas silver, and to a smaller extent gold also, always could be exchanged
at profitable prices (*Ways and Means: A Pamphlet of Revenues*, in
H. K. Dakyns, translator, *The Works of Xenophon*, London, Mac-
millan Co., 1892, II, 335-336). The durability and indestructibility
of the precious metals, particularly of gold, was already stressed by
Pliny (*The Natural History*, translated by John Bostock and H. T.
Riley, London: H. G. Bohn, 1857, VI, 96-97 and 111-112).

The extremely fertile literature of the middle ages and the six-
teenth century was carefully collected by Philipp Labbé (*Biblio-
theca nummaria, ex Theologis, Juris consultis, Medicis, ac Philologis
concinnata*, etc., Rouen, 1672). The collections of René Budel (*De
monetis et re nummaria*, Cologne, 1591) and of Marquard Freher
(*De re monetaria veterum Romanorum et hodierni apud Germanos
Imperii*, Lyons, 1605), contain many noteworthy publications of that
period (including the tracts of Nicolaus Oresmius and Gabriel Biel).
Roscher has discussed several of them in his *Grundlagen der Nationalökonomie* (Stuttgart, 1892, pp. 301-302, note 6) with great
scholarly industry. These tracts were chiefly concerned with the
practical problems of coinage, especially with the question of the
existence and the limits of the right of princes to change the metallic content of coins, and with the consequences of these changes
on public wealth. This problem had become important because of

frequent abuses of the coinage by government. In this context, several authors also take the opportunity of discussing the problem of the origin of money, which they solve on the basis of the findings of the writers of antiquity, with regular reference to Aristotle. See Nicolaus Oresmius (Nicole Oresme) (died 1383), *Tractatus de origine, natura, jure et mutationibus monetarum* (ed. with a translation by L. Wolowski, Paris, 1864, p. ix and p. xciv); Gabriel Biel (died 1495), *De monetarum potestate et utilitate libellus* (in Gaspar Antonius Thesaurus, *De monetarum augmento variatione et diminutione,* Torino, 1609, p. 1, also in an English translation, *Treatise on the Power and Utility of Moneys,* translated and edited by R. B. Burke, Philadelphia, 1930, p. 19); Carolus Molinaeus, *De mutatione monetarum quaestiones duo* (in R. Budel, ed., *De monetis et re nummaria,* p. 485); Didacus Covarruvias, *Veterum numismatum collatio,* in *ibid.,* p. 648; Jacobus Menochius, *Consilium XLIX,* in *ibid.,* p. 705; René Budel, *De monetis et re nummaria,* in *ibid.,* p. 10; and Jehan de Malestroit, *Les Paradoxes,* written in 1566 (reprinted in L. Einaudi, editor, *Paradoxes inédits du seigneur de Malestroit,* Torino, 1937, p. 97).

Summarizing the course followed by the investigations of these writers, they almost always begin by showing the difficulties to trade arising from pure barter. They next show how it is possible to remove these difficulties by the introduction of money. In the further course of their arguments, they stress the special suitability of the precious metals for serving as money, and finally, citing Aristotle, they reach the conclusion that the precious metals actually became money by the legislation of men. (Oresmius says that money is an "instrumentum artificialiter adinventum," *op. cit.,* p. xliv; Biel says that it is "vel ex sui natura vel hominum instituto," [2] *op. cit.,* p. 2; and Molinaeus says that "inventio et institutio monetae . . . est de iure gentium," [3] *op. cit.,* p. 486.) However meritorious the service of many of these writers in opposing abuses of the coinage on the part of princes, they did not therefore improve upon the views of antiquity so far as the question of the origin of money is concerned.

The early Italian and English writers are no exception. Bernardo Davanzati, writing in 1588, strictly follows the views of Aristotle and Paulus, and traces the origin of money back to the authority of

2. "either from its own nature or from man's design" (see Gabriel Biel, *Treatise on the Power and Utility of Moneys,* translated and edited by R. B. Burke, Philadelphia, 1930, pp. 20-21).

3. "the invention and institution of money . . . comes from the law of nations."

the state ("per legge accordata," see his *Lezione delle monete* in *Scittori classici Italiani di economia politica*, Milano, 1803–05, II, 24). Geminiano Montanari (d. 1687), does the same *(Della moneta*, in *ibid.*, III, 17, 32, and 118). And Lewes Roberts, whose widely read *The Merchants Map of Commerce* was first published in 1638, represents the economic views of England of the seventeenth century more accurately than any other work of that age, traces the origin of money to the same source (see p. 15 of the Third Edition, London, 1677).

Among the monetary writers of the first half of the eighteenth century John Law is preeminent for his researches into the origin of money. His contemporary, Boizard, was still attributing the origin of money to public authority, and Vauban *(Projet d'une dixme royale*, written 1707, republished in E. Daire [ed.], *Economistes financiers du XVIIIe siècle*, Paris, 1843, p. 51), as well as Pierre Boisguillebert *(Dissertation sur la nature des richesses, de l'argent, et des tributs*, in *ibid.*, pp. 396-398) did not go beyond stressing the necessity of money as a means of facilitating commerce. Law, on the contrary, most decidedly repudiates the contractual theory, and recognizing, as no author before him, the special position of the precious metals among other commodities, he derives the genesis of the money character of the precious metals from their special characteristics. Thus he is the founder of the correct theory of the origin of money (see his *Money and Trade Considered*, London, 1720, pp. 4 ff.; also his *Mémoire sur l'usage des monnaies*, written 1706–07, reprinted in Paul Harsin, ed., *John Law: Oeuvres complètes*, Paris, 1934, p. 167). Law is followed, in his opposition to the theory that traces the origin of money to a contract between men, by Antonio Genovesi *(Lezioni di economia civile*, in *Scrittori classici Italiani di economia politica*, Milano, 1803–05, VIII, 291-313), and A. R. J. Turgot *(Réflexions sur la formation et la distribution des richesses*, written in 1766, and reprinted in G. Schelle, ed., *Oeuvres de Turgot*, Paris, 1913–23, II, 558-560). Law's attempt to explain the genesis of the money character of the precious metals from their special nature, was taken up and admirably accomplished in part by Cesare Beccaria *(Elementi di economia publica*, in *Scrittori classici Italiani di economia politica*, Milano, 1803–05, XIX, 10-18); Pietro Verri *(Meditazioni sulla economia politica*, in *ibid.*, XXII, 13-19; and *Sulle leggi vincolanti principalmente nel commercio de 'grani riflessioni*, in *ibid.*, XXIII, 21); Turgot *(op. cit.*, II, 558-560; and "Deuxième lettre à l'abbé de Cicé" in *ibid.*, I, 143 ff.); Adam Smith *(An Inquiry into the Nature and Causes of the*

Wealth of Nations, Modern Library Edition, New York, 1937, pp. 22-29); and J. G. Büsch (*Abhandlung von dem Geldsumlauf,* Hamburg, 1780, pp. 279 ff.).

Among more recent writers in the same tradition are: T. R. Malthus (*Principles of Political Economy,* Second edition, London, 1836, pp. 50-60); J. R. McCulloch (*The Principles of Political Economy,* Second edition, London, 1830, pp. 129-136); John Stuart Mill (*Principles of Political Economy,* Edited by Sir W. J. Ashley, London, 1909, pp. 483-488); Melchiorre Gioja (*Nuovo prospetto delle scienze economiche,* Milano, 1815, I, 118 ff.); M. H. Baudrillart (*Manuel d'économie politique,* Fourth edition, Paris, 1878, pp. 252-262); Joseph Garnier (*Traité d'économie politique,* Seventh edition, Paris, 1873, pp. 309 ff.); and two German economists, Ch. J. Kraus (*Staatswirthschaft,* Koenigsberg, 1808, I, 61 ff.), and Aug. Fr. Lueder (*National-Industrie und Staatswirthschaft,* Berlin, 1800–04, I, 48 ff.).

Other German economists of the first decades of the nineteenth century show little interest in historical research, and the problem of the origin of money was almost completely neglected in the works of Johann A. Oberndorfer, Karl H. L. Pölitz, J. F. E. Lotz, Karl S. Zachariä, and F. B. W. v. Hermann. This situation continued until, with the reawakening of historical research in the field of our science, the question of the origin of money was again taken up by Karl H. Rau, Johann F. G. Eiselen, Wilhelm Roscher, Bruno Hildebrand and Karl Knies, as well as Karl Murhard somewhat earlier.

The monographs thus far published have furthered the investigation but little. Adam Müller discusses the desire of men for the state and thinks that the precious metals bring about this union, giving this as his theory of the origin of money (*Versuche einer neuen Theorie des Geldes,* Reprint Edition, Wien, 1922, pp. 78 ff.). Johann G. Hoffmann (*Die Lehre vom Gelde,* Berlin, 1838, p. 10) attributes the origin of money again to a contract between men. Michel Chevalier (*La monnaie,* in *Cours d'économie politique,* Paris, 1866, III, 5) does the same thing. Samuel Oppenheim's monograph, *Die Natur des Geldes,* (Mainz, 1855), is of greater interest, although its importance does not consist so much in a special view of the first origin of money (pp. 4 ff), as in an exposition of the process by which a commodity that has become a means of exchange loses its original commodity character and eventually becomes a mere token of value. Although I must emphatically contradict this opinion, I nevertheless find a clearly expressed thought (or rather an observation) in Oppenheim's argument which sufficiently explains why we encounter this mistake in the writings of many eminent economists. I refer to the observation that the character of money as an industrial metal often completely disappears from the consciousness of economizing men because of the smoothness of operation of our trading mechanism, and that men therefore only notice its character as a means of exchange. The force of custom is so strong that the ability of a metal used as money to continue in this role is assured even when men are not directly aware of its character as an industrial metal. This observation is entirely correct. But it is also quite evident that the ability of a material to serve as money, as well as the custom on which this ability is founded, would disappear immediately, if the character of money as a material applicable to industrial purposes were destroyed by some accident. I am ready to admit that, under highly developed conditions of trade, money is regarded by many economizing men only as a token. But it is quite certain that this illusion would immediately be dispelled if the character of coins as quantities of industrial raw materials were lost.

INDEX

Abstinence, criticism of doctrine that interest is payment for, 156, 172
Abstract value of goods, doctrine of (confusion of "use value" with "utility"), 116 n, 118 n, 118-19, 292 ff., 297-300, 307-8
Académie Française, 309-10
Accumulation of capital, 73-4, 109, 152-5
Advance provision, 68, 78-80, 87-9, 153 ff.; see also Economizing, Production, Requirements, Time
Advertising, 242 n.
Alternative uses, 58-63, 66, 85, 129, 162-3; see also Economizing, Complementarity, Production
Ambrosius, 286
Aristotle, 53 n., 277 n., 286, 295-6, 296 n., 305, 306, 315, 316, 317
Austrian Civil Code, 309

Bacon, Francis, 47
Bandini, Sallustio Antonio, 279 n.
Barter, 257-8
Bastian, Adolph, 281, 281 n., 284
Bastiat, Frédéric, 166 n., 308
Baudrillart, M. H., 319
Baumstark, Eduard, 310-11
Beccaria, Cesare, 318
Benecke, G. F., 313
Bernardakis, A. N., 257 n.
Bernhardi, Theodor, 289, 306, 307
Beulé, Charles E., 314
Biel, Gabriel, 316, 317, 317 n.
Bilateral monopoly (Isolated exchange), 194-7
Böckh, August, 264 n.
Boisguillebert, Pierre, 318
Boizard, Jean, 318
Books, market for scholarly 229, 243, 246, 251, 275 n.
Brocher, H., 304

Broggia, Carlo Antonio, 277 n.
Budel, René, 316, 317
Büsch, J. G., 310, 319
Business, mechanical character of, 63, 86, 225

Canard, N. F., 166 n., 303
Capital: definition, 155, 303-5; fixed capital, 66, 157, 278-9; held in form of money, 278; productivity of, 152-6; services of, 156, 157, 159 n., 172, 172 n.; see also Interest, Services
Carey, Henry C., 156, 156 n., 189 n., 304
Carli, Gian-Rinaldo, 279 n.
Carnap, 170 n., 257 n.
Causal interrelations: universal structure of, 51; law of cause and effect, 51, 67, 70; idea of causation related to idea of time, 67; see also Interdependence
Census, 91-2
Chevalier, Michel, 304, 319
Clavigero, Francesco Saverio, 269 n.
Clément, Ambroise, 290
Clienteles, 55, 242-3, 242 n., 250
Codex Juris (Justinian's Code), 309, 315
Cognition, 116
Coinage: as guarantee of fineness and weight of monetary metal, 281 ff.; coinage and legal tender, 283 ff.; government abuse of, 285; subsidiary coins, 284-5
Commodity: definitions, scientific and popular, 238-9, 308-9; history of concept, 308 ff.; distinguished from consumption good, 240-1, 259-60; demand for, 245; money as a commodity, 241, 262-5, 268-71; see also Marketability, Money
Commodity-character, nature of, 239, 240, 260